BRAC
8/2022

D1447309

2022

AUG

Praise for *The 60-Something Crisis*

"If you're considering 'what's next?' Barbara L. Pagano's book provides a thoughtful and compelling blueprint for creating a fulfilling last third of life."

—**Dorian Mintzer**, MSW, PhD, BBC-certified professional retirement coach and coauthor of *The Couple's Retirement Puzzle: 10 Must-Have Conversations for Creating an Amazing New Life Together*

"Brilliant, simply brilliant! Just when it appears life as we know it is coming to a close, Barbara illuminates how to enhance our intention, courage, and playfulness for the next 25 years!"

—**C. Richard Weylman**, CSP, CPAE international bestselling author, and yes, over 60!

"The awareness that came to me powerfully as I enjoyed *The 60-Something Crisis* is that this book is about more than strategic planning or defining a legacy. It's a book about *love*; and stepping into a greater love of life and love of ourselves."

—**David Hutchins**, author of *Story Dash*

THE 60-SOMETHING CRISIS

THE 60-SOMETHING CRISIS

How to Live an Extraordinary Life in Retirement

BARBARA L. PAGANO

Foreword by Jim Blasingame

ROWMAN & LITTLEFIELD
Lanham • Boulder • New York • London

Published by Rowman & Littlefield
An imprint of The Rowman & Littlefield Publishing Group, Inc.
4501 Forbes Boulevard, Suite 200, Lanham, Maryland 20706
www.rowman.com

86-90 Paul Street, London EC2A 4NE

Copyright © 2022 by The Rowman & Littlefield Publishing Group, Inc.

All rights reserved. No part of this book may be reproduced in any form or
by any electronic or mechanical means, including information storage and
retrieval systems, without written permission from the publisher, except by a
reviewer who may quote passages in a review.

British Library Cataloguing in Publication Information Available

Library of Congress Cataloging-in-Publication Data

Names: Pagano, Barbara, author.
Title: The 60-something crisis : how to live an extraordinary life in
    retirement / Barbara L. Pagano.
Description: Lanham : Rowman & Littlefield, [2022] | Includes
    bibliographical references and index.
Identifiers: LCCN 2021062440 (print) | LCCN 2021062441 (ebook) | ISBN
    9781538155752 (cloth ; alk. paper) | ISBN 9781538155769 (epub)
Subjects: LCSH: Retirees. | Retirement, | Older people.
Classification: LCC HQ1062 .P34 2022 (print) | LCC HQ1062 (ebook) |
    DDC 646.7/9--dc23/eng/20220110
LC record available at https://lccn.loc.gov/2021062440
LC ebook record available at https://lccn.loc.gov/2021062441

∞™ The paper used in this publication meets the minimum requirements of
American National Standard for Information Sciences—Permanence of Paper
for Printed Library Materials, ANSI/NISO Z39.48-1992.

For Liam and Lucy
To the promise of your long lives

CONTENTS

FOREWORD

The youngest members of America's baby boomer generation are up against their seventh decade (read: 60). As a card-carrying, leading-edge member of this cohort of 76 million, I've termed this as passage into the fourth quarter of life. (Not to be confused with the two-minute drill.)

As fledglings, we were forced to focus on answering the proverbial probe, "What're you gonna do with your life?" This first adulthood question was code for, "Are you preparing to deliver on society's implicit expectations and life's explicit obligations?" And the record shows that, against unprecedented odds, our generation stepped up and answered with performance and results.

Unprecedented because ours is the only generation whose careers straddled planet Earth's transition into the digital age, where professional survival increasingly meant analog-to-algorithm reinvention, marked by an opportunity/challenge ratio that was out-of-kilter—often not in a good way.

But now, our "fourth quarter" is straddling the third decade of the third millennium CE, and there's a new adulthood question that millions of boomers are asking themselves: "What's next?"

Yes, retirement is part of the answer. In fact, you'll start carrying a Medicare card at 65, and within a year or two, the federal government will insinuate its definition of retirement, complete with a Social Security check. But unlike many of our parents, most boomers won't be taking the gold watch and pension to the house. Indeed, for babies born between 1946 and 1966, retirement looks like yet another reinvention event.

But as prepared as we may be to accept this reality, that doesn't mean we can answer the new question with confidence because, like belly buttons, everyone's "What's next?" is different. Each of us will design our own unique fourth-quarter playbook.

The good news is there are inspiring examples that we can lean on.

- In his early 80s, Cato (234–149 BCE), legendary Roman philosopher, soldier, and statesman, decided to learn to read Greek. When asked why at his advanced age, he responded, "It's the youngest age I have left."
- After she had raised a family on a farm, in 1940 the world discovered the talent of Anna Mary Robertson Moses (1860–1961). That's right. As an octogenarian, Grandma Moses reinvented herself into one of America's most famous and collectible artists.
- In 1955, the year he qualified for a Social Security check ($105.00), Harlan Sanders (1890–1980) was broke. But that same year, the Colonel loaded his "11 herbs and spices" onto a 1946 pickup and drove across the country signing up new franchisees for his fried chicken idea.
- In her fourth quarter, with a successful career and family to show for her answer to life's "Can you deliver?" question, Barbara Pagano decided she and daughter Elizabeth should do something neither had ever done: sail around the Caribbean. That's right: two inexperienced women, sailing 2,000 nautical miles over six months. Successfully.

Why did these people do these things? It's because of what they all have in common: they didn't know their age was supposed to limit them.

My parents taught me the nobility of work. My first job was shining shoes in the fourth grade, 25 cents a pop. And true to my generation, I've reinvented myself professionally many times, including over uncharted territories on unassigned frequencies. When asked why I did it, or how, my answer was, "Didn't know I wasn't supposed to."

Now, at 72 and in my own fourth quarter, having defined retirement as "waiting to die," I imagined my carcass being hauled out of the office feet first. Refusing to be a barnacle on the keel of humanity, my

"What's next" answer is, "Continue to work, but now without deadlines." Besides, my ego thinks its owner has more to say.

The foregoing is historical, demographical, and personal validation of the very special and timely book in front of you. Author Barbara Pagano, friend and fellow baby boomer, is scary smart. But her intelligence, insights, experience, and courage are channeled here in such a way—a very human way—to be revealed as clarifying moments of wisdom for the rest of us.

As you read on, "Aha" moments will pop into your nodding head. Don't be surprised when you blurt out, "Hey! I hadn't thought about it that way." Or maybe, simply, "Damn right!" And don't worry. The notes you will take won't seem like homework.

In her 1974 book, *Passages*, Gail Sheehy said the thing she wanted most when she turned 40 was no more BS. In *The 60-Something Crisis*, Barbara is telling you no more wasted time. Fill the days focusing on your fourth-quarter values and goals, rather than expectations and obligations that you can now acknowledge are less relevant to you today and tomorrow.

Barbara devotes a section of this book to four giant life elements: place, yield, freedom, kinship. Alloying those four in my mind, I get fulfillment. This book will help you realize that fulfillment = happiness and happiness = a life well-lived.

The common thread Barbara weaves here is something I've long contemplated: the power of availability. And now, in your fourth quarter, make yourself available to new possibilities and find many more years of fulfillment. Like the rest of your life.

As Cato, Anna, and Harlan demonstrated, and Barbara reveals, you're never too old to reinvent yourself and seek a new definition of fulfillment.

Because today is the youngest age you have left.

Jim Blasingame,
award-winning author of *The Third Ingredient*
and *The Age of the Customer*,
futurist, and grandfather

INTRODUCTION

At 2 a.m. the knock comes softly on my cabin door. "Mom, it's your watch." I am awake and have been waiting for those words, keenly aware I will never hear them again in my lifetime.

This is the last night my daughter and I will sail a small boat through the sea. I try to take it all in—the sluicing sound of the bow parting water, the clatter of the halyard slapping against the mast, the rhythmic moan of the rudder, the hum of the wind through the mainsail, and the finish of uninterrupted time with a grown-up child I love. In less than six hours, we will drop anchor off the coast of Anguilla and end a six-month sailing adventure of more than 2,000 nautical miles. I want to relish this moment, when an ending is near, before I wrap it up into a memory. I want to remember it all.

We were not experienced sailors. If I took time to tell you all we did not know about sailing a boat, you, like so many others, would have begged us not to go. We were two women alone at sea who had never sailed at night and who took along a blow-up man for the cockpit to fool pirates. Ha!

We prepared as well as we could for the trip. Elizabeth went to sailing school for a week in Orlando, while I took a class in navigation (I flunked the final exam). We hired a Navy veteran to help us learn to dock the boat. We owe special thanks to the people at the Pensacola Yacht Club, who never once came running down to yell at us as we scrunched up against their dock—again and again. We stocked the boat with extra engine parts and books on weather, nautical maneuvers, and knots. I never did learn those knots.

"Weren't you afraid?" people ask. Well, yeah. There were moments I was scared to death.

But the truth of the matter is I was more terrified of a consequence bigger than hair-raising moments at sea, an outcome I knew would gnaw at me and would last a lifetime.

I was afraid of not taking a chance to *try*.

I wanted a go at it, simple as that. Turns out I was amazed I could do this. Sailing is hard work—days and nights of discipline, choices, misfortune, and mishaps. Tossed back and forth, just holding a course on a gorgeous but too windy day was difficult and exhausting.

I learned something new every day, and I changed. I learned how to ask for help, to make decisions based on the information at hand rather than the information I wish I had, and to always look for a better way (in some cases, as quickly as possible while someone yells at you very loudly to make sure she is heard over the wind). I now know the nighttime sky lights a pathway across the water as bright as day and lifetime friends can be found on wonky bar stools under thatched roofs.

We never got lost at sea. When there is nothing to see but water all around you, it's easy to lose your bearings. But it turns out, I'd lose my bearings in a different way. Long after I learned the importance of waypoints and markers, long after I successfully navigated deep waters, I got lost on land.

It was a staggering surprise.

When I turned 65, I had good health and I had choices. It seemed all I had to do was figure out the rest of my life. *What do I want to do now? How can I live my best life?* Every morning I sat on my office couch with good intentions and a cup of coffee, and believe me, I tried hard to figure that out. Despite graduate degrees in human behavior and many successful crossings into new life stages (I even preplanned a very successful midlife crisis for myself in my mid-40s), everything about this age I was now didn't fit me. Even the word "retirement"—the word we most use for a pivot, a time in life beginning when we turn 65—didn't fit me. Did I want to keep working? Work in a different way? Find new work? Travel? Volunteer? Bike the Pyrenees? Babysit the grandkids?

It shouldn't have been so hard, but it was. I never got depressed, but I was majorly confused about how to navigate the last third of my life. And I came to hate the question "What's next?" If there was a yellow brick road to happiness and joy, I wanted to be on it. But where was that road and who was I going to be now? What did I need to know, what did I need to do now, and how soon could I get started?

I wasted close to three years. That's precious time, folks. In due course, I ended up in libraries, bookstores, and classes and seminars to become a consummate learner of the current literature on aging, retirement, un-retirement, productive longevity, well-being, and happiness. Just like on that sailing endeavor, I learned something new every day. I buckled down and found a new way to ground myself and create a life in retirement—not just a ho-hum, be-thankful-for-what-you've-got life but an extraordinary one by my standards.

Six years later, that learn-by-doing approach yields significant returns.

Turning 65 and facing retirement had seemed more of an event. I was wrong. If I had given as much preparation to life after 65 as I did before I set out to sea, I could have navigated through one of the biggest transitions in life with a steady wind at my back to guide me. But I didn't think of it as a passage. Overnight, it came like a rogue wave disrupting my life, threatening to shake my identity and cloak the future in a haze that would require knowledge, markers, and milestones to converge and indicate the way.

A good sailing guide is indispensable when you head into a new, unfamiliar body of water to anchor your boat. You may be advised to head for the pink roof or the green bush, watch your depth, and pay attention to the prevailing winds—all before you drop anchor. The guide never tells you where exactly to drop that anchor. That's up to you. This book operates on the same principle—you choose your scaffolding, climb fast or slow, and create your own horizons.

There is wisdom and excitement in this book. But this isn't just an attempt to get you all happy and joyous in the celebration of aging into a long life. You are asked to demand more from this life stage and shift the conversation from "What's next?" to "What do I need to do now?"

Mature adults turning 60, now novices in an unfamiliar, uncharted landscape, can welcome a smart, well-written, practical, and poignant guide to hustle them forward. But *The 60-Something Crisis* appeals irrespective of age—it appeals to seasoned retirees who find something missing in life, to any individual interested in productive longevity, or to those pulled toward a higher target of well-being that endures.

This book is divided into three parts. Each part satisfies with advice, current and relevant information, keys to understanding, and inspiring narratives. Chapters close with "What Matters Most," presenting thoughtful and resourceful ways to explore ideas. Each section sets the stage for the next, creating awareness and interest and building motivation to do something.

The topics in part I, "The New Defining Moment," are conversations everyone should be having. This section begins with one of the most important questions for this time in life: "What happens when you don't give life your best shot?" Then another key question to ponder follows: "When will you leave midlife behind?" Chapter 3 is about finding the truth in our lives, and chapter 4 concerns redefining work for long life, a major issue when considering well-being as well as a finances. Chapter 5 turns attention to a key element that most of us don't understand: that this is not one transition you are making but a string of them all at the same time—and all of them can easily make you crazy.

Part II, "A Future That Is Truly Your Own," kickstarts high desire and discovery of a future life by way of four portals. The portal acts as a doorway—a single point of entry to knowledge, information, tools, and resources. The four portals are geography of place, yield, freedom, and kinship. Each portal is a definitive exploration of what is important to take with us from the past, who we are now in the present, and how we want to live the life ahead. You are never asked to reinvent yourself but instead are led to expand your known world into a life you envision and desire. These portals are the substance of daily living and the core of life ahead. They take us to familiar worlds that ask to be viewed in new and unfamiliar ways.

Part III, "Your New 25-Year Life," holds your feet to the fire and urges a commitment not to allow yourself to squander your last decades. Chapter 11 illuminates the winners—you, your children, your grandchildren, and all the generations that come to rest and face a long, long life.

If we truly understand what is required of us at the brink of this threshold, we can restore and renew ourselves. We can create extraordinary lives. We can take advantage of our extended lifespan to live deeply with fewer regrets. This book is a guide and resource to encourage this journey.

I will never again wait for a knock on my cabin door to hear those words spoken years ago, nor will I ever feel the flush of youth or experience the seamlessness of middle age. It's all quite fine. Because for now, time is still mine, just as it is for you. For us, the days ahead hold brightness and limitless possibilities, just like the dawns I saw from the cockpit, breaking over the water to embrace islands in the sea.

My wish for you is not remarkable. We all want meaningful, happy lives. May this work help you to live fully and well-intentioned.

Do your best. Godspeed.

Part I

THE NEW DEFINING MOMENT

1

WHAT HAPPENS WHEN YOU DON'T GIVE LIFE YOUR BEST SHOT?

> You know, some people say life is short and that you could get hit by a bus at any moment and that you have to live each day like it's your last. Bullshit. Life is long. You're probably not gonna get hit by a bus. And you're gonna have to live with the choices you make for the next fifty years.
>
> —Chris Rock, comedian, actor,
> writer, producer, and director

> The biggest surprise to me about aging is that you do deep changing. It makes you wonder. All the brilliant things we might have done with our lives if only we suspected we knew how.
>
> —Ann Patchett, *Bel Canto*

In last-minute preparations for the three-day sail across the Mona Passage, an infamous 250-nautical-mile passage from Hispaniola to Puerto Rico, we discover the solar light for the stern of our sailboat has quit working. Tim, a fellow cruiser, calls on the VHF to say he has several for sale. My daughter and I hop in the dinghy and head toward a small harbor right before the channel to the open ocean to happily purchase a refurbished solar light.

In the usual banter of cruisers, I ask Tim where he is headed. He hesitates. "Oh, been here for a couple of years," he replies. "Been waiting on a good weather window." Limited intervals of suitable weather conditions are critical for a sailor's decision to embark on the next leg of a journey. The pause between weather windows is days, not years.

The code in Tim's response was clear. He wasn't headed anywhere.

There is not a human being on earth who hasn't put in a good reason for delaying a passage. It often happens that in certain periods of our lives, you cannot awaken a desire or interest to get moving. In our 50s, 60s, and 70s, each of us has a chance to get more of what we want in life. We can demand more of ourselves, invest in opportunities to test our courage and to try one last time for the life we want. But even if you might have some wishes and dreams, you cannot find enough reason, inner strength, and motivation to act. And if life seems okay the way it is and there's plenty of time, why give a hoot about how it could be up the road? It will all be fine. Won't it?

There is no orientation to life after retirement. Most people are clueless about what to do in the last 20 to 30 years of life. Sixty-year-olds facing life after career, as well as those who have already retired, often succumb to the idea that a new future will be one of slow-moving ambition and then an easy, slow glide into contentment as the flush of freedom fades. This sets up a disheartening situation for a new phase that finishes a lifetime.

The decade of one's 60s is a crucial one full of weighty endeavors. The forever tensions between energy for professional lives and parenting, between care for parents and our own health, between growing into who we could be and finding comfort with who we are—these are real. Get into a brawl between spending time to figure out the future or handling the ever-present moments of our days, and there's a clear victor: "now" wins.

We value now. We are casual about the future because it's the future—a time very far away. The disconnection can seem even greater if we try to imagine ourselves in the future. Our brains act as if our future self is someone we don't know very well, don't want to know, or don't care about.

Maybe we're just scared.

The future is uncertain when you leave a safe harbor, and reasons to stay are many—often with crippling end results. Someone who arrives at the age of 60 has completed much of a full life's cycle. The last stage of life is glinting at you, but again and again we convince ourselves to overlook pivotal changes ahead. Why start now to shuffle through and arrange the rest of my life?

Don't get me wrong. Life can be dealt with at any time. But our sixth decade is on the threshold of preparing for an existence to live fully in a lifetime never before offered others. We have extra decades ahead. This is not only promising but also extraordinary. There is plenty of room to grow in strength and confidence and find much more meaning in life than in all our previous years. We often hear that this longevity is a gift. *It is.* But living long is also a problem to be solved.

We can give it a shot—our best shot. Or not.

There is a high cost for not trying. Today there is no map to follow for life in retirement, but the distance between happy and happier is felt by those in their 70s, 80s, and 90s. We can all do better. But the 60s are the first encounter—our first initiation—for the realness of retirement and what it means for us.

Like a bell for class to begin or the beacon of light beaming across the water to shine the way, moments in life's journey shape our future and define us.

This is your moment.

WHAT IS IT ABOUT OUR 60S?

What does it feel like to turn 60 years old?

We feel young. We are working hard. We are worthy of awards for mega-shopping and multitasking. We are comforted when notifications arrive on our Apple Watch showing closed activity rings. We're unsure about our readiness for retirement and concerned about missing the mark on the magic number for our retirement finances.

Our sixth decade brings the reality of aging each morning. Many of us find our parents staring back at us in the mirror. If not them, we often wonder who that is in the mirror. We may not be as pretty or handsome as we once were, but we still look and feel good. We feel differently about our face, hair, abs, and muffin tops—more accepting, less judgmental. Anyhow, everyone deals with this. And after all, age is just a number, and we are in reasonably good health and shape. We will work on that, we say.

We are sexagenarians, which is fun to say, maybe awkward, yet still better than "old." Many of us got a rude surprise in 2021 as the pandemic unfolded and experts warned that the elderly, starting at age 60, are extra vulnerable. "I turn 60 later this year, so I noticed that acutely," said Chip Conley, founder of the Modern Elder Academy, which he calls the world's first midlife wisdom school. "It was all of a sudden: I'm in a high-risk group, I'm perceived as elderly?"[1]

We've gone digital and feel savvy about being organized and connected through digital tools (68 percent of us own smart phones[2] and we're on them five hours a day[3]). We love MapQuest, watch YouTube for entertainment, and are big into Netflix. While some of us binge *Grace & Frankie* to learn now to make lemonade from lemons, the rest of us power up our addiction watching *Money Heist* to learn from "The Professor," a criminal mastermind.

At the tail end of the boomer generation, we are condemned to be driven. There may be an urgency about making a mark in our current professions, while others are bumping their heads as they navigate a next job or consider a career move. We may still be looking for purposeful work at the same time we think about putting our present work life behind us. Some have set a retirement date, which sometimes feels more like a warning than a fabulous time to frontload another lifetime.

If we have worked hard to establish a career and get kids out on their own, we may have more time for ourselves. We're happy about that flexibility and love having more time for fun and adventure. But there's a grandparent boom, so we may instead rev up our helicopter skills to be part of that. And even though there is not a better time to start working on a new phase of life, we'll put this on hold as we live vicariously through children's accomplishments.

We feel we have learned some things about life that those behind us have not. We see the benefits of "wait and see." We may be looking at our spouse or partner and thinking of what we'll do together in retirement. But we don't talk about it in detail, even when a sweet reference to "our golden years" makes one of us wince.

Most of all, we appreciate the present rather than anticipate the future. We can't envision ourselves as 80, so why be in pursuit of what you can't even imagine? Anyway, "old" is about 25 years away. Planning for it now would be a little like a 20-something mapping out life until their mid-40s. Who does that?

Are you turning 60 soon? Are you a 60-something?

If so, you are being seduced by the idea that the years ahead will be your best and you won't have to do a thing to make that happen. Looking back, you'll understand that you just faced down or got sucked up into one of the biggest transitions of your life. And you didn't even see it coming.

You'll wonder why no one waved a yellow flag to try to warn you that you weren't just facing one major life change but a string of them—all unmarked and ready to change the shape of your life. Could a retiree at least have whispered in your ear to tell you how much they regret that they walked out of the door after the retirement party into a space where they didn't know what they wanted? (Many do.)

Is this a crisis? Only if you don't want to finish your life knowing you've done your best.

The crisis of unfulfilled lives in the last third of life unfolds gradually, often with acquiesced boredom and a flimsy search for purpose. Our relevancy blows hot and cold as we age, and we too easily mistake comfort for contentment.

Boomers in 2022 are between the ages of 58 and 76. Many have already plowed into a future using an old model of success and never understood the fullness of the implications of longevity. While no one has cast a spell on the over-60 set to endanger their chances to live an extraordinary life, how many are *really* doing so? Retirees are defiantly cheerful; the kids want us to be happy, and society's creed of contentment as a high virtue is compelling.

Research shows that happiness falls sharply in one's mid-70s, just about the time elder suicide and loneliness increases.[4] The crisis crescendos. Over the past 50 years, research has shown that we all have common regrets at the end of life—not living my dreams and aspirations, not living a life true to myself, and not allowing myself to be happier.

We can change this outcome if we want to. We should want to.

THE BIG DEAL ABOUT YOUR 60S

As 20-somethings, we looked ahead to adulthood with high hopes, dreams, and excitement. But as 60-year-olds, we often bring low and vague expectations to create a substantial barrier to a life stage of won-der, hopes, dreams, excitement, and adventure.

Asked how one might imagine their life after career, a 2018 study finds that only 10 words were used to describe retirement,[5] just 10 words to dominate expectations about life after career—a period that often covers a full one-third of adult life.

"Relax," "happy," and "travel" are the top three words. Men talk about "hobbies" and "travel." Women talk about "calm" and "time."

Whatever the reasons may be, the words respondents offered show a trivial vision of life ahead. No words suggest any anticipation that life after work could be extraordinary, full of growth, change, and an eager-ness to de-ice unexplored potential. The reality of decades ahead for a 60-year-old invites new questions to ask ourselves as we lay dying. Two questions of relevance replace "Why did I spend so much time at the office?" to evaluate a broader concept of life:

1. Did I know myself?
2. Have I lived the life I was meant to live?

If we truly understand what is required of us at this age, we are blessed with enormous opportunity and we can enjoy limitless possibili-ties in a future life. We can renew ourselves. We can live an extraordi-nary life untethered to any prior life. And we have the opportunity to help future generations use us as a guide as they enter their own later years.

At any age, change happens. But 60 is the ultimate initiation where we now encounter longer years ahead with less time to live and at the same time we grow into old. If we act now, we won't end up lost and trying to figure it all out in our 70s. We *can* end up in a new decade dropping anchor smack into a life we love to the end of days. We have *just enough* time.

The decade is one of perfect timing and critical outcomes. That's the big deal about being a 60-something.

TWISTS OF THE SIXTH DECADE

Time-out is a form of behavior modification often used by parents of young children that involves temporarily separating a child from an environment where an unacceptable behavior has occurred. Even after 70 years of use, this parental disciplinary technique, though often hugely effective, is hotly debated. The short list of discipline tactics is redirect, distract, and time-out. To get gold-star behavior from children, parents will do whatever it takes. In time-out, a child is often told to "think about your choices and how you could have done it better."

The decade of your 60s could use a time-out to better understand the distinctiveness of this life stage and why the time is a perfect glide path for clarity and action into the retirement that's coming. This short decade serves as a place of introduction and preparation to something important.

While we have a necessary innocence in each season of life, in our 60s, five events happen to make this decade uniquely positioned to queue up awareness, find the discipline, and start heading into the last third of life.

First, the 70s Sneak Up on You

At 60, you'll feel it's too early in the process to apprentice yourself to old age. That's fine. But soon, oh snap! The gentle shock or mild surprise of being 70 could daze you.

Some say there is more change between 60 and 70 than other decades. At 70, aches and pains are a daily event and not because you had a good workout. As joint replacement happens, physical therapy marks up your calendar to disrupt that treasured travel at the top of the dream list. You'll learn more about medical conditions—yours and your friends'—as well as tests that you didn't even know about but suddenly need.

In your 70-something years, you'll give away more and more clothes and old pictures remind you that you were once very young, like the one at your 50th birthday party. You will find the power to feel it's okay if you don't feel like doing stuff you once did anymore. And you'll not care quite as much about what people think of you. When someone asks about sex, you'll be honest and say, "I miss it."

Nothing will surprise you more than being in your 70s. The years will begin to zip by, and you'll wonder who will take care of you if you become ill. You'll now understand the speed of life, and it will start going into warp drive. When Bruce Springsteen belts out "Glory Days," you'll think back on yours. You will learn that everything and everyone can all be taken away in the blink of an eye. You will talk to God on the way back from funerals.

You are no longer marketable in the working world, and most people are decades younger. You become aware that you have become invisible and wonder why you aren't willing to jump up like the self-helpers tell you to "feel the fear and do it anyway."

The comfort zone becomes cozy. Moving from this to that—relocation, new endeavors, new relationships—are evaluated on effort and risk, not on the possibility of triumph. You may be paralyzed from a myriad of options on what you want now from life or from a shrinking of self-confidence. Your wildness is tempered, if not by you, then others, and then by you.

What threw me and many others for a loop when we turned 70 was to even say the words, *I am 70*. How did this happen? This milestone event came with a distinct sense of difference—I was not 60-anything anymore.

Second, We Discount the Future

"Can anyone suggest a good fortune teller in the French Quarter?" Of all the answers posted on the Trip Advisor Forum for New Orleans, I love these two: "Go find 'Velvet.' She has colorful towels on her chair." And "Look for Voodoo Bone Lady."

A walk in the late afternoon across Jackson Square in New Orleans holds the magic and allure in a city nicknamed "The Big Easy." But there is nothing laid-back about the crowds lining up who earnestly want to know the future. People of all ages seek a glimpse of their lives beyond the present from fancifully dressed, bead-laden, turban-headed fortune tellers perched behind card tables with crystal balls and tarot cards arranged like a fan.

A sneak peak of life ahead may well be worth that donation of $50 because we are not good at divining the future. And when we cannot imagine our future selves, we can easily dismiss the motivation to care or plan for what this self might become.

We can easily channel the past. In a flash, I can clearly see myself wearing gorgeous white gowns on both of my wedding days and even recall what I was feeling. What remembered self and moment can you conjure up? Like Polaroid photos, our minds can summon pictures of ourselves in long ago moments and often with a story to flesh it out.

But we are not good at either imagining the future or connecting to our future self.

Last week, my grandson, age nine, received his allowance and dispersed the bills to the three jars in the pantry labeled "save," "spend," and "share." He returned 10 minutes later and took a $5 bill out of the "spend" jar and placed it in the "save" jar. Why? "I think my teenage self might want this," he said.

How much time have you thought about what your future self might want? Dan Gilbert, Harvard social psychologist and author of *Stumbling on Happiness*, works to help people see themselves in the future. According to Gilbert, "We love our present self." The present self is powerful and in control. The future self is not even around and therefore easy to lose track of.[6]

We have a fundamental disconnect to time perception. The future seems so far away that giving any headspace to a time other than the present seems a low priority. But that's not to say we never think about the future. Sixty percent of Americans think about the very near future—one month from the present—every day. Thirteen percent think about the future three years out every day with another 20 percent thinking about it several times a week. More than half of Americans rarely or never think about their lives 30 years out.[7]

The popular practice of mindfulness keeps us focused on the present and accepting of all that we have and all that we are. Mindfulness has intention, acceptance, and appreciation of the only place we can really live—the present. Looking into the future requires a lot more work than recalling the past or staying in the present.

Gilbert offers another reason why we neglect our future selves: we really don't believe we will ever get old.[8] Can we assist our imagination by using virtual reality to see our ourselves age? Sure. But we must know that the future will come.

Third, the Magic of 65

Something weird happens when we turn 65. People you know and people you just meet ask new questions. "When are you going to retire?" "What are you going to do when you retire?" "What's next?" In the beginning, you will shrug off the questions with a vague, encompassing answer—"I can't wait to find out!" and a tight smile.

Later, when you realize you have no good answers, you will make up answers. You may find a story line that will elevate your standing yet remain obscure enough not to prompt many questions. "I'm looking into being a volunteer at the Animal Rehab in the Amazon rainforest of Peru." Snarky responses to the dreaded and annoying question "When are you going to retire?" include "Why do you want to know?" "Is there some reason you're asking?" "That's between HR and me."

Like it or not, turning 65 has people thinking you are stepping off the playing field. All this will feel much more awkward than the AARP invite you received when you turned 50. Though our added years of life are not years of infirmity, people assume you will enter the cadence of slowing down and not doing all that much.

The magic moment of 65 means your preposterously long sense of youthfulness has really now arrived. People are moving you out. Change is in the air.

Fourth, "You" Are Unfinished

All of us are walking around with an illusion that the people we have become are the people we are meant to be—forever. If you think who you are now is who you will be in 10 years, you are wrong. Evidence from a longitudinal study shows that individuals underestimate the amount of future change they experience.[9] We also are not good at predicting how we will change. Most of us think we will change very little in the future, but research tells us that our predictions are off. We actually change a lot.

While one of the surprises about aging is that you keep changing, another surprise is that you might not even notice. Philomena, 75, found she was unknowingly a work in process. When Philomena's daughter, Elizabeth, and her son-in-law saw changes in Philomena, her daughter put it like this: "You know, Mom, Taylor and I have been saying we have never seen you quite so compassionate."

Philomena's response was "The nerve!" And then we roared with laughter. While I see my friend's compassion, she is, according to her children, growing into it.

We believe we have reached the peak of our personal evolution, but we may be wrong. And if the future is going to bring change, you might as well ask who you want to be and guide the process: What is the full measure of your greatness? Where is your courage? Will you be more generous in the future? Forgive yourself and others more easily? Reach out to others in need more often? Will you drink from a deeper well? Will you be less afraid and riskier? How about a new robust identity for yourself?

Life's movement is no different than the clouds moving through the sky. One of those clouds has your name on it with a tagline that reads, "On the way to different self." We are not overnight successes when we change ourselves. We may need time to try out new behaviors or practice until we get it right. Starting in your 60s to become the person you want to be means less regret in your 70s, 80s, and beyond.

Developmental downtime is not a good idea at any time in life and especially not now. It may be hard to accept that you are not finished. On the other hand, you might be tired of yourself (or parts of yourself), and that will make it easier to commit to change. Either way, you can be better than you are.

Defining moments have shaped you and your life. Time for a new one.

Fifth, Righting Regret

Daniel Pink is the author of six provocative and best-selling books about business, work, creativity, and behavior. He is always on the lookout for the next "Big Idea." "The right idea at the right time is life changing," says Pink.[10] His book *When* tackled the scientific secrets to the good time to help you flourish. His newest book grapples with regret. *The Power of Regret: How Looking Backward Moves Us Forward* spawned the World Regret Survey,[11] which has collected regrets from more than 15,000 people in 105 countries.

Regret *is* big and familiar. At every stage of our lives, we make decisions that often turn into regrets. Some, like tattoos and breast implants, come along with us each day. But regret is a feeling, so it is housed in a small almond-shaped structure called the amygdala in the downstairs part of the brain, along with other emotions like fear and anger. Sorrowful regrets hang out here.

Feelings of regret are not limited or confined to a prescription. What do we regret? You name it.

> *I quit taking piano lessons at age 12.*
> *I stayed in a marriage too long.*
> *I didn't go see Prince live.*
> *I wish I hadn't let myself get so trapped around money.*
> *I did not live my dreams.*
> *I did not share my love.*
> *I cheated on my husband.*
> *I wish I had not sent an angry e-mail.*
> *I played it safe my whole life. I wish I had not.*

Regrets can endure for a lifetime. But sometimes we can make it better.

When my brother divorced, I lost touch with my sister-in-law, Nina. My efforts not to take sides snowballed into 15 years of no contact and turned into one heavy regret. Nina is a lovely person—inside and out—and was a wonderful addition to our family. Ghostly memories of homemade ravioli at Christmastime would turn up. She is also one fabulous cook. But mostly, I just missed knowing her.

What would her reaction be to a call from me after so long?

Nina could not have been more gracious nor more accepting of my hand held out in friendship. Today, I still hold the regret of letting her slip out of my life. But I did try to put it right, so it's not in my top 10 regrets anymore. (Heads-up: Pink's research found that our regrets are often about friendships that we've lost not because of an event but because they simply faded.)

Feelings of regret don't go away with age. While some fade in intensity, others fester with fury. According to research, 90 percent of us have big, strong regrets.[12] As well, research agrees on this sting: we are haunted more by regrets of the things we *didn't* do. We can better manage the things we *did* that didn't turn out well. But *not trying* creates the bigger chasms of remorse.

What action might revive a friendship that has slipped away from you? What decisions can you make now to redirect any regrets that may come your way later? What wrong can you attempt to right?

While you can't construct a life that will shield you from regrets, you *can* begin in your sixth decade to embrace your power of choice. And while we can tackle regret at any age, our 60s offer time to reflect, rectify, and undo. Most of all, we have a chance to put something into motion that may take energy, perhaps money, and a plan.

Managing regrets is a critical life skill, and so far, we've not been successful. The biggest regret expressed in hospice beds today is the same one we've heard for 50 years. "I wish I'd had the courage to live life true to myself."

It's time to change the sorrow of this regret. Let the researchers discover that more and more of us are doing that deathbed scene saying, "I did my best."

Final Thought

Journey, a children's book by author–illustrator Aaron Becker, is one I choose regularly for nighttime reading with my grandchildren. It tells a story of a girl who draws a magic door on her bedroom wall and through it escapes into a world where wonder, adventure, and danger abound. Without a single word, the book inspires a careful examination of what is needed and a stirring sense of adventure. "Red marker in hand, she creates a boat, a balloon and a flying carpet that carry her on a spectacular journey toward an uncertain destiny."[13] It all begins with a drawing of a doorway to a magical realm.

We are always in a state of transition. But being in a very conscious state of transition is the best. You are 60-something. You are invited *now* to give life your best shot.

Make yourself a door.

WHAT MATTERS MOST

Retirement is not a feeling. But life in retirement yields a bushel of opportunities and chances for joy, love, serenity, amusement, pride, and amazement. While situations in life often just happen, more often we neglect trying to make them happen. Your 60s can be a declaration of trying. By establishing horizons to guide you, your future will not stall in transition. You may well do more in your last third of life than you or anyone expected.

That's Extraordinary

Just take a moment to think about what could make life in retirement extraordinary. Begin to ponder these questions: What might living an extraordinary life look like? What would I do for a chance to live life the way I really want? How high will I set my expectations for a well-lived life? How hard will I work to get it?

When the Trumpet Sounds

The more we dwell on regrets, the worse our quality of life tends to get. So I'm not advising you to make a list and agonize over it. But if we can learn, adapt, and self-mange, we can create better versions of ourselves and live fuller lives.

Regrets will haunt us until the end of our time. Our job is to improve our future. Ask:

Can you see yourself re-engaging with people or events?
What lost possibilities now have a lesson for you?
Overall, how might past mistakes complicate your future?

2

WHEN DID YOU LEAVE
MIDLIFE BEHIND?

I suppose it's like the ticking crocodile, isn't it? Time is
chasing after all of us.

—J. M. Barrie, *Peter Pan*

O ld is a hard sell.
The moment I ask individuals in their 60s or 70s when they
left midlife behind, their faces signal I may as well have asked when they
plan to leave for the moon. Truly, the transformative experience of leaving the earth for outer space may have greater appeal than leaving middle
age toward the farthest edges of a lifetime.

Brian, a successful architect, and his wife, Crystal, a prosperous
attorney, both turn 60 this year and raised their eyebrows when I asked
when they will leave midlife behind. "We are middle-aged," states Brian
flatly. "And intend to stay there," adds Crystal, with a tight, confident
smile.

Carol, a fun and vibrant 74-year-old with a brown-haired bob and
twinkling eyes, gives a show-stopper answer. She cocks her head to one
side and in sing-song fashion responds, "No, no, no . . . and never."
Then she leans forward and asks quietly, "Why would I want to do that
anyway?"

Indeed, why would she? Why would you? Why would *anyone*?

We have learned to love a symmetrical life with a beginning,
middle, and end. And boy do we love staying in the middle. One third
of Americans in their 70s think of themselves as middle-aged, and nearly
half of people 65 and older see themselves as middle-aged or young.[1]

While we may want to hang onto middle age for as long as possible, and while it may be impossible to locate the exact moment of the entry to old age, the first hurdle for an extraordinary last third of life is to *want* to jump—even roar—into a new developmental age. Yet that's not happening.

We are not comfortable being old.

In this chapter, you'll learn why our desire to stay in the middle of life seems justifiable; why an irresistible view of middle age hampers a future full of promise; how being youthful in our approach to getting older is a choice we can make; how some embrace a late-in-life chronological age without reservation; and why you'll want to make a dash forward into a new, exciting life stage.

Boomers are the first generation looking at retirements of unprecedented length and attempting a transition expressly to resolve how to live a windfall of 30-plus years. Are we ready?

Are *you* ready?

THE NEW TRUTH ABOUT AGING

Have you heard that life is short? My subconscious has absorbed that powerful phrase, *life is short*, and helped me seize the moment many times. I've heard it from my mom, a preacher, a warm-hearted professor, my divorce lawyer, good friends, and the saleswoman behind the counter in the upscale jewelry store in the French Quarter.

But standing in the doorway of an art studio on a cobblestone street called Quebrada, I overheard a phone conversation in which a diametrically opposite idea was presented. "Life is long. Do what you love," a talented contemporary artist in San Miguel de Allende, Mexico, Lola Pico, tells her 20-year-old son as he contemplates paths for his future.

That life is long has never been truer. The future of longevity is here. Look around. Many of us boomers will be here at age 90. More will follow with even longer lives. By 2050, according to US Census Bureau projections, one in five Americans will be 65 or older, and at least 400,000 will be 100 or older.[2] As populations are rapidly aging, the number of people over 100 is the fastest-growing demographic across the world.[3] Nothing like this has ever happened before.

Statistics might not be your favorite thing. But these statistics are *your* statistics, putting you on alert to be watchful about future decisions. As these remarkable shifts alter your children's futures and your grandchildren's, you are the pioneer and the trailblazer. A human life is whoever you were, whoever you are now, and whoever you will be. You have the story of the last third of your life to unfold in possibly rare ways. The kids will be watching and learning.

All in all, it's a stunner of a big picture view to digest and tackle.

The possibility that extraordinary life spans could become ordinary life spans is no longer far-fetched. A recent issue of *National Geographic* magazine, for example, carried a picture of a baby on its cover with the headline: "This Baby Will Live to Be 120."[4]

But come on . . . living to 120? Do we really want to be that old? "Maybe not," say some boomers. For others, living to 100 suits them fine.

Given the option, most Americans would choose to live longer than the current average, which in the United States is 78.6. Almost 70 percent of American adults would like to live to be 79 to 100 years old. The median ideal life span is 90 years.

Relative to whites and Hispanics, blacks are especially likely to say they would choose a longer life span (median of 94 years). Asked their median ideal life span, men and women show no significant differences. And there are no significant differences in the median ideal length of a lifetime by education.[5]

So it seems we may not want to see our 120th birthday, but we do want long lives.

We just don't want to *be old*.

How's that working for us?

On the one hand, like Brian, Crystal, and Carol, we may choose to push off being "old" for a good, long time and with respectable reasons that you'll soon discover. Yet staying in the middle of life is impossible, and seeing yourself as middle-aged while in your 70s may curb your enthusiasm for advancing into a new life stage and keep you believing that you have all the time in the world, which you do not.

How can we move over and out of middle age? How can we embrace the years ahead, wrapped in the joy of aging? How can we change what being old means?

THE BACKSIDE OF 50

Recently, when my husband needed to pay our cable bill, I offered to stop by the cable company's office on my bike ride and take care of it. The office is located about two miles from our house. I planned to pay the bill and then log another 18 miles on my three-times-a-week bike routine.

In case you think I'm bragging about being an avid cyclist, let me assure you I am not. I *bicycle.* I live in the Florida Panhandle. It's flat. I do, however, wear cool cycling outfits.

I parked my bike outside the cable company and paid the bill in an office deserted of customers. As I turned from the counter to head out, a man who looked to be in his 60s, wearing jeans, a cowboy hat, and boots, sauntered in the front door.

"Wow, look at you," he said, tipping his hat. "Congratulations."

I nodded, then asked, "Why are you congratulating me?"

"Well, hon," this good ol' boy replied with a smile, "you are no spring chicken. And look at you . . . on a bike!"

The three girls behind the counter, whom I don't know, start clapping, and one shouted, "Leave her alone. We love her."

I'm pretty sure all this amounted to a kind of compliment. But here's the point. Though I have worn well over the years, no cute bike outfit, helmet, or sunglasses hides anything from a stranger who tallies my years at a glance.

We boomers are not young.

You and I check in on our years of living in various ways—a child turns 50, your mom now resides in assisted living, a high school sweetheart who no longer looks like you remember contacts you on Facebook and it takes you back to a time that seems 100 years ago.

We have other ways to track our lives. Moments occur when you realize that no matter how hard you try, you're never going to be fluent in Spanish, do anything about your neck, start a new business, or go live in Paris.

No, we are not wasting our time away. But it may mean that we are sweeping past the idea that we are no longer young enough to have time for everything.

Most of us feel lucky to be alive. We count our blessings and feel, perhaps not overjoyed, but "okay" about how old we are. We aren't hiding from age. We are hiding from a chronological sequence that marks us.

"Let's say I am 73," I said to the audience of successful business owners in Baltimore one hour into my presentation about "The New-New Rules of Retirement." They knew immediately that this was make-believe because I didn't look 73. At least I don't think I looked 73. Anyway, I was not 73, yet.

"If I am 73, am I old?"

The crowd was reluctant to answer. They murmured to one another. Finally, a brave man shouted, "Yes, you are old."

The audience grumbled at his truth. The age label of "old" wasn't playing well. Frankly, some looked sorry for me. The room turned quiet again. Finally, and resolutely, one late-50s executive declared, "Nah, she's not old."

"Then, what am I? Am I middle-aged?" I asked.

Another audience member raised her hand, needing clarification. "Are you asking if you are middle-aged at 73?"

"Yes."

This lively discussion mirrors what we must determine for ourselves. *When is old? Am I old? Did I leave middle age? When am I leaving middle age?*

AGE BY THE NUMBERS

On the face of it, the concept of age is straightforward; a small child understands it. Lucy Mei, my grandchild, knows exactly how many more days before she is eight. She *cannot wait* to be eight. Chronological age has power, and Lucy knows that eight is better than seven.

Chronological age determines when you can consume alcohol, drive a car, qualify for Social Security or Medicare, get married, be eligible to vote, apply for military service, or when you must commence with required minimum distributions from qualified retirement plans.

The passing and accumulation of years is a natural rhythm and structure of your life narrative. While not all cultures celebrate a birthday, most of us have grown up with traditional festivities—the cake, blowing out candles, the Happy Birthday song, and gifts.

There are multiple theories about how this all started. The Romans had the first celebrations to honor the day of birth for family and friends; the Greeks baked round cakes to symbolize the moon and topped them off with candles as a special way to pay tribute to the moon goddess; and the smoke from the candles carried prayers up to the gods, according to some ancient culture.

The cake, especially for children, is the one tradition to gain enormous attention in our culture today. The German bakers were the first to market one-layer cakes in the 15th century for a child's birthday celebrated modestly. Today those bakers would do backflips in delight.

My grandson's seventh birthday cake was an owl that looked like a real owl and cost $250. My daughter tells me no one admits to spending that much for a child's cake. But, she added, "some probably do."

For the past 10 years, smash cakes for a first birthday are an increasingly popular trend. These small 4- to 6-inch cakes are put in front of a child for them to wreak havoc on while parents snap away. Rising from this is the adult smash cake craze reported by *The Washington Post* as social media's most precious new trend.[6] Adults turning 30 hire professional photographers for the grown-up-smash-cake ritual. Women don poufy skirts and tiaras while men are bare chested in front of a small, usually gorgeous, cake. It's the perfect social media show-and-tell.

We tend to make the most of the celebrations when our birthday ends with zero. When my brother turned 50, I had a black funeral wreath delivered to his Phoenix office where he was going over dismal sales numbers with his team. His team mistook it for the topic at hand. But he knew this was a marker for an over-the-hill theme still celebrated for 40th and 50th birthdays.

When my husband turned 70, I sent an e-mail invite to friends for a surprise happy-hour celebration at The End of the Alley, a local pub in Pensacola, Florida, that spills to an outside area reminiscent of New Orleans with fountain statues, iron work, and lush potted palms. I would pick up the tab for drinks from 5 to 7 p.m. One of his golf buddies offered to handle the invitations to the golf group. Little did I know the "golf group" would include all 80 members from the Northwest Florida Senior Group who would never think of turning down free drinks. My budget for that birthday celebration was shot! But it was fun.

I celebrated my 60th birthday with a well-planned adventure hiking the Inca Trail for five days to Machu Picchu. At the top of Dead Woman's Pass (13,828 feet) in a tent with my daughter, my sister, and eight women friends, I blew out candles on top of a chocolate cake, lopsided from the altitude and baked by one of the Sherpas.

We all have birthday celebration stories. Whether you celebrate birthdays with elaborate festivities, travel to exotic places, give yourself a party, or go out for dinner, birthdays will always be important. And when people ask, "How old are you?" the answer will always be your chronological age.

But today, that number says less and less about us.

The lifestyle trends of baby boomers defy age as a determining factor in choices we make. People now return to school at age 60, have children at 45, start encore careers at 55, enter their first triathlon at 66, and remarry at 70 or 80 or 90. Maddy Dychtwald, cofounder of Age Wave, the nation's foremost thought-leader on the workplace and aging trends, proclaims boomers as trailblazers in her book Cycles: How We Will Live, Work, and Buy. She states, "The members of the rule-breaking baby boom generation are revolutionizing the conventional model of maturity."

We are changing things up—finding a late-in-life groove to suit who we think we are or want to be, even as the rest of the world still calls us "seniors" or "elders." (We dislike both references, and we are weary of "golden agers.")

At a certain age, we may know we are getting older. But we don't feel old. That's a good thing.

Isn't it?

AS OLD AS YOU FEEL

Accumulated years on this earth can ambush our image of ourselves.

My high school class of 800 graduates canceled a 57th-year reunion due to the coronavirus. The many e-mail responses that followed were less about disappointment in the cancellation and more about the fact that we all had 75th birthdays that year.

Sue Ellen Bordwell, an active cyclist and community organizer in Maine and one of my best friends in high school, told me, "Birthdays have never been big days for me. But when I turned 75? All I could say was, 'How did this happen?'"

She was far from alone in asking that question. Still in touch with many of her 1967 Keuka College classmates, they had a Zoom party to celebrate turning 75. "The collective theme," she explained, "was that question, 'How did this happen?'"

How indeed! Growing older is mysterious. As we age, some look youthful while others do not. Some feel creaky in the mornings while others embrace a routine holding a downward-facing dog for longer than it takes my microwave to thaw frozen meatloaf.

We don't forget how to feel young. While driving my mom, then 75, to lunch on a visit home in Ohio, I stopped at a stoplight and out of the blue Mom said, "You know, Barbara, I don't feel old." She paused and our eyes met. Then, reaching down to get her purse from the passenger floor mat, she added, "I only feel old when I look at my hands." She put her purse in her lap and slid her hands underneath it.

Most 50-, 60-, 70- and 80-year-olds, like my mom, feel younger than they really are. Into our 80s, we can feel we are only 64.

One study reports that most of us feel about eight years younger than our chronological age; other research shows consistently that we typically view ourselves as feeling a decade or more younger than our chronological age.[7] The news gets better.

William Chopik, an assistant professor of psychology at Michigan State University, surveyed more than half a million Americans via the Internet to find that as people got older, they felt *much* younger than their chronological age. "Sixty-year-olds felt like they were 46," he wrote. "Seventy-year-olds felt like they were 53. Eighty-year-olds felt like they were 65."[8] People know that they are aging, he concludes, but they are evaluating themselves and their lives reporting feeling about 20 percent younger than their current age.

The passage of time is swift and, from the standpoint of our interior landscape, often seems mismatched. We feel younger than our years, and that complicates a decisive move from middle age to old. Why leave middle age at 70 when you feel 50?

Choosing to be "old" is made more difficult as each of us wrestles with our place in a youth-oriented culture. It is cool to be young; it is not cool to be old. In 2019, AARP's study of online media images found older adults are seven times more likely to be portrayed negatively as younger ones and the portrayals are heavily stereotyped.

Dozens of companies are using Facebook to exclude older workers from job ads.[9] In advertising, marketing, hiring, and firing, ageism prevails. Our ambitious expectations to remain young are a way to combat being marginalized or sidelined.

Nowhere is the driving force in the resistance to move from middle age to old more apparent than in how we spend our money. Whether you are a boomer who feels young or looks youthful or not, we are great consumers for being active, healthy, and hip. Consumers aged 50-plus constitute 33 percent of the population and consume 52 percent of personal health-care products, 55 percent of physical therapy sessions, 57 percent of health club memberships, 68 percent of over-the-counter drugs, 74 percent of vitamin consumption, 77 percent of prescription drugs, and 82 percent of home health-care usage.

Does all this sound like a group who wants to leave middle age?

Music has been telling us for years that we want to be and feel young. In the 1992 Grammy-nominated country song, "I Don't Need Your Rockin' Chair," George Jones declares we not only don't want the rockin' chair but also Geritol and Medicare. "Glory Days" by Bruce Springsteen idolizes the good old days of high school, and Emmylou Harris and Rodney Cowell confess in harmony to fighting it (aging) every day in "Back When We Were Beautiful."

For almost 50 years, Bob Dylan, a songwriter of unparalleled talent, has made us happy to hear a 1973 song written as a lullaby for his son Jakob Dylan, the youngest of four children that Dylan had with his first wife, Sara. The lyrics of "Forever Young" may create a lump in your throat or a secret wish that Dylan might show up in your family tree.

The song endures as a classic and encourages all of us not to want to be old.

BODY AGE

Chronological age is a force that logs our time on earth with the most power. But in case you haven't heard, we humans have two different ages—chronological and biological.

Your cells do not celebrate your birthday. Whatever age you say you are, your body may beg to differ. Even though two people may both be 60 years old, one of them could have a biological profile that is closer to 40, while the other may have a biological profile of 70.

Biological age reflects a combination of your genetics, accumulated lifestyle factors, demographics, diet, and exercise habits. There are a range of age-related biomarkers, from blood pressure, lung capacity, and grip strength to the length of one's telomeres (the "bumpers" that protect DNA from damage)—all this determines a "biological age."

Some of us like the marker of biological age better than chronological age. First, biological age is a stronger predictor of longevity than a birth certificate. Second, unlike the number of candles on your cake next year, you can lower your biological age.

Say you lost 30 pounds, quit smoking or drinking, and started eating healthier food. You have a chance to lower your biological age.

Being in charge of biological age may be a new challenge for many of us. Others have taken it on with gusto. We all know or have read of individuals late in life defying age in what you and I may think of as outrageous, seemingly impossible ways. Soccer, mountain climbing, ultramarathons, triathlons, and the trapeze are only a few of the places seniors are making their mark—a new mark—and blowing our minds about what it means to grow old.

We are part of a generation of older adults who pursue a passion for succeeding and maintaining active lifestyles—and the thrill of competition.

At 4:55 a.m., on June 17, 2017, Pat Gallant-Charette, then 66, entered the ocean at Shakespeare Beach, just south of Dover, England. The water was cold. For 17 hours and 55 minutes, her son Tom counted her strokes, tracked her food intake, and watched for signs of hypothermia. He also watched his mother become the oldest woman to swim the English Channel. She's done it twice.

In February 2019, Gallant-Charette's second attempt to swim the 16-mile-wide Cooks Straight in New Zealand would serve as her final leg of the Oceans Seven Challenge. She failed with three miles to go. After 26 miles and more than 12 hours of swimming, it was over. If she could swim faster, she might have beat the currents and winds that pushed her backward, making it impossible to swim.

In December 2019, she said, "I am training, losing weight, and I am getting faster." There is a four-year-long waiting list to swim Cooks Straight. At almost 69, Gallant-Charette told organizers she would be on a plane if anyone cancels.[10]

Biological age could dramatically impact every facet of retirement planning and life insurance in the future. The financial industry cares more about your biological age than your chronological age because health is the biggest wild card in growing older.

Andrew J. Scott, professor of economics at the London Business School, and Lynda Gratton, professor of management practice and a fellow of the World Economic Forum, say it's time to question chronological age as a kind of numerical determinism. In their book, *The New Long Life: A Framework for Flourishing in a Changing World*, they describe in detail a culture that needs to be blown up and encourage us to become "social pioneers."

We may not be the ones to help government, policy makers, and corporations institute cultural change. We hope they do! For certain, anyone over 60 should not wait for a society to catch up.

Deep within this current reality, you and I find ourselves in a world that can classify us in a flash and doesn't expect much from us past a certain age. But we can create an awareness that chronological age begets a bias and is worthy of enlightenment. Based on what you've read so far in this chapter, if someone asks how old you are, you could say, "I'm 75 with a biological age of 60 and I feel 50."

Armed with self-awareness, knowledge, and current reality, living an extraordinary life begins with understanding the *shape of growing into old* in today's world, how certain periods of life are set forth, and what's under way.

AGE BY THE STAGE

So far, we've looked at age measured by time, age measured by biology, and age measured by you—how old you feel or want to see yourself. But beneath every life are constructs that quietly provide a foundation for how we live. Developmental psychologists study how people grow, develop, and adapt at different life stages.

This is where the idea of "middle age" finds roots.

Until a century ago, there were three life stages—childhood, adulthood, and old age. Simple. But during the 1920s, a fourth developmental stage called "adolescence" was recognized as a fiery period of rapid change and raging hormones that occurs between childhood and adulthood. The associated ages with these four life stages were: childhood (birth to 10), adolescence (begins around age 11), adulthood (begins around age 18 and lasts an exceedingly long time), and old age (begins around age 60).

All this held steady until the year 2000, when a new stage— "emerging adulthood," proposed by Jeffrey Arnett, professor of psychology at Clark University in Massachusetts—was added to reflect the fact that people in their 20s were not becoming adults on schedule. They were not following the norms. They were not (as previous generations before them) leaving home, finishing school, and finding jobs. They were not marrying and having children on the previous time schedule but instead taking about 10 years to explore their options. They eased into adulthood around age 30.

Perhaps your children mirror these changes in growing up, and the life stage of "emerging adulthood" is one with which you are well acquainted. You may have lived through it with impatience and anxiety. Or maybe it was so subtle you didn't notice this was a phenomenon of grand scale and notable to the academic world.

Life stages may or may not be added as rapidly as we make changes in the way we live. Even if the differences seem profound, changing the cycle of human development is a rarified event. You may be living the cycle, with dramatic changes taking place right before your eyes, before it even has a name.

The difference in how we now live is apparent when I compare my life to my daughter's. I did not ease into adulthood; I jumped. Boomers like me, married at 19, took on mortgages and gender roles dictated by the 1960s, began professional careers, built businesses, and started families—just like the new adults we were supposed to be.

Contrast that with my daughter's choices. After graduating, she backpacked in Europe then forged her career for 18 years, married at 40, had her first child at 41, and adopted Lucy Mei from China four years later. She and her husband, John, are doing at age 50 what I did in my 30s.

Today, the five life stages that remain stable are childhood, adolescence, emerging adulthood, adulthood, and old age. Currently the chasm between adulthood and old age is thorny, and the middle of that adulthood stage is being stretched. And it all starts with boomers doing what they've always done—shaking things up.

When boomers decided not to stop working at age 65 and settle into being old—poof! the beacon guiding prior generations dimmed. Nowadays the relevance of retirement is challenged and undesired by many. The beacon is no longer dim but a mere flicker.

Choosing to fit work into newfound freedom also prompts an examination of how to best live the last third of life. Relationships take front and center, as do buckets full of dreams. We are asking ourselves critical questions on a variety of fronts.

Boomers changed family life with a glut of divorce in the 1970s and a national divorce rate that peaked in 1980. Today, most of us are not couples on tandem bikes riding ocean boardwalks. We're asking: How do we honor our marriages when individuals want different things? How can I find a partner to share the remainder of life? Can I find the courage to leave a partnership that is no longer good for me after all these years?

Maybe we raised latchkey kids, but grandparenting is extremely important. "Boomers are taking grandparenting to the next level," states Richard Eisenberg, managing editor of *Next Avenue*, the PBS digital platform for boomers. We are spending more time with and money on our grandchildren than previous generations. Lori Bitter, author of the book, *The Grandparent Economy: How Baby Boomers Are Bridging the Generation Gap*, writes that, since 2000, grandparent spending has outpaced general consumer spending at an average rate of about 8 percent annually. Hate to admit it, but there is joy in seeing my grandchildren in $60 shoes.

But there is even more joy in spending time with them. With years ahead abbreviated, we are faced with trade-offs. We wrestle with time for our dreams and realities while yearning to be in the lives of grandkids. How can we be terrific grandparents and still go live in Mexico? How do we manage the cost of airfare to three different locations where our grandchildren live?

Finally, living out the last third of life brings the realization that we want vastly different things than our parents did. After climbing the ranks of government administration while raising four kids, my mom retired at age 65. "Why are you doing this?" I asked. "It's what we do," she replied. She traded negotiating $1 million purchase orders to supply America's defense system for a Bingo card. That's what she wanted.

Achieving our aspirations requires self-confidence and sometimes money. Where do we find the chutzpah and cash to enroll in law school at age 60? How can I travel the world on my small pension? Just like those 20-year-olds in the late 1990s who forged ahead not paying attention to norms or acting their age, we have big questions for our futures. We are making life bigger. We are refusing to be "old" in the previous sense of the word. Some experts now say old age does not start at 60 anymore but instead begins as late as age 85. (Some of you just cheered.)

All to say, life stage development has not kept up and is clearly poking along. No definitive or acceptable new life stage has emerged. There is no named life stage after adulthood that is uniformly accepted or has become a part of the literature.

Well, that's not exactly true. Academics and scholars are *trying*. Thomas Armstrong, PhD, wants the new and improved last three decades of life to be called "Boomers 3.0." Armstrong proposes "12 Stages of Life"[11] (12!). The last three are:

- Midlife (ages 35–50);
- Mature Adulthood (ages 50–80 or 65 to death); and
- Late Adulthood (age 80+ followed by death and dying).

As you can see, "old" has vanished, which could be good news. But otherwise, I'm afraid I see nothing exciting going on here. Mature adulthood doesn't sound keen. Gail Sheehy, author of the renowned book *Passages*, proposed we put a new life stage smack in the middle of life and called it "A Second Adulthood."

A second adulthood sounds like something I'd like to avoid. The Third Age, established in the positive aging theory of the 1980s, is accepted by many and, I believe, has possibilities. But is it a captivating new life stage to usher us into our new supersized lives? A named stage to focus on those of us who have the possibility of living nine, 10, or more decades with breathless anticipation for our time ahead? Not quite.

In a world where social norms do not fit us and with nowhere to go between middle age and old age, more of us want to extend the adulthood stage—stretching the latter part of it out slowly and carefully, like saltwater taffy. We'll take even longer to think of ourselves as "old."

The developmental stages we once relied on to gauge our passages through life are no longer reliable. Bamboozling age labels cheat us out of jobs and whittle away at our self-esteem. Choosing to stay in the middle of life happens not because we don't want to move on but because of a shortage of life constructs.

In this extraordinary era of aging, it is past time to tell a new story.

THE NEW MAP OF LIFE—WOW

"To make full use of longer lives, we need to radically change our thinking about how we live our lives from beginning to end. We cannot achieve what we cannot envision," states Laura Carstensen, director of the Stanford Center on Longevity and author of the acclaimed book *A Long Bright Future.*[12]

Stanford University's Center on Longevity has taken on the challenge to blueprint longer lives and began a five-year project in 2019 for "The New Map of Life" by convening experts across numerous disciplines—health, gerontology, pediatrics, economics, investment, education, and finance. Their ultimate task will be to develop a detailed and idealized map from birth to death that maximizes the quality of life with models that can help to achieve them.

The center acknowledges that existing norms no longer work because they evolved for lives that were half as long as current ones, and the traditional three-stage life course—education, work and family, retirement—is outdated. The project includes redefining the concept of "work" and "retirement" as well as a more meaningful appreciation of the link between early and late life.

The November 2021 initial report, *The New Map of Life: 100 Years to Thrive*, unveils the new map as a long, curvy road with guideposts that include lifelong learning, working more years with more flexibility, living in longevity-ready communities, and a future where investing in centenarians delivers big returns. A scenic overlook has this signage: "Prepare to be Amazed by the Future of Aging."[13]

All in all, there's much to be enthusiastic about.

You and I may or may not be around to live in a world that fully embraces a new map of life. While we can applaud the effort to advance this new narrative that redefines what it means to be "old" and values people at different stages of life, the likelihood that this will directly benefit us is doubtful.

Culture change is a long road, often taking 40 years or more before a world embraces and supports an idea. Meanwhile, some are taking on the gauntlet of becoming "old" in every sense of the word. I did.

In a blog post titled "The Goodbye Moment to Middle Age from a Once Beautiful Woman," I described, to myself, the moment when I readjusted my personal narrative.

I am old. Shall we get on with it?

Each of us is going to have to reconceptualize our time on earth and how we want to live. You have a dimming awareness of old age, and each day we are a little less removed from middle age. I am not presumptuous enough to suggest you leave your middle age. I am not trying to inspire you to brand yourself as "old."

No one can tell you when it's time to do this. Some of us never will. Some may want to, but hate good-byes as big as this.

In her book *A Short History of Myth*, Karen Armstrong makes the point that every time humans take a step forward, they revise and update their understanding of the world. Yes, there is a new story to tell about aging. But take all the time you need to revise your understanding of yourself and call yourself "old."

HOW LONG LIES THE ROAD

In ways still unnamed, the worst global health crisis of our time has changed our perception of human life. Because of the COVID pandemic, we understand more than ever that tomorrow may not be ours to live. Life is what we have always known—fragile, hazardous, and precarious.

Uncertainty is your companion—it always has been. Ambiguity is never easy to walk into, but you did. Look back at the turns in your life that you thought were the end of the road but were actually the beginning of something. You have survived it all.

Each stage of life is a beckoning—a call to move from this to that. I still ask people the question, "When did you leave middle age behind?" Not to judge the answer but to incite an awareness that life is a tidal and seasonal movement of becoming.

So for now, do what you sometimes do when you find yourself in the middle of a curve on a gorgeous mountain parkway and see the sign "Scenic Overlook." Pull over and take the moment in stride.

Did you leave midlife behind? It matters not. Nothing matters except to understand you are not done.

WHAT MATTERS MOST

We cannot create a perfect place to start the transition into the last third of life, but we *can* start where we are. Take a little time for yourself to become more aware of how you are standing at the center of life's narrative—looking both backward and forward.

Does it matter when midlife begins and ends? Maybe not. But knowing you are passing through the midpoint is a chance to choose *how to view* the road ahead. Now *that* matters.

Admire the First Half of Your Life; Behold the Second

Name the two or three things that distinguish the first half of your life. Now, ask yourself: Can I imagine taking some wild risk in the future? Why or why not? What might that risk be?

Apprentice Yourself to a New Identity

Become a student of longevity. Look around and find people 10 or 20 years older than you whom you admire. Or remember an individual in their older years—a grandparent, great-aunt, professor, or neighbor—to whom you looked up at some point in your life. What about these individuals captured your admiration? Describe their spirit. How did they meet the challenges of aging? Now, imagine yourself and your life in your late 80s. What can you learn from them? What do you want people to say about you in your old age?

Meet Your Resistance

Begin a conversation with yourself and others by asking, "When did you leave midlife behind?" What reluctance rises up? Can you enumerate all the ways and reasons for the resistance? Can you clear a space in your mind and create a good reason for leaving or staying in middle age?

Reimagine Time

Often, we are focused on payoffs and events closest to the present time. Bring up your calendar on the screen of your phone or computer. See the moments, days, and years ahead laid out alongside one another. Take a long view of all this time ahead. Might there be more future than you imagine? It is not the time to map out anything but to tweak your perspective of time. You have time.

3

WHERE DID THE TRUTH
IN YOUR LIFE GO?

All human beings should try to learn before they die what
they are running from, and to, and why.
—James Thurber, author and playwright

I urge those of you who cling to your dream of the "good
old days" to take a nice long nap and dream on, dream on.
—Parker Palmer, *On the Brink of Everything:*
Grace, Gravity, and Getting Old

Those leaving the workforce and choosing traditional retirement
often describe their future as "time now for me." Many others want
to rewrite the rules of retirement and begin a lifestyle that includes work
or utilizing talents in some way. In both situations, "freedom" is a hall-
mark described by most I interview as "time to do what I want to do."

All the anticipation of what lies ahead is enough to make a 60-year-
old giddy. In award-winning research based on national and international surveys, Ken Dychtwald, a visionary on active aging, and Robert
Morison, researcher and senior advisor with Age Wave, define the late-
in-life American Dream. "What they want is health for life, freedom to
be one's authentic self and a chance to pursue one's purpose and personal
version of happiness."[1]

Advancing toward the winter of life does not diminish the winds of
fortune. You *could* have it all or . . . it could be worse than you expect.
Health is a wild card for everyone. Running out of money is a worry,
and at some point, the kids could take away your car keys. All this is
speculation, but what remains is not. You *do* have a chance to choose
what to do in life.

Having it all is a concept that will mean different things to different people. In any case, one thing is certain: the person in charge of finding a new life and lifestyle will be *you*—not that younger 20-, 30-, or 40-year-old you but this older you. The one looking at the shorter road ahead. The one with baggage. The one with memories of high-flying moments. The one who has been let down. The one carting around potential, dormant dreams, and a promise of time for the best life, better than ever imagined.

We must bring all we are to this moment. You are the only answer, and there is no shortage of advice on how to begin. The drums beat loudly for finding purpose, following passion, and seeking authenticity. What does all this mean and where does it leave us? What if we can't find our purpose? How do we consciously come to know and understand our character, feelings, motives, and desires so we can live an extraordinary last third of life?

In other words, how *do* we make the most of this time ahead? In this chapter, we examine how our "Me" generation grew up with cultural aspirations of self-fulfillment, alternatives for how to begin the most pressing late-in-life identity challenges, and how best to reconsider ourselves before we try to change and reemerge.

WHAT DOES FINDING THE TRUTH IN YOUR LIFE MEAN?

"I betrayed myself," said Nancy, 73. "I focused my time and attention on being a great parent, a successful entrepreneur, and a good wife. I forgot about me." Nancy led a busy, productive life. After the business was sold for a handsome profit and her two kids were on their own, she did not slow down. Instead, Nancy juggled a gig in real estate and pursued certification as a physical therapist. Now, years later, she realized that checking in with herself had gone missing, buried perhaps in high achievements and good intentions.

The purity of this honest, straightforward self-assessment held an ache. Maybe you wouldn't use that word—*betrayed*—but we've all overlooked, argued with, or failed to listen to that voice inside our head at certain times.

Nancy has lived a good life and accomplished much. But she lost herself as well. Losing touch with *what you wanted to do* with your one life is easy. We give up dreams for the practicality of a paycheck, surrender time to parenting, accommodate partners, take care of aging parents, and work our tails off in our own businesses, as decades fall on top of one another.

Most of us have diminished dreams for awfully good reasons. My college choices were based on finances, not my heart's desire. When the star-spangled job that would boost my career was offered, I couldn't take it because it involved travel; I was a single mom responsible for a five-year-old. I chose to live in the right school district rather than in a funky bohemian Atlanta neighborhood that I loved.

But while circumstances dictate much of life, what often gets in our way is us. "I have lived my life for others" is one of the most common looking-back comments from people in their mid-60s. Double-crossing oneself by putting others' needs above your own may be something you're not sorry for. And although pleasing others may have gotten you off track, you still care what people think about you.

An invite for a Friday beer from your millennial boss translates into victory in overcoming generational barriers you worked hard to earn. Mom's endorsement of us continues to carry weight, and when she's proud of us, we're over the moon. The volunteer board position at the nonprofit where they love you once gave you meaning but presently takes up way more time than you like.

Now that you have the chance to live differently, you're thinking you just want more of your life back. We go through life adjusting ourselves to others and to become more of who we want to be, all the while constrained by invisible boundaries and patterns of behavior.

I'm convinced it may be harder for us late in life to chip away at roles, break habits of a lifetime, disconnect from those who don't honor us, and smother the drive we have to "fit in" and rebel against expectations for the sheer selfishness of doing it our way. But I know we can change no matter how many years we have lived.

Will Nancy continue to sell out her future and live feeling cheated? Let's hope not.

If each of us can stand on the brink of this new life and reestablish what we want for ourselves, the future will be truly ours—fewer regrets, more joy, deeper relationships. If we pay attention to being alive, then we can live the truth of who we are and do what we are meant to do.

Finding your truth starts with conscientious attentiveness. In *Untamed*, Glennon Doyle writes how her truth was revealed in her life: "There, in the deep, I could sense something circulating inside me. It was a Knowing. I can know things down at this level that I can't on the chaotic surface. Down here, when I pose a question about my life— in words or abstract images—I sense a nudge. The nudge guides me toward the next precise thing, and then, when I silently acknowledge the nudge—it fills me."[2]

Living in accordance with our truth creates this sense of "knowing" and bumps us up closer to the bones of who we are. This benefit of understanding your truth is monumental because it is the core of self-trust, which is apt to become a little more wobbly as you age.

A person's level of confidence and self-esteem typically follows a bell curve that gradually rises during midlife, peaks, and tends to decline after age 60.[3] Research says the main reason for this pattern is that midlife is when people typically occupy the highest positions of power, status, and importance. They are working, involved in relationships, and more adventurous about trying new things. In contrast, older adults often not only lose these roles in events such as retirement but body changes, health issues and loss of loved ones continue to diminish confidence after 60.[4]

Another reason older adults lose confidence is ageism—the socially pervasive idea that you are too old to do certain activities. In fact, studies show that age stereotypes diminish in older adults the ability to perform tasks *even if they possess the proper skills.*

Research published in 2016 in the *Journal of Applied Gerontology* found that adults ages 65 and older exposed to negative stereotypes had much lower self-report confidence in their driving ability, even when they performed well on the driving test. This means that prowess in your computer technology may have less to do with your capability and more to do with beating down a belief that older individuals just can't manage those technology skills.

Confidence in oneself creates an inner strength. Finding truth is a choice you make, and *keeping your truth close* allows you to say what you mean and do what you say, take action, and live your values. You will feel it.

For Doyle, the *Knowing* "feels like warm liquid gold filling my veins and solidifying just enough to make me feel steady, certain."[5]

At no other time in your life is the courage of your convictions more important than now. Finding truth offers wisdom, flexibility, and integration to all of who we are. But one of the most important aspects of living your truth is that it creates self-trust and brings alignment and congruence, making us happier, more balanced, more powerful.

You don't create truth; you find it. And you don't have to work hard to find it.

TRUTH VERSUS PURPOSE, PASSION, AND CRYSTALS

Why aren't we using truth as the guiding principle for going forward now? Here's why. When I ask bookstore staffs for the location of the section on aging and well-being, the answer is usually, "Oh, that sounds so interesting, but we don't have a section for that." Then I am walked over to the very grand self-help section, which is right next to the spirituality section, where I am bombarded with advice on finding purpose and passion and how to open the windows to my soul. What's disheartening is that the conventional and tired textbook guidance we've all heard—find your purpose, discover your passion—is awful advice.

It is clear, both in popularity and practice, that purpose and passion work for millions of people. Still, both have severe limitations and are overrated as pathways for designing a life.

Let's unpack these two approaches to learn about their shortcomings.

Finding Purpose

A clear sense of purpose has the power to focus you on what matters most. While some advocate one purpose statement for everything you do—work, relationships, investments of time and money—others advocate that you can have as many purpose statements as you like. Some call these "mission statements."

When I interviewed Mel, 68, he told me that, yes, he did create a life purpose but couldn't exactly recall it because it was 17 years ago. Three days later an e-mail arrived from Mel informing me excitedly that he had found it. "I still like this," he said. "It's pretty good, don't you think?"

It was a nicely written purpose statement. But how well had this statement served Mel? What difference had it made in important life decisions? What excitement had resulted? In Mel's day-to-day life, had the document mattered for 17 years?

Creating a life purpose statement to guide a life has challenges for many, and the premise elicits concerns. Could it be that life purpose was one thing in your 40s, another thing in your 60s, and still another in your 90s? So we will need to keep them current? Will a messy divorce, loss of health, death of loved ones, or another kind of painful experience cause us to overhaul that purpose? Is purpose enough to make you happy, or is it the *sense of purpose* that is more important?

These elements of purpose as a life design tool are worrying:

1. If you aren't able to find your purpose, you can feel inadequate.
2. You can waste time searching for the elusive purpose.
3. A couple of statements are too narrow or broad for a life. How am I to incorporate all of who I am, who I want to be, my hopes and aspirations, into one or two statements?
4. As a rule, life statements do not drench everyday life with vigor and verve. Most are either totally boring and generic or ridiculously grandiose, rendering them unattainable.
5. Life is change. One's life purpose statement is constantly up for revision during a lifetime.
6. The Internet offers "life purpose statements you can adopt," which seems the ultimate insult for this practice.[6]

When I turned 65, I sat for hours with a pad and pen trying to write a life purpose statement. It took me three days to decide this wasn't working for me. Searching my soul and coming up empty-handed in the end disheartened me. Purposeless is not a good feeling.

While life purpose works for many people, the rest of us struggle. Many turn with success to an equally touted way—follow your passion—as their best way to go forth with meaning. In the same way we are pushed to find purpose, designing life through passion is wildly popular, sounds more arousing, but also comes with drawbacks.

Follow Your Passion

The premise of "passion" is to find something you love to do, keep learning, and work toward mastery. This will give your life the ultimate meaning.

"Follow your passion" is a phrase that has increased ninefold in English books since 1990 and has an admirable history. Before that people were saying "find your genius." According to Carol Dweck, professor of psychology at Stanford University, "That was so intimidating. It implied that only people who were really brilliant at something could succeed." Dweck explains that "'find your passion' feels more democratic, because everyone can have an interest."[7]

There are volumes of writing online and in self-help circles about the idea that we need to find our passion in order to be happy and successful. But according to Cal Newport, PhD, a best-selling author and assistant professor at Georgetown University, "It's an astonishingly bad piece of advice." In his book *So Good They Can't Ignore You*, Newport explains that "follow your passion" assumes you have a preexisting passion. Many people don't. He advocates *cultivating your passion*.[8]

Newport tells the story of Steve Jobs stumbling into Apple computer (a scheme to make a quick $1,000) at a time when he was "passionate" mainly about Eastern mysticism. When Jobs sensed that his scheme was bigger than he imagined, he poured his energy and pivoted into building a company around selling computers. He *cultivated* passion; he didn't follow it.

Passion is deeply embedded in our culture and highly prized as a life design tool. What are your passions? Are you passionate about teaching English as a second language, recycling efforts in your community, or reading to young children? Are you zealous about a hobby, an adventure sport, or living in Italy?

Following any one of these wonderful ideas will not transform a future into a life well lived. You may be halfway to happy, but you'll still have to figure out where to live, how to create deep friendships late in life, and how to stay healthy.

Passion is energy and is a motivating force, but "follow your passion" could be a disastrous oversimplification for an individual who still needs to garner an income during the last 30 years of life or who wants to extend their working years before tapping into a nest egg. Your art may not boost your checking account.

The common wisdom of "find your passion" to design a life often starts when we are asked to choose a profession or major in college. In declaring pre-med as my major, my heart sang despite earning a C- in high school chemistry. I tried hard, but I hated that class. When the college professor of my freshman biology class informed me that I would narrowly pass the lecture part of class and would definitely flunk the lab, I thought long and hard about having three more years of science-based classes. Suddenly, I didn't have an affection for pre-med so much. Could I have stuck with it and made it work? Was it truly a passion or did pre-med sound cooler than elementary education? Reality can change passions.

Despite the popularity of letting passion rule your life, these shortcomings are noteworthy:

1. If you have numerous passions, do you pick just one?
2. Can you hold on to a high level of passion and make it last? What if the process, like my having to take more chemistry and biology classes, is really, really hard?
3. If you seek income, passion may not provide.
4. If you have to do it every day, the level of passion could change.
5. Passion may *feel* good but not ultimately move you forward into well-being.

Some people have turned away from purpose and passion to more alternative ways of guiding their lives. What used to be thought of as weird and woo-woo—tarot cards, astrology, and crystals—are now going mainstream.

If you have a life purpose that works for you, wonderful. If your passion is your guide to life's meaning, great. If you find peace of mind with crystals, cards, and the stars, I'm on cloud nine. And if you can't articulate your purpose or passion in less than 30 words (and I certainly can't), there's nothing to feel bad about.

All this brings us back to suggest that *find the truth in your life* is the best way to investigate and plan a new 30-year life and live doing things daily that bring you joy and happiness. In reality, *finding your truth* can be suspect to many. After all, purpose and passion are cemented into the popular culture and sound a bit more substantial, whereas a search for truth may sound like metaphysical woo-woo.

Take a closer look. Finding truth is a position you take, a stand you make—not something written down on a piece of paper to put in a box or file. Living as true to yourself as possible trumps purpose and passion for these reasons:

1. The truth in your life functions within the whole narrative of your life—past, present, and future—and integrates all that you are and have been.
2. Truth is adaptable. All you do—anytime, anyplace—is ask, "What is my truth here?"
3. Truth integrates in totality—values, roles, desires—with no limiting boundaries.
4. Truth is definitive. Purpose and passion get you to the round-about of happy life, but truth tells you where to turn on that roundabout.
5. Truth builds trust. Trust builds confidence. Confidence builds courage, and you need both of these more than ever.
6. Finding truth and living it is exciting.

Truth is also comfortable in a way that other avenues to personal growth are not. You may lose touch, but sooner or later, you'll hunger for this companion. At the end of this chapter, you'll learn that the prerequisite to truth in your life is a high level of self-awareness that you can renew, rebuild, or meet for the very first time.

Joe and his wife, Marge, carved out successful careers working from home in adjacent rooms in their New York City apartment for more than 30 years. After Marge died of cancer, Joe, 68, set out to travel as an antidote to intense grief. It didn't work. When we met 18 months later, Joe often wept telling me about the "good life" he had with Marge.

Then one sunny day on a park bench in a coastal town in Portugal he added that he'd been reflecting on the "good life" and realized it was not one he had much say in. "She called all the shots," he shared. "I just went along."

Asked where the truth in his life had gone, Joe thought a moment, then looked at me and said, "I must have left him behind in a ditch somewhere and now I realize I have missed him so."

HELLO IN THERE. HELLO.

Conventional wisdom tells us that, no matter where we have been in life, if we want to discover more of ourselves, we should ask, "Who are you?" That may seem a chilling question. It was for me.

As a 25-year-old graduate student studying for a master's in counseling and human behavior, I was required to attend small group sessions with nine other graduate students. The philosophy was that you can't help anyone with their lives until you've put yours together . . . or mostly together.

The first session required us to answer the question "Who am I?"

I didn't hesitate with my answer: "I am the wife of Ray, the mother of a beautiful daughter, the oldest of four siblings, my mother's favorite, and a teacher." The room was so hushed I heard a janitor's rolling trash bin going down the hall.

"Is that it?" asked one of the PhD candidates. I nodded. Eyes went to the floor. I was stunned when one woman raised her head, locked eyes with me, and said, "That is such bullshit."

Full-throated sobs at traffic lights while driving home did not ease my pain. Yes, I was embarrassed. But mostly I was confused. I told the truth. Why wasn't that a good enough answer?

Perhaps you can see the trouble my peers had with the answer I gave. I listed the roles I was playing in life. These roles were part of my identity, yes, but only a small part. I had not yet discovered other aspects of me. What did I dream for myself? What did I yearn to do? What were my hopes and aspirations? My challenges to overcome? My burdens, roadblocks? What was the promise for my life?

Who knew all this? I, for sure, did not know.

Finding your truth requires self-awareness, and I had lived the bulk of my life with little of this. I followed rules and pleased others. What I wanted in life and the sum total of "me" was locked inside an unexplored interior landscape.

I owe that group tremendous gratitude for challenging me—actually they forced me—to go deep, requiring me to do the difficult work of introspection. They also insisted that I track down "me" not just for my professional success but also for my personal well-being. For the entire semester, I did not miss a meeting, and honestly, there were a couple I dreaded.

In my work with pre-retirees and retirees, I ask vital questions central to unwrapping a life and expanding insight into a future. Answers often expose a foggy, ill-defined, or unexplored self.

"No one ever asked me that before."
"I've never really thought about it."
"I'm not really sure."
"I don't know."

Are we good at being self-aware? No, we are not. Self-awareness is a critical tool that positively correlates with higher levels of overall happiness. Yet, as one study estimates, only 10 to 15 percent of people are truly self-aware.[9]

Benjamin Franklin, who began life as a poor printer, is one of the most important founding figures in American history. If you fancy an electric car, you can thank this guy, the Father of Electricity. If your Warby Parker eyeglasses have lenses with bifocals, thank him again for inventing these.

Franklin was an inventor, scientist, businessman, statesman, and philosopher. By the age of 42, he became the richest man in Pennsylvania. He left us with many meaningful life lessons. "Virtue is more valuable than gold." "Honesty is the best policy." "Hide not your talents." "Early to bed, early to rise makes a man healthy, wealthy, and wise."

But Ben Franklin missed the mark on one life-changing message. In his *Poor Richard's Almanack*,[10] he observed the great difficulty of knowing one's self: "There are three things extremely hard—steel, a diamond and to know one's self."

Take heart. This is terrible advice. To know yourself—it's actually not that hard.

THE TASK OF TRUTH FINDING

Self-awareness is not something that you intensely focus on every moment of every day. It's not even an annual requirement for living well. Instead, self-awareness becomes woven into the fabric of who you are and emerges at different points, depending on the situation. In my graduate school example, I needed the credit for the group experience so that my advisor would not hit the ceiling. I also was overdue for some personal identity work.

When in our 60s, we are usually getting ready to step out of something known into something unknown. Life gives us a transition, so we need more self-awareness than usual. Finding truth is using your highest level of self-awareness as a guiding force to navigate your way ahead.

On July 7, 2012, a group of neuroscientists convening at Cambridge University signed a document officially declaring that non-human animals, "including all mammals and birds, and many other creatures including octopuses," are conscious. Humans are more than just conscious; they are also self-aware.[11]

To be conscious is to think; to be self-aware is to realize that you are a thinking being and to *think about what you are thinking*. Sound amusing? Some agree. You may find self-awareness admirable, or you may find it self-indulgent navel gazing.

But becoming *self-aware* is a way to gain personal insights. You may already have a true vision of yourself, but if a truer vision is possible, I wouldn't call that a bunch of hooey.

What exactly is self-awareness and where does it fall on the continuum of truth finding? The American Psychological Association defines self-awareness theory as "the consequences of focusing attention on the self,"[12] which is certainly not mind-bending. Self-awareness means having a deep understanding of one's emotions, strengths, weaknesses, needs, and drives.

Self-awareness is one of the most important psychological traits you can develop within yourself for life. Its benefits extend to everything—whether it's managing your emotions in conflict or being realistic on what you can accomplish. Every step of the way, self-awareness is necessary to make it happen. People with strong self-awareness are honest—with themselves and with others.

Unfortunately, we make light of this whole *knowing ourselves* business. On T-shirts, Etsy rings, face masks, iron-on patches, embroidered caps, and tattoos, you see "Nosce te ipsum"—the Latin phrase for "know thyself." Wayfair sells a "Know Thyself" large poster for $89 with free shipping.

You are as likely to see the advice "Know Thyself" in serious philosophy textbooks and well-grounded research studies as you are in wacky self-help books. But if we take the importance of trying to live our best life in the next 30 years seriously, it's not an option.

Self-awareness theory, developed by Duval and Wicklund in their 1972 landmark book, *A Theory of Objective Self Awareness*, has been around for several decades, giving researchers plenty of opportunity to test its soundness. Psychologist Daniel Goleman helped to popularize emotional intelligence, calling "self-awareness" the foundation of emotional intelligence.

Here's what you need to know:

1. **You are not born self-aware.** Researchers suggest that children progress through a series of levels of self-awareness between birth and age 4 or 5.[13]
2. **Self-awareness has big benefits.** When we see ourselves clearly, we build self-trust. We make sounder decisions, build stronger relationships, and communicate more effectively.
3. **Self-awareness isn't one truth.** It's a delicate weave of experiences, values, desires, and expectations.
4. **Self-awareness is not going to make you whole or fix your life.** Change through action based on truth that aligns with values changes lives for the better. Self-awareness alone does not.
5. **We make a conscious choice to become self-aware.** It's like turning the throttle on an electric bike, which, in turn, creates a kind of kick into a more powerful ride.

6. **You can improve your self-awareness.** The good news is that the more you practice self-awareness and work toward it, the easier it becomes.

Just as we've heard a lot about "purpose" and "passion" as strategies for a fulfilling life, we've also heard of the "authentic self" or the "true self." It may seem that we should jump into the hot bed of self-awareness asking, "Who am I?"

That would be a faulty way to begin.

A MATTER OF IDENTITIES

The truth in your life is not going to be found in the idea of only one "self." Just think about all the ways you have changed throughout your lifetime. Most of us have multiple perspectives on who we are. As we move forward in life, there are some parts of us we want to keep and others we might want to lose.

What did you love about your 30-year-old self? What part of your 16-year-old self have you lost? What do you want to be sure to take with you as you find your 70-year-old self?

To find one's truth, the concept of "possible selves" needs to be explored. This model asserts we are not "one true" self but many selves and that those identities exist not only in the past and present but also, and most importantly, in the future.

On the faculty of Harvard and professor of organizational behavior at INSEAD, an international business school located in Fontainebleau, France, Herminia Ibarra reveals, "We all carry around, in our hearts and minds, a whole cast of characters, including the selves we hope to become, think we should become or even fear becoming in the future."[14]

"Who am I?" according to Ibarra is the wrong question to ask. Instead, she invites answers to:

Who is the self I might become next?
Who do I think I should be?
Who do I hope to become?

Who do I fear becoming?
What do I risk losing in the process?

Most of us have multiple perspectives on who we are. Life circumstances often result in identities we never wanted for ourselves. Many never asked to be a widow/widower, divorced, unemployed, or a cancer survivor. In contrast, we often relish identities hard-won through achievement as highly successful executives, winning entrepreneurs, renowned surgeons, great teachers, and respected community leaders.

Sometimes identities are part luck or timing. You're big-time lucky if you are born in the United States, birth a healthy child in your 40s, or receive wealth from a trust fund.

We latch onto identities because they help us define and shape who we think we are. We create identities in the process of living and trade selves as we grow up and change. The truth in your life is part of all these identities.

The deepest part of our sense of self is based on a foundation of variables. What constitutes our sense of self/selves is found in:

- abilities/disabilities (funny, shy, smart, bad at math, a slow reader, etc.);
- affiliations (e.g., book club, golf, volunteer);
- family relationships (e.g., mother/father, sister/brother, partner/spouse, etc.);
- hobbies (e.g., musician, singing, athlete, etc.);
- occupation(s) (e.g., lawyer, farmer, teacher, electrician, business owner, etc.);
- spirituality (e.g., Catholic/Christian, Buddhist, etc.); and
- notable attributes (e.g., hardworking, honest, dishonest, attractive, lazy).

You will continue to be many selves in the future. Who you want to be and how you want to live at 60, 70, and 80 starts with slowing into a discovery of who you were, meeting that person you have become, then moving forward to who you want to be.

If we want to truly understand ourselves now—and we should want to—we must grow into a wisdom of ourselves not by an intense academic study of personality and identity, but through taking a joyful trek inside ourselves. In part II, the Four Portals guide you to a new life, possibly an extraordinary one. Each Portal demands self-awareness and truth. At this critical juncture in our lives, let us hold on to our curiosity, our desire to seek, our yearning to know everything we can about ourselves.

I've met and worked with many people who show me the results of this journey. Whether beginning, in the middle, or nearing the end of the transition of life after retirement, they demand much of themselves and tackle change with a mindset of curiosity and growth, commitment to moving forward, self-honesty, high aspirations, and clarity of confidence.

IMPROVING OURSELVES TO DEATH

These days, health clubs are filled to capacity with sweating bodies, yet not long ago the kingdom of self-improvement was packed with pop-psychology. The 1970s was the golden age of introspection, perfect for baby boomers who would begin the sexual revolution and skyrocket divorce rates. The watchword was *change*—in women's rights, gay rights, civil rights, and music. This generation's playbook of cultural shifts included aspirations of "self-realization" and "self-fulfillment." Ascribing high importance to these created a heyday for teachable moments and stoked a full-blown industry of self-improvement.

The majestic landscape of Big Sur surrounds Esalen, an institute founded with the intention of promoting "human potential." More than a hippie commune, this was a respite for anyone in search of a greater understanding of oneself in the early 1970s. Perhaps the most successful self-improvement guru ever, Tony Robbins's rise to the top of the heap started in the 1980s and awakened thousands to their full potential as they literally and figuratively walked through fire in the 1990s. Currently, you can bypass that experience and choose a life coach, master class, book, online course, or app.

Self-improvement often has a substantial psychological basis. The word *psychology* literally means the "study of the soul" with names you easily recognize as legendary contributors to the field—Freud, Maslow,

Erikson. I cut my teeth in graduate school not in the psychology department but in the counseling program, where more value was placed on helping someone by listening rather than analyzing them. Still, the prevailing and popular theories in psychology influenced the counseling curriculum, and I leaped into the personal improvement movement just like some of you.

Most of us recall the engaging discourse of transactional analysis in one of the four life positions—"I'm Okay, You're Okay." Transactional analysis (TA) was a kind of movement used in business as well as personal development and elevated cocktail party talk to a tier above casual conversation that was mostly accepted with amusement. TA was also used in conflict resolution to channel effective communication. Like all pop-psychology, it didn't always work. I remember being met with a chilly reception when I said "I'm Okay, You're Not Okay" to my then husband in the middle of an argument.

Also in the 1980s was Albert Ellis's rational emotive behavioral therapy (REBT), another significant but less well-known contribution to popular self-improvement ideas. Ellis commanded attention across much of the discipline with loud, colorful language; a provocative, blunt approach; and Friday night seminars. Labeled a "maverick," Dr. Ellis would invite members of the audience onstage and skillfully guide the volunteer through the steps of using REBT to think, feel, and behave in a less distressing and more rational way. As an audience member in a packed local theater in Akron, Ohio, I recall the experience as lively, intimate, and too wild for my young budding self. I got home at 3 a.m., received credit in my course work, and, no, I did not go onstage.

Ellis's theories are considered today as the foundation of cognitive-behavioral therapies. The American Psychological Association named him the second most influential psychologist of the 20th century behind only Carl Rogers. Rogers was big into self-actualization and believed that all human beings sought to fulfill one's potential and achieve the highest level of "human-beingness" we can. If someone has ever annoyed you with the phrase "What I hear you saying is . . . "—that's part of Rogers's reflective listening technique.

Today the self-improvement field continues to boom. Statistics reported by MarketResearch.com state that though the "personal growth" market, like many others, took a hit in 2020 due to the pandemic and recession, a 7.7 percent rebound was estimated in 2021, to $11.3 billion. The forecast is 6.0 percent average annual growth to $14.0 billion by 2025.[15]

With a focus on making life better, recognizable personalities and their best-selling books influenced us through the past 40 years and still do:

- Tony Robbins—*Awaken the Giant Within*
- Stephen Covey—*The Seven Habits of Highly Effective People*
- Barbara Sher—*Wishcraft: How to Get What You Really Want*
- Richard Carlson—*Don't Sweat the Small Stuff and It's All Small Stuff*
- Susan Jeffers—*Feel the Fear and Do It Anyway*
- Julie Cameron—*The Artist's Way: A Spiritual Path to Higher Creativity*
- Glennon Doyle—*Untamed*
- Dalai Lama—*The Book of Joy*

Are we self-improvement obsessed? Sometimes it seems that way. It's not enough just to feel you'd like to live a life that still matters; we require concrete advice. The most common self-improvement areas are fitness and beauty, finding purpose, acquiring more skills for success, improving personal relationships, and doing more with our lives. This decade's break-out self-help star is queen of clean, Marie Kondo, who motivates people to declutter and to ask if the item in question "sparks joy." In this sense, we organize our stuff to become less overwhelmed and, by extension, change our lives for the better.

There's little doubt you can improve life by losing weight, tidying up, or even not giving a f*ck. Living a good life using this counterintuitive approach, according to superstar blogger and author Mark Manson, is the answer. *The Subtle Art of Not Giving a F+ck* has sold more than six million copies and is for some an inspiring book about purpose cleverly disguised in vulgarity and doom.

But the goal in your 60s, 70s, and 80s is to make the *rest of your life chock-full of your ideas*. This is a bigger self-improvement project than cleaning out your closet or starting a social media diet. Personal growth late in life poses unique questions. Is there such a thing as the dawn of a new, improved "me" at my age? What are the real chances life can be extraordinary in our final chapters? What are we looking for now that's different than what we looked for when we were younger?

Having already lived the bulk of our lives, efforts to improve ourselves and our lives are not unfamiliar. But the idea that at our age we are *good to go* and will be fine in the years ahead without much thought to a looming transition comes with a danger sign. Tending to your psychological portfolio and working toward well-being after the "sugar rush" of retirement is critical for high levels of happiness.

A new 30-year-plus life that holds a bright future requires focus and new tools if we are to glide through the transition ahead. We are well experienced with transitions. Life in retirement involves an emotionally painful time where activity shifts and identity wobbles, demanding full attention to big questions:

- How ought I live?
- How do I fit into the world?
- What should I do to have a happy, fulfilling, and meaningful life?

Sounds and feels daunting. The strategies of purpose and passion, while flawed, are concerned with the goal of helping you live a well-lived life. Who doesn't want that?

We all want that. But trying to narrow down your purpose or identify passion as a precursor to actionable living can get you nowhere. While these concepts work for many people, they won't necessarily afford *you* the best way to move forward.

Is there a better way? There is. Forget your purpose; find your truth. Ignore the search for a passion to center your life; find your truth. Don't write a purpose statement, narrow your passions, or mind-map your future life. Find your truth.

How *do* you find your truth? Return time to yourself, rediscover all of the selves you bring to the threshold of launching into an unknown of 30-plus years, and become the spokesperson for your life. Then, with clarity and conviction, you can establish clear horizons in this new way to grow old.

There is a truth inside you. That truth has a voice. It is your best guide.

WHAT MATTERS MOST

As you age, an important goal is to build a stronger and grander version of yourself. Self-knowledge and self-improvement are useful tools for creating this new story. That's the insider work of finding your truth. But, also, be aware of what goes on around you.

Ageism in the workforce has been illegal since the Age Discrimination Employment Act of 1967, yet it remains prevalent. We also face ageism outside of the workplace—your family, the grocery clerk, members of the book club or rotary, and your best friend all have attitudes about aging.

Behold Aging Advice Everywhere

Recently I twisted my ankle playing Nerf guns with the grandkids. Hearing how I did this, the orthopedic surgeon never said a word, but my friends did. Most e-mails and conversations had little to do with well wishes for recovery, but everything to do with age. "You are a grandmother. Only do slow things." "Maybe your Nerf gun days are over." Even people who love you have strong beliefs about aging, and they'll willingly share these beliefs.

How are you experiencing ageism in your life? Who is overemphasizing your age and choices? How might this influence how you're seeing yourself?

Self-Inquiry Experiment with an Invisible Companion

If you feel out of touch with yourself or would like to test out your self-awareness, do this: Take 10 minutes a day for the next five days. In a quiet spot, ask how things are going for you. What's working today? What's not? What's working in your life? What's not?

I have a bluebird who is my companion in self-inquiry. He sits on my shoulder and asks, "How ya doin', Barbara?" I'm serious. Yes, he's invisible, but this bluebird is a mighty friend I created to ask me important questions. Sometimes he's invited; other times he just appears. You might want to invent yourself a companion if you don't want to go it alone.

Stop Fooling Yourself

Use these probes to scrutinize and learn more about yourself: When in life have you been most confident? When did you not listen to yourself and wish you had? Are you willing to fail at something at this late stage of life?

4

REDEFINING WORK
IN RETIREMENT

I have been impressed with the urgency of doing. Knowing is not enough; we must apply. Being willing is not
enough; we must do.

—Leonardo da Vinci

When I stand before God at the end of my life, I would
hope that I would not have a single bit of talent left and
could say, I used everything you gave me.

—Erma Bombeck

My father lived to be 96 with a sound mind and a history of work
unique to his generation. As a young man in his 20s, he worked
in the mines for five years in his hometown in eastern Kentucky, traveling each day two miles underground to dynamite a shelf of coal in his
"room." With a pickaxe and a shovel, he filled as many coal cars as he
could. The small room was three feet high; he worked on his knees.

Working in the mines was the best work around to provide a living. He hated it.

So like thousands of Kentuckians he migrated with his family to
Ohio, where work on a Frigidaire assembly line beckoned. After 35
years and rarely missing a day of work, he retired with a plaque and a
pension.

His "work" in retirement was two large gardens—one extending
the full perimeter of the backyard in Ohio and the other on a couple
of acres in a holler adjacent to the white-framed house built by the coal
company where he grew up. Photos of an old man, trim and smiling in

a dirty white T-shirt and dirtier pants under a weeping willow, remind me of afternoons he zigzagged a push lawnmower on a hillside, stopping often to remove his cap and wipe the sweat off his forehead with a handkerchief from his back pocket.

He liked to try new things, like growing grapes on the arbor he built weaving down the center of a plowed field. That didn't work. But there was always a bumper crop of zucchinis and multitudes of colorful zinnias.

Years later, on a fall afternoon visit to his nursing home, I sat by his wheelchair watching the World Series and talking baseball. During the commercial, Daddy changed the subject.

"Barbara, do you have a car?"

"Yes. Why?"

"I need a job. Could you drive me around and see what I can find?"

"Daddy, why do you need a job?"

"Well, I think I might be running out of money. Anyway, I like to work. I miss it."

"You are 96 years old. Who do you think would hire you?"

"Barbara, I'm a good worker. Someone would hire me."

What we think about ourselves matters. That afternoon my dad didn't see himself as elderly, shaky on his feet, or impaired with arthritis that gnarled his fingers. Through the lens of work, he regarded himself as someone who could be productive and add value—a good worker.

Work—the intentional commitment of time and talent whether paid or unpaid—shows us what we are capable of being. I call the shape of earnest, wholehearted engagement the act of doing "work in retirement." When this work is chosen, it is not a job.

Work is a fabric of our lives. Work satisfies the drive to engage and pays dividends in identity, social interaction, health, worth, and financial security. As more of us face longer years ahead, the implications of work *in* retirement take on greater significance.

Work matters. In the last third of life, work is a mindset, not a job. And "work" in retirement is on every boomer's mind. *Do I want to work? Do I need to work? What will I do? What do I want to do?*

THE SEARCH FOR WHO KNOWS WHAT

There is no easy way to say this: retirement can be one of the most disappointing times in your life.

Our "retirement lives" are now an experiment we are all participating in—one with unexpected and sometimes worrisome outcomes. Accomplished and challenged, we are not. Over half of today's retirees say they are "bored and restless."[1] We can feel lonely and isolated and struggle to be relevant.

Whiz! Bang! Retired! And all of a sudden, we sit on the sidelines watching life go by while filling calendars with activities that make us "busier than ever" yet far from fulfilled. Often, we are simply confused.

"I'm thinking I should take piano lessons," said Harold, 73. "We're supposed to learn new things in retirement, aren't we? That's what I heard."

The changeover—from working to not working—is seen as an easy move from one life box to another. But in fact, retirement is a major disruptor. Repeat: *retirement is a major disruptor.* The possibilities of becoming bewildered, muddled, dazed, and perplexed are foreboding tones as we enter the "golden years."

Since life after a career covers a full third of life, this looming batch of misery should concern us. What many have failed to understand is that happiness in later life is jeopardized as retirees experience the tension between freedom, a sense of social connectedness, and personal fulfillment.

"For many people, retirement is supposed to be the ultimate goal and reward after a lifetime of work. Yet for some, it can be incredibly disappointing, frustrating, intimidating, and even more overwhelming than starting a career," states Michelle Silver, assistant professor in the Department of Sociology at the University of Toronto. In her book *Retirement and Its Discontents: Why We Won't Stop Working, Even If We Can,* Silver writes about the dissatisfaction associated with retirement as a sentiment that has been ignored and glossed over.[2]

Nothing gives a more chilling picture of casualties than the comment from a reader made to Arthur Brooks, a contributing writer at *The Atlantic,* professor of management practice at the Harvard Business

School, and host of the podcast *The Art of Happiness with Arthur Brooks*: "Since I quit working, I feel like a stranger to myself."

Losing a sense of oneself is an understandable side effect in a retiree's hunt for a good life, especially when Brooks characterizes it as a search for—"well, they're not quite sure what." In a transition that stirs up high needs to create structure and confidence and find a new identity, retirement is a hell of a time to *not* know what we want or are looking for.

While no period is better suited to inner growth and development than retirement, we typically do not return to the idea that "work" is what is now crucial for future health and happiness. Yet it is just that. While there is joy in freedom *from* work, *work* provides more of what we need—a solid sense of self, possible financial returns, structure, and even excitement. The chance now—maybe for the first time in your life—is to choose what your work will be and experience the outcomes with elation and high regard.

What could "work *in* retirement" be for you? There are a thousand good ways to live productively until age 100, and throughout this chapter, you'll see examples of how others work *in* retirement. (Figuring out your "work in retirement" as well as the big-picture look at retirees at work is explored in chapter 7, "Yield.")

For every pre-retiree or retiree, the takeaway is this: throwing away "work" as you create your life ahead is neither self-enhancing nor smart. Individuals who fail to redefine "work" and include it as part of the essential platform for daily living in retirement face a life crisis and gamble on future well-being.

We are at the beginning—just the beginning—of learning how to successfully journey and live to age 100. What we now know about a personal passage to a fulfilling retirement is more than we've ever known. Through my coaching work and in more than 150 interviews with pre-retirees and retirees, many stories unfolded into a larger narrative where future "work" was viewed negatively and not a good fit for the carefree retirement life. Work was often seen as a competitor of newfound freedom.

Yet, for a well-lived life, work and play as equal partners is perhaps a better vision to hold in your mind.

FISH OUT OF WATER

The bobbing bait looks good to the hungry fish. He takes the bait, and he's hooked.

Similarly, the lure of retirement as a well-deserved rest, the great payoff, and the "best time in life" hooks us. Freedom promises idle days spent traveling, golfing, and puttering around the house. But with an estimated "fifty trillion hours of leisure to fill,"[3] retirement can be brutal.

Don't get me wrong. If you work every day for most of your life and then one day, you don't work at all, you're likely going to feel like the luckiest person alive. Most do—but only for a little while.

In a short time, the positive aspects of retirement—freedom and leisure—can lose their glow. When a person "retires" and therefore no longer participates in paid employment, they frequently take one of three possible paths:

1. The Honeymoon Path is characterized by acting as if one is on vacation indefinitely. Men and women become busy doing many leisure activities they never had time for previously, especially travel. On this path, retirement can be a bit of a showoff with journeys scheduled hither and yon. Others use time for ordinary things such as dental work, cleaning out the garage, or sorting photos.

2. The Modification Path is adopted by those who continue to have a full and active path similar to what they were doing with alterations in time and responsibilities. They could also try something new like turning a hobby into a business. These individuals easily establish comfortable schedules soon after retirement.

3. The Rest and Relaxation Path after retirement is a period with a definite turn away from work but with a sense of wanting to do "something" in the future. People who have had busy careers with limited time to themselves frequently choose to see this time as a gap year and a sabbatical. Others relax into an agenda of waiting for "what's next" to come along, which then turns into a lifestyle of just that—waiting.

These paths are temporary stopovers, rarely providing the essential scaffolding and new grounding for a productive long life of well-being. How long does this period last? Not long. Research shows, on average, it's less than two years.

When retirees become disenchanted with this stage of life, they battle the feeling that something is missing in their lives. Days lingering with this "new normal" wear on them. Retirement guilt can result. Some experts recommend the way to overcome this is to think of your retirement as an act of generosity that will give a younger person a chance to make a mark. Good for them! Meanwhile, disappointed and confused, many retirees keep trying to find meaning in the art of doing nothing.

As the emotional high of retiring wears off and feels less exciting, retirees settle into an uncomfortable place where past identity begins to disappear, but a new one has not yet been established—where the security of the past is left, but the success of the future remains unknown.

Then, retirement may be viewed as a "monster curveball"—a term used by Bruce Feiler in his book *Life Is in the Transitions: Mastering Change at Any Age.* "You enter one place, go through an elaborate squiggle, then come out in another," he writes, noting that life does not just extinguish itself at the end of the squiggle.[4]

The new retirement strategy for working in your 60s, 70s, 80s, and beyond is blending *some kind of work* and leisure. While there is nothing wrong with enjoying freedom, a long life ahead demands more.

FOR THE LOVE OF WORK

In 1977, "Take This Job and Shove It" was a huge hit for Johnny Paycheck, hitting number one on the country charts for two weeks, then spending 18 weeks on the charts. The song, written by David Allan Coe, was immediately something that every working person could connect with. It was a song about a man who worked hard at a job for a long time without much recognition or reward.

It was Paycheck's only number-one hit.

The phrase became popular. Today a revolution is sweeping America of front lines of people fed up with unfulfilling jobs and who are rethinking careers. *Free Agent Nation: The Future of Working for Yourself*, an oldie but goodie by best-selling author Daniel Pink, maps the landscape of a new work model.

But many people definitely do not love work. In fact, if they had the chance, they'd like work to be erased from their lives. The resistance is clear; the objections potent.

When I talk to clients about "working" in retirement, reactions are swift and snappy:

I do not like that word.
I'm trying to get far away from work.
You have got to be kidding. No way do I want to work after I retire.
When you tell me I need to keep working after 65, I don't even want to listen to you, Barbara.
I don't need to work. I have enough money.

It took me a while to understand the intensity against working. I have always enjoyed my work—except for one summer job as a 16-year-old salesperson in women's apparel at an Elder Beerman store in Dayton, Ohio. Mr. Beerman, CEO, once spotted me standing next to the sweaters on one of his random walkabouts when there were few customers in the store and none in my department.

"Straighten those sweaters," he said, pointing to the perfect stacks I had just finished. "Always look busy," Mr. B barked. "And the next time I see you, you will look busy." I didn't like that job.

Today a whole lot of people are desperately unhappy at work. They have overbearing, petty, or incompetent bosses. They have incompetent coworkers. They are overworked and underpaid. They are tired. They receive no recognition, are unable to grow a career, and become demoralized in a culture of pressure to achieve at all costs.

Research reaffirms work is a place of disconnectedness and misery. Most employees are not engaged or are actively disengaged. Gallup's *State of the Global Workplace: 2021 Report* identified global employee engagement of 20 to 34 percent in the United States and Canada.[5]

Pandemic working conditions pushed worker discontentment into a new orbit. For millions, the opportunity to remap priorities in the work-life equation incited action: they quit their jobs. "Some describe a long-simmering but barely tolerable state of discontent in which the pandemic abruptly cranked up the heat, making the situation 'jump or boil,'" writes Karla L. Miller, columnist for the *Washington Post*.[6]

The Great Resignation, also known as the Big Quit, is the trend of high employee turnover after the COVID-19 pandemic. More than 4.4 million workers quit their jobs voluntarily in September 2021, up from 4.3 million in August.[7] Gallup data show it's not an industry, role, or pay issue. It's a workplace issue. The highest quit rate is among not engaged and actively disengaged workers.[8]

We might want to think these large numbers of unhappy people must be the ones in cubicles doing boring work with low salaries and living with their parents. Not so. Resignation rates are highest among midcareer employees.[9]

Disappointing work experiences are not easy to overcome. If your experience with work has not provided fulfillment, let alone much happiness, it is easy to understand that the idea of "work" as an essential part of life after retirement makes you queasy.

But this is the situation: a life worth living has to be built on something more substantial than the prospect of 30 years of leisure. While trying to escape numbing corporate politics or dull-as-dishwater work, we can eliminate work from retirement life only to find we become wedged into accepting much less from ourselves than we might be capable of.

Ultimately, in our final decades, we settle for much less than life offers. We don't have to let this happen.

YOUR WORK, YOUR WAY

The best possible future for a thriving life is based on five distinct factors of well-being. These elements are the currency of a life that matters and describe aspects of our lives that we can do something about. The five broad categories are: career, social, financial, physical, and community. According to a Gallup study, while 66 percent of people do well in at least one area, only 7 percent are thriving in all five.[10]

Career is arguably the most essential of the five elements of well-being.[11] If you don't have the opportunity to regularly do something you enjoy or get paid to do, the odds of your having high well-being in other areas diminishes rapidly. People with high career well-being are more than twice as likely to be thriving in their lives overall. Work shapes identity and well-being. Work is a choice. For some 60-year-olds, that means a paycheck for the very first time.

Kelly, an attractive, petite blonde, is an introvert by nature. As a dutiful corporate wife for 30 years, she handled the intricacies of 18 moves, often settling her family in faraway places like Africa and India. A long stint in California finally gave her the time to be active in her community, where she took charge of a huge nonprofit.

Now 61 and divorced, Kelly is building her concierge business in Nashville. The financial rewards are part necessity, but just as important is the contribution to her identity. Kelly's father always introduces his children by way of their work. "This is Kyra [Kelly's sister]. She runs her own health-care business in Phoenix." "This is Robert. He's an attorney." When it comes time to introduce Kelly, he says, "This is Kelly. She's the pretty one." Now that she's a business owner, will Kelly's father introduce her differently? "Doesn't matter," says Kelly with a twinkle in her eyes. "I know he loves me and right now having my work has other advantages. Out on the dating circuit, the men I meet can spend a good 20 minutes telling me about their work. Now I can too."

Work is not just about being fearlessly ambitious, making money, or merely pumping up a fragile self. A part-time job that *you sorta like* to make a little money could be your best choice. When money isn't a motivator, some are driven by a leisurely pursuit important to them.

In his book *Master Class: Living Longer, Stronger and Happier*, author Peter Spiers encourages retirees to use hobbies as a building block to successful aging and cognitive health. Genealogy is currently the second most popular hobby in the United States.

After a long successful career as a health-care executive in New York City, Dennis Kord traces his family history with a sense of "duty." His parents, Czechoslovak Jews, had almost all their family members murdered in the Holocaust. Who these murdered people were or even their names were never discussed as he grew up. Dennis only knew that his mother and his father's sister were slave laborers in Auschwitz-Birkenau and were rescued by the Swedish Red Cross in 1944. He also found out that his father walked to Russia as a 14-year-old and eventually joined the Czechoslovak Army in the Soviet Union.

"My goal is to reconstruct the world that they came from and, most importantly, find the name of each person and child who was killed," he told me. "The Bible exhorts the Jewish people to remember [*zahor*], and I feel that it is my duty to attach names to all those who died nameless."

For the past seven years, but especially since the beginning of the pandemic, Dennis spends six or more hours a day using the many online databases and the assistance of various archives in Slovakia and other countries. He has assembled the names of more than 2,000 extended family members, stretching back to the 18th century, and learned about the details of their lives and where they lived.

"All of these people, some of whom even lived a 10-minute drive from us in New York, were people I never knew existed," he said. "Finally, I can tell myself the story of my family."

Work in retirement life is often fluid with an ebb and flow due to changing circumstances, natural endings, or waning interests. These retirees have work that currently aligns with the time they wish to spend, needs, or customer demand:

- Jen, 74, tall and athletic with a rugged can-do spirit, would love to travel but instead spends her time caring for Ted, her husband of 25 years, who was diagnosed with Parkinson's 12 years ago. "It's what I do for now," she says. "Wouldn't have it any other way."

- Dee Dee, 68, lost her husband 15 years ago, and that ended a sailing life aboard their 50-foot trimaran where she was the go-to weather person. Today, Dee Dee volunteers her financial talents to the AARP Foundation Tax-Aide Program, which provides tax assistance free of charge to taxpayers who are 50 or older or who have low to moderate income. This work requires training and IRS certification. "That test is hard!" she said. Her work is seasonal—January through April 15.

- Beverly, 76, mother of three and devoted grandmother of two, revived her artistic endeavors during COVID, created a website, and now has an Instagram following. Painting on heavyweight paper and manipulating it to create multidimensional, many-layered surfaces creates art that people want to buy. "I receive awesome comments, and I am selling!" she writes.

While stories of late-blooming entrepreneurs, octogenarians pushing physical boundaries, and 90-year-old love birds create headlines for what it means to live longer, you and I need to focus on a more surefooted path of well-being and add work to life. Unpaid and meaningful perhaps. How about a paid side hustle? Even better if finances need bolstering.

One person who describes his retirement as "feeling like a teenager with a little money in my pocket" prompts us to remember those times. That was then. This is now—a time in life that requires much more loose change than we may ever have imagined.

IT'S THE MONEY, HONEY

"You can be young without money; you can't be old without it," wrote Tennessee Williams.

Some people will want to choose an intentional commitment to an activity that produces income. Retirement is the biggest purchase of a lifetime. Retirement costs far more than all of life's other big-ticket items—buying a home, raising a child, or paying for college. The average "cost" of retirement is over $1,000,000.[12] The costs keep going up, not only with inflation but also with longevity.

We can bolster retirement funds after 65 by working longer, creating a phased retirement, finding part-time or seasonal work, or becoming entrepreneurial with our interests and hobbies. Why work for money? Foremost because financial stress can have negative consequences on your health, which is the ultimate retirement wild card and we all know it. New research from Merrill Lynch, conducted in partnership with Age Wave, found that 81 percent of retirees cite health as the most important ingredient to a happy retirement.

Facing up to money issues in advancing years preserves not only our health but builds self-esteem as we continue to build a life. Boomers' wealth is 12 times greater compared to millennials. Are we boomers really worried about going broke? Yes, we are.

At the top of the list of retirement concerns is running out of money, maintaining their lifestyle, and rising health-care expenses. The Center for Retirement Research at Boston College estimates that half of the households that are age 65-plus are at risk of being unable to maintain their standard of living in retirement. Already the consequences are happening. A growing concern is the bankruptcy rate for 65-plus households, which has tripled over the past three decades. People age 65-plus now account for over 12 percent of all bankruptcy filers, a dramatic rise from 2.1 percent in 1992.[13]

Did we do something wrong? So, okay, we could have saved more money. It's also true, according to some financial experts, that there is no 40-year career that will fund a 30-year retirement.

Assumptions about life expectancy have dramatically changed retirement strategies. A growing number of financial advisors are now creating financial plans that keep assets in place until at least age 100. So those charts with the red line swoop indicating you are going to be out of money at age 90 aren't going to look good anymore.

But even with retirement planning, many are caught between a now longer-than-expected lifetime and the fear of outliving our savings. We are stressed.

We should talk about this, but we aren't. Nearly half of retirees say they don't discuss retirement savings, investment, or finances with close family or friends. This is a personal matter, say 92 percent of Americans, and many are more comfortable talking about their end of life than about finances.[14]

Nest eggs go poof in a variety of ways—cost of living increases, housing needs, health care, and so on. Years ago, I had an annual meeting with our financial advisor, Donna Jordan, CEO of Money Professionals in Pensacola. She said, "Barbara, you should be fine." Then she paused for what I thought was a long time before she added, "Unless something unexpected happens."

"Whoa. Like what would that be?"

"That would be like, now you are raising your grandchildren, for example."

I didn't have grandchildren then, so my immediate thought was "Who's doing that?" According to Lori Bitter, author of *The Grandparent Economy: How Baby Boomers Are Bridging the Generation Gap*, 2.7 million grandparents are raising grandkids. This growing number of "grandfamilies" is happening because of substance abuse, the death of a grandchild's parent, and extended military deployment.

I am now a grandparent, and I can wax on about how that experience enriches my life. Even if we aren't raising them, we are spending more time with grandkids than previous generations, and this is good. Sixty percent of us are also spending down our retirement savings on them. Hate to say it, but I love to see my two grandchildren whiz around on those pricey Segway hovershoes. Sounds crazy even as I write it.

As parents, many boomers are also financially supporting their adult kids. More than 7 out of 10 parents say they put their children's interests ahead of their own, according to a 2018 Merrill Lynch–Age Wave study.[15] These parents are spending twice as much on adult children (those between the ages of 18 and 34) as they are contributing to their own retirement accounts. For many, generosity extends to the need to help parents or siblings who have their own money struggles.

Obviously too much generosity isn't a good long-term strategy, but that's a decision each of us has to make.

Retirement also holds unexpected things that can throw you for a loop—hurricanes, wildfires, a health crisis—and that are just around the corner. And pension dumping is on the rise. Married couples now wanting different things in retirement can implode a financial plan. (We cover this in chapter 8.)

There's plenty of good resources with advice for financial planning in retirement. This book is not one of them. However, if financial security is a concern of yours, one of the best course corrections is keeping paid work in retirement. The benefits of work that we've already covered can extend to more financial security and alleviate stress.

A MORE FITTING LEXICON

Being "retired" used to mean you stopped working. Not anymore. What exactly does it mean?

Some people bristle at the word "retirement." In his blog post "Why Retirement Is a Dirty Word," Michael Hyatt, author and expert in leadership development, called the idea of looking for fulfillment in the pastures and not in work as "a way to murder your heart."[16] Others grin at the word "retirement" and count down to its beginning—"one year, 3 days and 45 minutes."

We live in contradictory times, and boomers made it so. About half of the massive boomer generation are now "retired." As boomers head into retirement in droves with a growing interest in pickle ball and a penchant for travel, many will also seek paid work as part of this stage of life, marking a deviation from the traditional concept. Others will make a slow departure from the world of work for a variety of reasons—financial gain, love of work, or an unreadiness to slow down. Retirement is not the correct word for this time in life.

The word "retirement" is a total misfit, whereas the word "work" simply requires rethinking. Work usually means something you are paid to do. Yet this chapter inspires you to expand this definition to include what you are choosing to do with your time, talents, and needs in retirement, whether paid or not paid. Not everyone is going to understand quite what you mean when you say your "work in retirement" is getting healthy, being a super grandparent, climbing mountains, or raising chickens. That won't sound like the work they know.

The word "retirement" will be with us for the foreseeable future, and the confusion about what it is to be retired today will continue. The words "retirement" and "retiree" will likely linger for another decade or so. Experts today acknowledge that the word "retirement" is imprecise, and plenty of people are desperately trying to find another word for the stage in life.

Serious academics, thought leaders, and professionals have suggested these replacements for "retirement":

- Arrivement
- Next Act
- Boomers 3.0
- Jubilation
- Unretirement
- Encore Career
- Happyment
- Yippeement

See anything you like? I didn't think so. A new word for retirement could pop up tomorrow because that's what words do. They arrive and each year the Merriam-Webster dictionary adds them. Bingo. New word.

In January 2021, the Merriam-Webster dictionary added 520 new words. Among the new additions were "long hauler" and "Second Gentleman." The coronavirus pandemic changed the term "long hauler" from a transport term to a person who is still having some sort of symptoms 28 days or later after they were first infected. "Second Gentleman" defines the term as the husband or male partner of a vice president.

While these two terms have instant acceptance, other new words take a while. A good example is the word "stewardess," a term used to describe glamorous women in the aisles of aircraft for more than 50 years.

In the 1970s, when Southwest stewardesses wore hot pants, National Airlines spent $9.5 million on a 1971 campaign that read, "I'm Cheryl. Fly Me," which they later expanded to include "I'm going to fly you as you've never been flown before." While many people were outraged, National claimed that it saw a 23 percent bump in passenger traffic as a result.

But a substantial shift took place, and by the end of the 1970s, the term "stewardess" began to be replaced by the gender-neutral alternative "flight attendant." This term also gave recognition to their role as members of the crew and new roles in safety.

You may have made that change in your vocabulary quickly, but I needed help. Whenever I used the term "stewardess," my new airline-pilot-husband would touch my arm and gently say, "Flight attendant, hon. They keep you safe."

Eventually I got it right.

Someday we'll have new words—better words—to help us describe ourselves and view the world around us. Today we can marvel that we are at the frontier of a giant change in what it means to be "retired" and what it means to "work *in* retirement." I read somewhere that "working in retirement" is either an oxymoron or a brilliant idea.

Let us dare to make it a brilliant idea.

WHAT MATTERS MOST

If online dating for seniors feels awkward, so does the question "What do you want to do with your life?" Doing what we can with what we've got makes for a good shout out. But we do have to build a future life. We have to dig deep for a life that matters. If you're unsure of the next step, proceed slowly. Invite yourself to a conversation and grow into more self-awareness and into a life of work and play.

Connect Work to Life

Nothing offers more challenges than the discovery of "work" in retirement. We can grow into our work or upgrade activities to elevate their significance. What could be your work? Raising grandchildren? Teaching cello? Selling your artwork? Caring for your 90-year-old father? Working at a coffee shop for a little cash? Name the ways that work gives deep meaning to you and your life.

The Money Talk

Money and aging are sensitive topics. You've already learned that many avoid talking about their retirement financial plans. You don't have to be one of them. No matter if you have a lot of resources or not very much, adult children will be impacted by your future plans for money. You can prepare them for change. Will you sell the house? How about long-term care? Will you work for money late in life? What are the children's roles and responsibilities? Will there be an inheritance? Financial clarity can contribute to healthier dynamics between your loved ones and your new chapter.

A Place Called Retirement

A road is used to get us from one place to another. What would you name the road you will take immediately after retirement? If you have already retired, what is the name of the road you're on? If you were to come to a fork in the road, what would be the name of the other road—the one you aren't choosing? Name the road someone else is on that you think is bold. Name a road you would like to avoid.

Words say something about us. What are you learning from the names of your roads? How will that influence you?

5

CRISIS CRAZINESS

Navigating a String of Transitions

We steer the boat; we don't alter the river.
—Josephine Earp, wife of Wyatt Earp

A river is the ultimate metaphor for life. Life, like a river, always changes course, always flows. A journey down a fast-flowing river in a small craft has moments that will get your heartbeat up, teach you lessons, and move you forward. Similarly, shifts and transitions in life shake us to the core in often unpredictable ways and force us to make changes.

Rapids in rivers are clearly marked passages that are named with their difficulty predetermined. Unlike life's journey through changes, you know some—but not all—of what you're in for, in a thrill ride of uncertainty.

The Futaleufu River in Chile is known in white-water circles as one of the most stunning and challenging rivers in the world. It is exhilarating white water, a power storm with a life force of turquoise, champagne-like water. The river's name is derived from a local Tehuelche Indian word meaning "big, big river," and it lives up to its namesake in every respect.

I rafted that river as the oldest in a group of 10 women and one of two who didn't get thrown from the raft (pure luck). White-water rafting is fun and dangerous. Sections of a river where the water moves very fast, often over rocks, produces turbulent water, and a person can get trapped underneath them under water.

Whenever someone goes rafting or kayaking on white-water rapids, it is vital that they have a good idea of what to expect from the river. To clarify and simplify this process, all white-water rapids are rated on a scale of I to VI. The rapids receive ratings based on a combination of difficulty and danger, not fun. While not an exact science, most commercial outfitters and experienced paddlers are able to agree on the ratings of particular rapids.

For simplicity, Class I rapids are described as "easy," and a "novice" can handle them. Class II rapids are clear, open passages between rocks and ledges with regular waves. Some maneuvering is required. After that, things get trickier. Class III rapids are moderately difficult with high and irregular waves, and more expertise and attention are required.

Class IV rapids are difficult, and Class V ones are *extremely* difficult, with big drops and violent currents. Now it becomes serious. Scouting is necessary; rescue preparations mandatory. In Class VI rapids, the difficulties of Class V ones are carried to extreme. These highest-rated rapids are nearly impossible, very dangerous, and generally considered "unrunnable."

The names of the rapids on the Futaleufu paint a picture that is not for the faint of heart: Perfect Storm, Gates of Inferno, and Wall Shot. On the last morning of rafting, a local family of four stands on a swinging bridge, looking down, and they all wave as our inflatable rafts cross under. The two children shouted in English over and over, "Don't go! Don't go!"

Every day on the river gave us a new challenge. We were never outstanding in skill, but we never fell apart. We made it through. Does anything feel better than doing something you're not sure you can do? I don't think so.

On the fifth day, Matt, our river guide, maneuvered the raft into an eddy from his commanding stern seat using his long paddles. We relished a short, well-deserved break after being on the river for five hours. Our wetsuits smelled funky, our muscles ached, and we were weary. As we chewed quietly on protein bars in our assigned raft positions, Matt climbed a nearby boulder and communicated with two other guides who have scouted the river ahead. He returned, took his high seat, and just above a whisper, summed up our future.

"Ladies," Matt said, "I know you are wet and tired. I know you are thinking you don't have anything left to give." Then he paused in a way that you knew the most important part of this speech was coming. "But, ladies, around the corner is Terminator [another pause] . . . and

I can't do it by myself. So when I yell, 'Dig,' I want you to reach deep inside and find a way to bury your paddles into that water and dig like you never have before."

No one said a word. We nodded our dog-tired heads, gripped our paddles, and headed out to meet the monstrous, hole-infested, long-as-hell Terminator Class V rapid. Many pros suggest this is the most challenging commercially run rapid in the world.

Later that evening, Matt told us he was nervous running Terminator. "I'm always nervous before running that rapid. It's scary and difficult," he said. He gave all the credit to the two guides who had scouted the rapid. From high ground, they provided a big-picture view of the rapid and a plan for the best approach to run it.

I tell this story so you can imagine the life transition you now face as a Class V rapid on a big, big river—one full of big, big changes and unknowns. Retirement is a passage where the decisions you make and the perspectives you choose can determine a life in which the impact of mistakes last long and there is potential for having to claw back from the edge of situations. On the other hand, you may arrive living more aligned to your personal values and hopes than in all your previous decades.

Life after 65 will move forward one way or another. But just ahead . . . do not underestimate what lies ahead.

PILE-UP OF SIGNATURE EVENTS

Most of us treat retirement as an event—a happening where work is over or revised. But retirement is not an event.

Retirement is a late-in-life process that comes with an additional series of events conspiring together to give a nice, big bucking bronco ride. At no other time of life could these events happen, and their timing initiates a passage that can be chaotic, emotional, and intense. These signature events are obvious because of age. They are quiet but not soft in effect.

Transitions can be noble, beautiful, or exciting. And hard. The three changes accompanying the life stage of retirement below are all of these—noble, beautiful, exciting, and . . . hard. I call them "signature events." They overlap, yet each involves a fundamental shift in life's meaning or direction and reshapes the way we think about ourselves.

Three Signature Events That Accompany Retirement:

- Last Chance
- 30-Year Bonus
- The Young Old

Last Chance

When Lucy Mei, my eight-year-old granddaughter, gets down to the last dice rolls in a Sorry game that she's close to losing, she squeals, "Oh, I'm so scared!" Most of us are not freaked out as we face the last third of life, but what can move the needle on our thrill-and-chill meter is the feeling of a last chance.

In your 60s and 70s, you have lived the bulk of your life, and as always, the future is uncertain. What is certain is that time is running out. While the feeling of a new stage of life ahead is not new to us, this journey to your future falls at a different place on the timeline—closer to the end of life. This last-chance feeling is a major differential characteristic from other life transitions.

A time alert resonates within us—not a clanging gong but an underlying gentle operative. Life has moved us along to a strategic point, and whatever might be important to do now may need to be decided, planned, and begun. If you want to paddle an ocean, get a law degree, take your grandson to Paris, make yourself healthier, seek reconciliation with estranged family members, or live by the sea, this is your chance.

All of us have faced oncoming traffic at an intersection where we want to make a left turn. While the light is green, we watch for the safe opening in oncoming traffic. But often that does not come, and the light turns yellow. Now we have a choice to make because this is our last chance on this light to move forward. We may be anxious, excited, jittery, or unsure. Will we go or not?

Last Chance is subtle yet profound, providing an entirely new perspective and part of the process of retirement that elevates this transition not only in importance but in challenge. How will we sort and prioritize happenings? What will get done and what will not get done? Whether or not it will be truly a "last chance" for some things may be in question. But we have all wandered in cemeteries; we know how it ends.

We may always want to see the world in terms of having another whack at life, but the reality and the mood change as the clock ticks in our late 60s and 70s.

30-Year Bonus

Reaching 100 years of age used to be sufficiently rare that many countries took steps to recognize it. In Japan, for example, anyone reaching 100 was entitled to receive a silver sake dish, a sakazuki. When this practice was introduced in 1963, there were just 153 centenarians, but by 2014, more than 29,350 were issued sakazukis. In 2015, the health ministry said it would stop giving commemorative silver cups because its super-aging population had made the tradition too expensive for the state. Using a cheaper material such as wood or just sending letters are being considered.

As the first generation to have a chance at 30 more years of living, you are not simply planning for 10 to 15 years of leisure. A long life has so many exciting possibilities: more hours to spend; more opportunities to grasp; more identities to be explore; and more time for break-ups, remarriage, and new grandchildren. University of Penn psychologist Martin Seligman argues that humans are the only primates able to plan ahead. He sees us as "homo prospectus," the forward-looking ape, and argues that the best the other species can do is look for the next banana, whereas people can imagine far into the future.[1] Still, we are unexperienced in planning and thriving into a long life.

In the past, when time in retirement was perceived as constrained, we were more likely to invest in sure things, deepen existing relationships, and find satisfaction in the status quo. The challenge today is to increase our self-awareness, evaluate risks, refuse to settle for less, and plan a long, bright future.

Last Chance implies time is running out and is in contrast with the signature event of a 30-Year Bonus, which tells us time is on our side. The dichotomy of "last chance" alongside the "plan another lifetime" employs a bit of crazy factor to this retirement transition.

There are scores of ways we can use these bonus years now tacked on the end of life. Asked about aspirations for living to 100, Laura L. Carstensen, professor of psychology and director of the Stanford Center on Longevity, laments that typical responses are: "I hope I don't outlive my money" or "I hope I don't get dementia." She writes that if we do not begin to envision what satisfying, engaged, and meaningful century-long lives can look like, we will certainly fail to build worlds that can take us there.[2]

The speed with which life expectancy has increased leaves us unprepared with knowledge, infrastructure, and social norms. While the world catches up, you and I are left to find the joy and make our way into another lifetime. We have a lot of time to get things right that we didn't get right before. What does living to 100 mean for you? How might you be in the future? This is redesigning life. This is not easy. But the greatest risk of failure is setting the bar too low.

The Young Old

The "golden years" of adulthood are now considered by many to be the Third Age and are generally defined as the span of time between retirement and the beginning of age-imposed physical, emotional, and cognitive limitations. Today that would fall between the ages of 65 and 80-plus.

Aging has no set pattern, sequence of events, or progression of steps for navigating this life space. The Third Age is relatively new to human history, and there is little social understanding about it or general guidance yet. For individuals, this Third Age can last a few years or as much as two decades or more.

It is a period of developmental ambiguity, a time of life that is both old age and not old age. Stephen Barnes, professor at San Diego State University, characterizes the Third Age as a paradox—a point in chronological time when adults can experience life more positively while some basic cognitive functions continue to undergo slow deterioration.[3]

We, the young-old, show strong continued performance in areas of resilience.[4] That sounds good. But we are aging, and life losses such as loneliness, health, and finances are more concerning now than ever before. The COVID pandemic has amplified the collective sorrow of losing loved ones, the loss of safety, of social connections and personal freedoms and security. All of those are likely as we age. While there are positive outcomes relative to aging, there are declines and obvious changes. And people notice. Calling an older man a "Silver Fox" or woman a "Glistening Vixen" may sound sexy to some but ridiculous to others. In a youth-oriented culture, our age contributes to slights—subtle and not so subtle. A retired, well-regarded business consultant, 70, who commanded high fees with audiences in the thousands now finds her relevance and intelligence questioned. "You can expect to be ignored or not listened to," she says.

Another individual laments that, as he grows older, his children have become much more protective, annoyingly so. "They question my ability to drive or travel alone and want to hold my arm when walking," he says. "All in a caring way, perhaps, but quite unnecessary in my opinion. I think the older I get the worse it will be."

In the context of the transition experience of retirement, this marker of Young-Old is an emotional marker accompanied by inevitable change. We've explored how leaving middle age is an individual decision. As you approach your late 60s, you won't be able to keep aging at bay forever. You are getting older—young-old perhaps for a while—then *old*. And that's a trail journey all its own.

In the late 1990s, Andy Grove, CEO of Intel, coined the term "strategic inflection points" to refer to change that was 10 times more significant than a typical change encountered by business. In a lifetime, we can expect periods of forceful bursts of change that lead to a period of upheaval, transition, and renewal. Call this what you want—a lifequake, pivot, turning point—they are not the minor routine disruptors in life.

The major change of retirement brings a transition laced with these three signature events that prompt a feeling of mortality, a challenge of planning a future, and the reality of aging. In his book about mastering change, author Bruce Feiler calls it a pile-up.[5] I love that word. This, then this, and then this and then this—all fitting together to signify a transition on steroids—one that can present a monstrous calamity that can upend a life of even the smartest, spoil a future of potential, and/or waste precious time.

Leaning into a transition is a ride that begins with a long good-bye, a messy middle, and a new beginning. Transitions work. Choosing retirement and then choosing the "just keep paddling" approach will lead to less-than-optimal results. If understood, separated, and navigated, each of these three signature events can add to the richness of building an extraordinary life. You can do this transition better and more effectively than any other that you have faced.

LETTING GO OF IDENTITIES THAT SERVED US WELL

So here we are in our 60s or 70s, long after we thought we'd figured most of life out, facing a new space in our lives with important consequences—one where the framework of our identities requires new scaffolding.

As much as we'd like to, we simply cannot systematically plan and program our way into a simple straight-line process of reinvention, especially when it comes to a new definition for ourselves. We are on the threshold of a new identity that often is blurred and unfolding.

Kate Peterson wrote in a response to one of my blog posts about her initial foray into retirement, "Each time I have left corporate life, it has been well planned and my new, next identity has been both clear and very appealing. This time I'm self-employed and the possibilities are unclear and feel much more evolutionary—picking up on the purpose-filled threads of previous identities."

Experts agree that successful transitions begin with letting go. If that sounds easy, I assure you it is not. Letting go can be a drawn-out affair. My ex-husband and I dated for a year after our divorce. Does that sound like letting go is easy? While I can look back at how crazy that seems, I also can acknowledge that for both of us that marriage and the love we had shared was hard to let go of.

In life we often get identities we never wanted for ourselves. We become empty-nesters, widow/widowers, divorced, unemployed, caretakers, or cancer survivors. On the other hand, we have latched onto many identities that we love—and I mean really love. Unhappily, we now face having to relinquish roles we cherish.

In retirement, parenting, marriages, and friendships will be reshaped. Joyful, valued roles as parents and grandparents change as we age. We wield less influence as sons and daughter mature, and our status as cool grandparents lasts until time with friends is chosen over time with us. Either through death or distance, we lose friends—often best friends—those who have known us longest.

Many of us are no longer wives, husbands, or partners in life with anyone. We are on our own—alone. Marital roles often change as couples remain married but concoct different lifestyles in different geographical places. We may not be losing a partner but re-creating a married-but-living-apart lifestyle that will alter a sense of self and shelve many shared activities.

Identities help define and shape us, but the life stage of retirement challenges us to dislodge past lives of professional success, soaring financial rewards, or dependable monthly income. This is hard for many. These are positions in life and hard-won roles that provide us with identities we relish. Through high achievement, earnest work, and courage, we create identities of highly successful executives, winning entrepreneurs, renowned surgeons, great teachers, and respected community leaders.

Intellectually we may appear to swap out identities from a lifetime with ease. But remnants of treasured professional identities, parental roles, and youth are often kept for years, signaling a great attachment. Deanna has kept every Mother's Day card from her two daughters and three grandchildren for more than 50 years—*every* card. Kaye has boxes of every letter sent to her since college, organized by date in a storage unit. My husband's Delta uniform hangs in his closet, and an Emergency Flight Instruction Manual for a T-37 from his Air Force flying days is on his bookshelf, alongside a faded Penn State beanie.

After my mother died, I found my tap-dancing chicken costume along with a small envelope labeled, "Barbara's first taps." The chicken costume was a gem but ratty and had to go. But I still have the taps. What do you hold onto from roles of your past?

We have become many selves during our lifetime. With new space in our lives, we can swap out one identity for another several times more. While each of us will discard and swap in our own way, it is important to honestly admit the strong attachment we have to past identities.

For instance, is there a younger self we would like to be again? Do I want to be the Barbara of my 30s—divorced, educator/counselor, working mom raising smart daughter, master of a green Volvo wagon that often refused to start when it rained and discovering the core of her identity would strengthen to spawn a confident, courageous sense of self? Would I want to be her again? Yes. She was one of my identities that served me well. She was a favorite. I had a tough time giving her up. She wouldn't be the last identity hard to shed. The sailing Barbara, the travel-all-over-the-world facilitator, highly paid executive coach, and woman who wore three-inch heels. I miss her too. I miss many of my previous identities. Which ones do you miss?

In our 60s, we can begin to reconfigure the full set of possibilities in our lives, but we will limit our creative powers if we cling to old, wonderful roles. We can love them, cherish them, let them go or fade away, knowing full well that this can leave us lost and confused when they are stripped from us. Letting go is an ambiguous process.

When we can acknowledge what once was will no longer be, we honor the hope of the transition facing us. We can more easily fall into step with everything that is waiting for us.

Thomas Moore, in his classic *Care of the Soul*, gives us good reason to let go in the face of this late-in-life transition with gentle reproach. "The only way to nurture your life is to reach out beyond it."[6]

INVITATION TO CHANGE

In her book *Wintering: The Power of Rest and Retreat in Difficult Times*, Katherine May describes unexpected times in life as a fallow period when you can feel cut off from the world, rejected, sidelined, blocked from progress, or cast into the role of an outsider.

"But wintering," she writes, "is transformation." Plants and animals don't fight the winter, she explains. They don't pretend it's not happening and attempt to carry on, living the same lives that they lived in the summer. "They prepare. They adapt. They perform extraordinary acts of metamorphosis to get them through," states May.[7]

Most of us begin thinking about retirement, often anticipating it, even before the magical reset button seems to appear at 65. Pre-retirement—the stage before you actually retire—*is* the first stage of the major transition of retirement. This can be 5 to 15 years or more before your actual retirement date when you being to entertain and imagine a new life. We may be uncertain about the future but don't imagine that we will carry on the same lives. But do we prepare? We do prepare financially but not emotionally. What is our best emotional preparation? Reading this book can change your perspective on the transition to retirement, and learning how it is different than the transitions you've already faced is a good beginning. Part II leads you into the Four Portals to create not a definitive map but rather new horizons for life in retirement. Uncovering those clues will be advantageous in your planning.

But beyond that what can we do? Is there a best first step?

In our 60s, when we feel like we are heading toward retirement, even when there is no place to go, we can take one of the most important steps in a successful transition. We can *grow our expectation of change.*

Sailors on a three- to four-day sail from one island to another have plenty of time to anticipate a new experience. Departing land for a deep ocean passage, one feels excitement—going to a new destination, a sense of adventure into unknown weather, possible seasickness and unexpected troubles. You pull anchor and leave behind a country, people, land birds, and safety.

Throughout the voyage, you wonder about this new island and all it may bring you. An anchorage of good holding? Fresh vegetables? Who will you meet? How will this island be different?

Days and nights traveling on a small boat in a small space toward a new destination increase your eagerness. Ahead are new people, new foods, and new adventures. Wow. Fatigued from standing watch through the nights and increasingly nervous if there's bad weather, excitement continues to grow and grow. How many more nautical miles is it? Can we trim the sails to increase speed?

Far away from the smells we are accustomed to on land, one actually smells land before you spot the distant haze or string of trees of your destination. The smell is like dirt and can be quite strong. Sighting land after being at sea is glorious. It is only now that we begin the preparation for landfall, checking depths at the entrance, laying out lines, attaching fenders, grabbing the guidebook and binoculars.

In our 60s, we can feel a change coming even though we are not in it yet. Before standing on land again, the sailor spends time wondering about this next island. Pre-retirees can wonder and imagine more. They can imagine what's ahead in terms of change. *How will this turning point shape me? What will be the outcome? How can I learn to find joy and meaning through this transition?*

In the book *The 100-Year Life: Living and Working in an Age of Longevity*, authors Lynda Gratton and Andrew Scott describe a set of intangible assets as part of an individual's endowment as they begin to plan for long lives. "While money is indeed important," they write, "intangible assets—a supportive family, great friends, strong skills, a set of skills and knowledge and good physical and mental health are just as important." But the one intangible asset that brings the positive dynamic required to successfully achieve change in transitions is "openness to experience."[8]

Making a transition, especially this one, is something to really get excited about—building a new life truer to your values, becoming more of who you want to be. We can begin to open ourselves up for change. We can feel its beat. We can get high on a sense of our own becoming.

While planning a new life is touted as important—and it is—we can take time to grow in anticipation of change long before we start making a list of to-do's or exploring options. If we are already retired, we can recalibrate, go back, get the measure of the possibilities in our lives, and begin again to feel the beat of a future story.

I am encouraging you to find and mark this moment.

WHAT MATTERS MOST

Retirement is one of the most important decisions we will ever make. We often get it wrong. Regretting your decision to retire fuels even more regret. Tolerating retirement as simply "your lot in life" means missing out on a phase of life that could be extraordinary. A little soul-searching as well as being proactive before you retire builds your emotional framework and can make a big difference in your success with this transition.

Look Now to Work Possibilities

Would part-time work for a more gradual retirement be better for you than an abrupt cold-turkey option? Transferring your skill set and experience to a part-time position within your company or becoming a consultant in your industry works well for many. Could this be for you? If so, you will want to do this before you retire. One of my clients presented the idea about a part-time position within his company the week of his retirement. "This is a great idea," said his boss. "But we should have been looking into this months ago. It won't work now."

Who Do You Think You Were?

Emotional preparation means recognizing how we have changed through the years and how changes in the future are inevitable. What is one of your identities that you cherish? What specifically about him/her do you love? What parts of this identity can you take into a future one? A successful life in retirement requires building a new framework for the person you will become as well as building a new life. The past shows us a collage of selves—some we miss more than others—but we can gain and grow in awareness from them all.

Choose Your Beast

This chapter describes a pile-up of transitions called "signature events"—Last Chance, 30-Year Bonus, and Young-Old. Each of these changes can be noble and inspiring. All affect us in different ways.

Which signature event significantly alters how you think about life in retirement? Which one will reshape how you think of yourself? Is there one signature event that holds more concern? Getting retirement right means plunging into all aspects of this life change and challenging the idea that retirement is just one event.

Part II

A FUTURE THAT IS TRULY YOUR OWN

6

THE FIRST PORTAL

Geography of Place

The mountains are calling and I must go.
　　—John Muir, "Father of the National Parks"

Young martins and swallows return to their nest after first
flights. Young swifts do not.
　　　　—Helen Macdonald, *Vesper Flights*

The place I've loved most was on a tree-lined street off Merriman
Drive in Akron, Ohio. Saying good-bye was tough. My husband
kept the motor running on the U-Haul while I did a final walk through
the house. Standing in the doorway of each room, flooded with memories of a scant three years, I bawled.

On our way to Atlanta, I drove an old beige VW wagon and followed the moving truck to a new town where the sun shines 150 days
more each year and it doesn't snow in May. From her car seat on the
passenger side, my four-year-old daughter gazed at me from time to
time. I cried all the way to the Tennessee border.

How many places have you lived? How many places have you
loved?

Throughout most of our lives, where we live is determined by
career, family, and responsibilities. However, as we enter our 50s and
60s, there is a substantial shift as we begin to cross what a Merrill Lynch
study reveals to be the "Freedom Threshold."[1] When where you live is
no longer determined by responsibilities, you can choose to live wher-
ever you like.

There hasn't been another time in life when you've had this kind of
freedom. But now you do. Can you imagine where you might want to

live? Your place may be a cabin in the woods or an international flight away. Or maybe you'd rather just stay where you are.

Surprisingly, many people don't give a lot of thought to where this might be. Sure, they ask themselves cursory questions—especially about the weather and affordability. But they rarely delve deeply into this high-stakes decision—one that will make or break future well-being.

Where am I going to live?

Where to live will be one of the most important decisions you'll ever make.

THE INTERSECTION OF HAPPINESS AND GEOGRAPHY

In his captivating best-seller, *Stumbling on Happiness*, Harvard psychologist Daniel Gilbert writes that "most of us make at least three important decisions in our lives: where to live, what to do and with whom to do it."[2]

In happiness studies of the past, "place" was often the missing link, but that's changed. Many experts, like Richard Florida, author of *Who's Your City? How the Creative Economy Is Making Where You Live the Most Important Decision of Your Life*, now attest to the overwhelming importance of "place" to happiness and well-being.

Florida partnered with Gallup to conduct a major US study confirming that "place" forms the third leg in the triangle of well-being, alongside personal relationships and work.

"This makes Place a predictor of our all-around personal happiness," argues Florida.[3]

An even more vocal and popular advocate of the importance of place to happiness is Dan Buettner, author of *The Blue Zones of Happiness*, who teamed up with National Geographic and traveled to parts of the world where people live the longest and report the highest levels of well-being.

If you want to be happy, Buettner has a long-lasting solution. Move to Denmark. Or Costa Rica or Singapore or any of the places that rank among the happiest in the world.

Buettner explains that, while popular positive psychology tactics such as mindfulness and cultivating gratitude can increase happiness, their effects tend to be short-lived. They generally stop working once people stop practicing them. But he finds that places—happy places—nudge people to live lives filled with lasting happiness.[4]

Even with all the research, do you think moving to a happy place will make you happy? I don't. Chances are you don't either. Those happy lists are dizzying, often mystifying, with infinite variables that may or may not have importance. Do you care how many bike trails there are if you don't ride a bike?

I do find it interesting when Buettner says that just moving to a happy place gives us a temporary lift in happiness. At certain times in life, all of us can use a boost in emotional well-being . . . even if it's fleeting. But late in life, most of us are not willing to haul old paint cans out of the garage to take to the dump in a rush to move for a moment or two of bliss. Temporary happiness isn't worth the effort.

What we care about most is registering a high degree of sustainable and long-term well-being. If where we choose to live plays a critical role in happiness and well-being and we are entering the "freedom zone," then bingo. We couldn't be in a better place to begin to shape our future.

I don't know about you, but I'm all for stacking the deck to garner well-being points for the last third of my life. Let's choose where we live with as much care and thought as we did naming our children or our cats.

THIS FREEDOM THRESHOLD

Have you ever dreamed of living somewhere else? I have and likely so have you. This idea becomes more than a pipe dream in our late 50s. By age 61, according to the recent Merrill Lynch study *Home in Retirement: More Freedom, New Choices*, most people feel free to choose where they most want to live.

For the first time in our lives, where we live doesn't have the push and pull factors that underpin previous lifetimes. The short commute, the best schools, proximity to your partner's workplace, the size of the house, the city center—these drivers are much less important in a new life stage.

If you have not yet retired, you may dream about a time when living where you want could happen. But the dream becomes a reality after you leave the workplace. Sixty-seven percent of retirees are more than twice as likely to say they are free to choose where they want to live, yet only 30 percent of pre-retirees feel the same freedom.[5]

And just because we feel free to move, do we really clean out the attic and make it happen? Many do just that. Sixty-four percent of retirees have moved or anticipate moving.

When individuals cross the Freedom Threshold to determine where to live, they often go on a hunt; others ease into the situation.

- ReAnn, 70, housesat in 17 different countries for almost four years before she entered the Peace Corps for a nine-month stint in St. Kitts. She spent the next year crisscrossing the United States, stopping to work and volunteer along the way. Finally, anxious to settle down, ReAnn chose a small town in Mexico.
- Mary Jo's business card lists two addresses with the designated months she and her husband, Jim, live in each home. What works in this second marriage is a combination of residences— one in Highlands, North Carolina, and the other in Sarasota, Florida—because he loves the mountains, and she loves the beach.
- Richard scouted countries outside the United States for a community of bridge players and low-cost Alzheimer's care. With his medical history (both his father and grandfather had Alzheimer's), Richard carefully searched for places to meet these needs. Ecuador and Panama were his last two stops.

Not everyone considers a different place to live. Some simply go look at paint chips at Lowe's for a new garage color with no intention of leaving where they are. While roughly two-thirds of retirees are likely to move at least once in retirement, the other one-third anticipates staying where they are throughout their retirement years.

Why stay where they are? Top reasons include a deep emotional connection with their home (54 percent), proximity to family (48 percent), and the presence of friends (31 percent).

- In his early 50s, Tom, now 73, built his home in upstate New York. His three married daughters along with his six grandchildren live within five miles of one another.
- Don, 79, retired from cattle ranching and now lives in the corner of a pecan grove in Louisiana where he was born and raised. "No way will I ever leave," he told his new wife of two years. "This is it."
- For more than 30 years, Adrienne, 70, a textile artist who teaches classes all over the world, has rented a large Victorian home outside Boston. "I love my community," she says. "Honestly it's beyond me to think of living anywhere else."

Growing numbers of Americans see retirement as a chance to try living outside the United States. The countries they choose most often are Canada, Japan, Mexico, Germany, and the United Kingdom. "While many people are interested in stretching their dollars, many are interested in seeing the world," said Olivia S. Michell, director of the Pension Research Council at the University of Pennsylvania's Wharton School.[6] The number of expats leaped by 40 percent between 2007 and 2017, and the trend is expected to continue as baby boomers retire. Just over 413,000 American retirees are now living abroad, according to the Social Security Administration.[7]

The gateway to unprecedented freedom for choosing where to live is open and real for millions of us. The destination is a beeline to future well-being. You're here to jump down this portal to discover what might be your best options for where to live.

Where in the world is the best place for you to live?

Is your best place one you already love? Or a place you need to find?

What do you need from this place?

Where will you thrive?

Ahead in this chapter, you'll discover answers, find a fixed place on the horizon, and create options to guide you to your best place. Where to live may seem cerebral, like rating all the variables that go into one of the "best places to retire" lists (cost, location, available housing, climate, number of city parks), and to a degree it is. But the decision hinges, more than you might think, on intuition, perception, and emotional connection.

So how about just a place you love? Wouldn't that be your best place?

OH, THE PLACES WE LOVE . . . AND HATE

Some of us have lived all over the world, while others never left their hometown. Yet we all have experienced connecting to a place. We know when we love a place, and we know when we don't.

Have you ever put a fishing line in a familiar body of water or strolled down the streets of place you've never been before and thought, "I love it here"?

If you're like me, you've said this more than once in your lifetime. I've professed love of a place on a secluded beach in the South Pacific; on a mountain trail above Durango, weary from the weight of a 25-pound pack; and in the cool, creepy basement of my grandmother's house in Kentucky, reaching for canned beets where there were spiders.

Ask us why we love a place and we'll tell you about the climate, people, happenings, proximity to family and friends, vistas, or the food. But you still might not understand. Who hasn't been confused when another's love of place doesn't seem to add up in logical ways for us?

- "This place just makes me happy," says a woman who smiles as buses billow exhaust fumes and inch by in the daily bumper-to-bumper traffic of a hot, dusty, mountain town miles from nowhere.
- "I love where I live," my friend in New York City tells me as we stand in line hoping for affordable theater tickets on a freezing January day.
- "Isn't this great?" I ask my husband on Thanksgiving Day as we pant and trudge uphill on cobblestones past empty flatbed trucks to find a family-owned restaurant in a Mexican hilltop town I've learned to love. He doesn't get it.

Why do we love places? When we can't rationalize, it hardly matters. We just know how a place can make us feel. And sometimes, instead of love, we feel hate.

Geography is powerful. Our response to environments that don't inspire us can be indifferent: "It's an okay place, nothing special." But when a place is perceived to damage lives or wound our spirits, we feel it deeply. Geography connects to our hearts and souls. Even beautiful places with peaceful vistas caught in a timeline of experience are not exempt from loathing.

In her 40s, sitting in a porch swing in the coal mining region of eastern Kentucky where she grew up, my mother looked up toward the hills on a spring day when the forsythia glistened and said, "I can't breathe in these hollers anymore." Quietly she added, "I hate this place."

Mom's suffocation wasn't for lack of air but lack of opportunity. For reasons we do understand, some places are not good for us. There's more than happiness at stake when choosing a place to live. Some places promote health and longevity more than others; some places fit our personalities; some places are safe; some places are cheap. Some places are cheap and safe.

You love the vistas and culinary adventures in San Francisco, but living there will cramp your finances. Atlanta is affordable with fabulous weather, but the traffic affects daily living. Your hometown is a good place but cannot provide a revenue stream. You absolutely love New Zealand, which has everything you need, but it means being far from family.

Place must hold the makings of what we can use to create a lifestyle good for us. Loving a place is not enough. Neither is choosing a place just because it's where you are now or have been living for a long time. Neither is choosing a place based on logical factors alone such as afford-ability, weather, how close the grandchildren are, or how high a place ranks on one of those lists.

YOUR GEOGRAPHY OF PLACE

I use the phrase "geography of place" to help people envision a destina-tion for their future as they begin to create a new life stage. Geography of place describes a location that helps you live the way you want to live, doing what you want to do, becoming more of who you want to be. A geography of place is somewhere between your psychological wants, your needs, and what a community can offer.

While it's not just about the topography of land or a cityscape, in the end it is a location on a map. This place you choose will determine much about you in your next 20 or 30 years, like what clothes are in your closet, what's on your calendar, and who is in your life. Will you keep making friends with people like yourself or cultivate a diversity of people to add to your life? Will you find a community to support your love of aviation as well as stimulate a curiosity of goat yoga? Will you add Day of the Dead as a celebration to share with your grandchildren?

Geography of place joins together aspects of your life and arranges sensations into a composition that has the feeling of love but is even more nourishing. It's more than a view from your kitchen window, even if that view is so spectacular it takes your breath away. Geography of place is not just the mountains but how you feel when you're lacing your hiking boots. Geography of place is not the sound of the gurgling creek in your suburban neighborhood but what you see on your grandson's face when you help him catch a fat baby salamander.

Geography of place combines location, supports lifestyle, and fills needs. Once, your geography of place may have been a prestige office of a storied career, but now it's the sound of clinking beer bottles with a hot-shot millennial and colleague in your new co-workspace in Cincinnati. The markers of our geography of place are dear to us: Sunday morning church in your usual pew, a greeting from your favorite vendor at the farmer's market, the annual holiday gathering of your senior golf group.

Some people wake up in places that give them a sense of privilege, while others are thrilled with a deli down the street. For some, it's more about a theater or pickleball community; others just want sunshine. An intellectual community may be a high priority, or you may be giddy with joy in a redneck bar. Finances certainly play a role, and there will be trade-offs. But, somewhere, there's a fit for you.

You'll want to love this place or like it well enough. You'll delight and feel joy each day. You will feel blessed. It may be hard to find, or it may not.

Moving may be one of the significant happenings in the last third of life your life. But choosing happens to everyone, often more than once. This choice triggers more questions:

What really matters in choosing our geography of place?
Will we know it when we see it?
How long will it take us to find it?

WHAT WE VALUE IN PLACE

What really matters to people in the places they live? Research finds people value five things—physical and economic security, basic services, leadership, openness, and aesthetics.

While each factor matters a great deal, the top two are aesthetics and basic services. I have lived for a year and a half in San Miguel de Allende, Mexico, where I disinfect my fruits and vegetables with 10 drops of something called "KillerBac" for 20 minutes in a water soak and transport drinkable water upstairs to my bathroom in a small ceramic pitcher so I can brush my teeth. It's a pain. Each day these annoyances disappear when I walk outside and see the pink spires of the baroque cathedral in the main square against an azure sky.

That pine tree outside your window, the green space in your neighborhood, and the changing color of the marsh can matter more than climate or clean air. We want to linger in beauty when we can. When it comes to beauty and outdoor space—created by Mother Nature or talented city planners/architects—people experience serenity, joy, peace, mindfulness, or any other feel-good emotion you can name. We crave physical beauty in the things that surround us and especially in the places we live.

After the basics and beauty, we crave communities where we are welcome and can easily meet new people. (On the list of "friendliest cities,"[8] Glasgow, Scotland, is number one; Moscow is number 60.) People want to feel energy in places they live. Certain people want to feel a vibe—around the music scene, the arts, food, or technology.

We have high expectations for the places we live, and we should. "Place" underwrites our lives in three very important ways:

1. Place is a major source of excitement and creative situation, an essential component of our psychological well-being.
2. Place gives us an environment in which we can cultivate our individuality. People derive happiness from being themselves. Self-expression, say sociologists and psychologists, is a major source of happiness.
3. Place gives us belonging, pride, and attachment.

We presume to know a lot about why people choose to live where they do, why they move or stay, and who is happy where. The research shows interesting realities, pointing out where you and I might be a little "off" in our thinking:

1. The widely held assumption that people in rural areas are happier than those in dense city centers is only slightly true.
2. Assuming homeowners are happier than renters is not true either. Renters are a little bit happier.
3. "Roots" matter more than you imagine. Many people stay in communities because of the pull of family ties and lifelong friends. One study found that seeing friends or relatives in person almost every day is worth more than six figures of additional income.
4. Just about two-thirds of respondents in Richard Florida's study were happy where they are. More than a third of respondents are ambivalent.
5. Expats are the happiest retirees.
6. Nature—the sea, mountains, woods, or an expanse of prairie from your living room window—provides a connection that often predicts happiness regardless of other psychological factors.
7. Personality matters. If you are an introvert, you may want to head for the hills because you'll find more happiness there. Different personalities are drawn to different physical terrains, according to new research. The stereotype of the quiet, introspective mountain loner and the beach-going partyer may have truth to it.
8. The lure of the long-distance grandchild is a powerful draw that plays into the retirement living decisions of many seniors.

Children may have different ideas about their parents' retirement than parents do. They might think it would be better for their parents to move closer to them. But the parents might have friends and a social network near their current home they would lose if they left. Think it through carefully, say voices of experience.

Richard Florida describes "quality of place" as the intersection of three key elements: what's there (natural and built environments); who's there (the people); and what's going on (what people are doing, our relationship with the natural and built environments).

That may sound simple enough to help you determine your best place. But if you're married or in a committed relationship, what matters to you may be different than what matters to your partner. For couples, a geography of place can become a geography of places—one for you . . . and another for me.

MARRIED BUT LIVING APART

"You don't want to go, do you?" I asked my husband.

"No, I don't. But you should go."

So I did.

Living in a Mexican mountain town is wonderful for me but not so much for my husband. Herb likes but doesn't love San Miguel de Allende. He loves our home overlooking Santa Rosa Sound on the Gulf Coast. With narrow, winding cobblestone streets, San Miguel makes him feel closed in. I get it. So here we are, still very married and devoted to one another after 35 years—but living apart.

Each of us has found a different geography of place.

And apparently, we're part of a gently escalating trend of more and more couples in retirement, happily wedded but with different notions about how and where we want to live. Couples who now choose to live apart.

The Center of the Study of Long Distance Relationships (yes, one really exists) estimates that more than 3.5 million married couples in this country are apart for "reasons other than marital discord."[9] Most people live apart because of their jobs, and while this may also be the reason for some couples later in life, jobs are not usually the reason boomers choose this lifestyle. Respect for the needs of one's partner, support of differences, and keeping the promise of commitment guide couples to make "alternative" arrangements workable.

For the last seven months, I've collected names and contact information of couples married-but-living-apart and have filled an entire single-spaced page in my notebook. Chances are you know a someone who is doing this or thinking about it.

This arrangement flies in the face of marriage experts who advise that couples in retirement "should never do anything without 'enthusiastic agreement' between the two."[10] The long embraces between me and my husband at the airport, saying good-bye, seem to defy any enthusiasm for living apart. Along with the financial challenges of the situation, our lives have omissions. My husband misses the magical appearance of groceries; I miss having the bed made. More often, we just miss each other.

Still, this nontraditional marriage arrangement gives back more than it takes away. The time we spend together is special, and we enjoy one another more. My husband laughs about my Mexican adventures. And I can't wait to see his smile when I show up before my usual fourth-inning arrival to the baseball game in June when I visit.

If you think living apart sounds like a woman's idea, you're wrong. Men as well as women are asking for a marriage to stretch so they can live where they want.

When John, 72, told his wife of 30 years that he wanted to live 2,600 miles away in a condo in the Northwest, she was planting spring flowers in the yard of their big, lovely home in Alabama. She wasn't happy and is still reluctant to tell her friends. "It's working out fine, but I don't know. I just don't want people thinking our marriage is in trouble because it's not."

Married-but-living-apart is not some sort of grudging compromise. In chapter 9, "Kinship," we look closer at how this decision is made and who's doing it. Couples are working together to determine a lifestyle that both enjoy, and this trend for retirees is on the rise. Roberta Taylor and Dorian Mintzer, authors of *The Couple's Retirement Puzzle*, say, "We're going to see more living together apart."[11]

MORE THAN ONE GEOGRAPHY OF PLACE

A career change in her late 20s landed Jill in Southern California, where she fell in love with the weather, the geography, and the people. Eventually, she headed back to her New England roots with locked-in memories to act on 25 years later. Jill and her husband, Dennis, divide their year between their homes in Palm Springs (seven months) and a small town in Vermont (five months). "Not only do we both feel so blessed to experience both coasts of the US," said Jill, "but we hang with a diversity of people now instead of just New Englanders. We feel better adjusted!"

For some people, living in two homes is part of living the dream. The advantage affords opportunities to experience different climates, people, food, and activities. Sometimes, the birds make it all worthwhile. "You just wouldn't believe the diversity of birds and animals between Palm Springs and Vermont," says Dennis. "It's fabulous." Having two geographies of place may be a lifestyle of two homes, but there are variations. Extended RV travel, boat cruising, or a permanent camping site create ways individuals divide up their time to choose "place" in ways that work best for them.

THE NOMADIC LIFESTYLE

Some retirees view their newfound freedom as an opportunity to pull up stakes and adopt a nomadic lifestyle. And they do. With a flexible definition of "home" and an expansive geography of place that extends often to the entire world, many choose to broaden travel into a way of life.

In 2013 after three months of Excel number crunching, Michael and Debbie Campbell from Seattle, Washington, determined that yes, they could have that one last adventure of travel. They retired; sold their home, a car, and a sailboat; filled a small storage space, stuffed a couple of rolling duffel bags to the brim; and bought two bed pillows ("one of the best decisions we ever made"). They have been in 85 countries and 270 Airbnbs. Debbie explains a philosophy that makes this lifestyle work for them: "As long as we stay healthy, on budget, learn something, and are still in love, we are good to go."

Because they were in San Miguel for a long stretch during COVID, I asked Debbie if they were thinking of settling down. "Well, I did buy a rice-cooker that I love, but no, not a chance," she replied. "This is our lifestyle." The couple's agreement is that if one of them at some point doesn't want their nomadic life anymore, they will quit.

Whether traveling the world by plane or boat, hitting the open road in a van, or booking back-to-back world cruises, more and more retirees are creating lifestyles that defy rootedness. Their sense of place is being where they are on any given day. And if where you want to be is in wildly disparate landscapes, you can make it work. In a blog post, "The Honest Truth about Van Dwelling," Michelle Schroeder-Garner describes how a boat and a van give her life the "best of two worlds"—mountains and beach living.[12]

But for many, the itinerant life is a necessity not a choice. The golden years are indeed wander years for a growing number of post-recession refugees from the middle and working class in Jeeps, campers, and repurposed buses. They cobble together a life on wheels that turn through self-sufficiency, determination, and human connection in search of work in beet fields of North Dakota, the campgrounds of California, and at Amazon's CamperForce programs.

In the 2021 Academy Award–winning film *Nomadland*, based on the book by Jessica Bruder, Francis McDormand grieves the life ripped away from her when the gypsum plant closes. Hitting the road in the van she lives in, she discovers wandering tribes who call themselves "houseless," not "homeless." The film illuminates the idea that one's best geography of place may simply have to do with vast blue skies, fresh air, shelter, and transportation. The itinerant lifestyle offers privacy along with a lending-helping-hand community, richer perhaps than a life in suburban tract housing or in an upscale downtown high-rise.

While there is no clear count of how many people live nomadically in America, anecdotally the numbers at the Amazon camps are growing with alarming speed, and Rubber Tramp Rendezvous near Quartzite, Arizona, an annual winter "pop-up metropolis," attracts tens of thousands in small vans and large SUVs parked snugly for educational seminars.[13]

All of these nomadic lifestyles celebrate creativity as well as independent choices for a place or places one can live a best life. If you don't feel a need to hit the road or walk a jetway to find your land of enchantment, that may mean you're already in a place you love.

A place you never ever plan to leave. As far as you know.

PARADISE LOST

Innerarity Point is a Florida peninsula protected from the Gulf winds by two barrier islands, Perdido Key and Ono Island. The natural beauty of land "where towering treetops filter euphoric, perpetual light, and where spirits soar with the lively creatures that surround us" is captured by Christy Emmanuel in her award-winning submission to the 2018 writing competition sponsored by the Perdido Key Chamber of Commerce.

"I have a love affair with trees," Christy tells me. Innerarity Point is her chosen geography of place, where a small brick home in a sanctuary of soaring and gnarly trees along the Intracoastal Waterway is part of an 80-year-old family compound.

> There is something profoundly enchanting about the forested landscape fronting the Intracoastal Waterway that invigorates the senses. The howling winds that course through the tree tops in the winter. The clamoring birds they attract in the spring time. The sun's rays they filter at dawn and at dusk. The motion of shadows they accentuate as broad winged pelicans, ospreys and herons fly overhead. The dew their leaves drop like rain on foggy mornings. The aromas they release to please the senses. The life emanating from the majestic oaks, pines, cedars, hickories and magnolias is utterly captivating.

This is now an ode to the past. "Those trees! No more," says Christy.

Hurricane Sally hit the Gulf Coast in 2020 on the same day, September 16, as Hurricane Ivan did 16 years before. Christy recalls losing 55 trees from Ivan including several glorious, majestic pines. In the wake of Sally, renewed devastation includes the loss of magnificent heritage oaks and magnolias as well as a Southern oak propagated in 2005 from the sprawling octopus-like "Treaty Oak" in Jacksonville, which is estimated to be 250 years old. Christy and her husband, Rick, had eagerly watched their branch grow into a beautiful tree with a six-inch-diameter trunk.

Cleanup and replenishing the washout on the waterside with truckloads of dirt and tree plantings are only the beginning of laborious, time-consuming, and costly work. Christy and Rick are seven months into doing the painstaking process refurbishing the land, then "praying that the grass take root and holding our breath that it all works." The tree removal cost alone for Ivan and Sally is $13,000.

Natural disasters—floods, wildfires, tornadoes, earthquakes, storms, and hurricanes—are billion-dollar catastrophes and are on the rise. These misfortunes can change the environments we love to the point where we've had it either financially, emotionally, or both. "That's it for me," said Jeannette, 70, who just got walloped by Hurricane Sally. Jeannette will leave living on the water in search of another geography of place. Her home is for sale.

Christy is staying, for a while anyway. No longer under a forested canopy, she strives to reframe her view. "The dense canopy of trees, some older than any of us alive, will not be witnessed here for generations to come. Likely never again. But it is still beautiful in its own way. A different way. Not the way I prefer it, but it is a blessing to be here, one with nature all the same."

You may have found your paradise last year or 40 years ago. But as Mother Nature fuels her fury, many will face anguished choices when the beauty and offerings of place and lifestyle become defenseless, fragile, and dramatically transformed in ways that no longer fulfill our needs or stir our souls. Finding a geography of place is a critical component of a future life and for those who have never yet sought out, found, and loved a place—a galvanizing quest. But leaving a place you love to go find *another* place to love is bittersweet and often a change we didn't see coming.

Speaking of things we didn't see coming, did we ever know that pandemics could provoke enough chaos in a community to make us leave a place we love? In her well-written article for *Outside Magazine*, "When the Techies Took over Tahoe," Rachel Levin describes in detail how California's first statewide COVID-19 lockdown freed a population of people from cubicles and work commutes, a migration of thousands, laptops in tow, to mountain towns all over the West, transforming them into modern-day boomtowns know as Zoom-towns.

In Lake Tahoe, these outsiders bring trash, traffic, noise, and what some call "uppity attitudes" to settle in cul-de-sacs alongside individuals who relish a low-key outdoor lifestyle and sneer shamelessly at shiny puffer jackets. Decades ago these locals staked their claim on place with a breathtaking blue lake surrounded by snowy mountain tops and established a small mountain culture—their geography of place—forever. Or so it seemed.

Resentment to this influx of individuals who blow through intersections in Teslas and don't seem to know much about living in the woods has many locals questioning if they want to remain in a place once beloved or relocate.

Cultural differences and tensions aside, residents like Dee Dee Kincade, a single 66-year-old, finds her biggest loss in the supportive community of neighbors of 30 years, many of whom "caved to astounding sums of money in exchange for their homes." This hole in a close-knit group of neighbors is a loss as deep and profound as the devastation of a hurricane.

From Sun Valley, Idaho, to Stowe, Vermont, a resettlement of urban dwellers is changing beloved mountain towns. But will this migration dramatically transform the character of these mountain communities? "The pandemic shook everything up," writes Levin. "Neither Tahoe nor the world will likely return to what it once was."[14]

Hearts can fall out of sync with our surroundings. The pleasure you feel today in your view of azure water, early morning sounds of a city awakening, a canopy of towering trees, a front yard of blooming azaleas, or your neighborhood book club is irreplaceable, until it is not. Feelings aside, a beloved geography of place may have to be forsaken because of many reasons—health, nature, age, finances, bad neighbors, safety, or simply suitability.

And so we will look once more for what we know is one of the most important decisions we make in the last third of life—where will we live and the place we will call "home."

WHAT MATTERS MOST

After the intermission of a musical performance in San Miguel de Allende, a talented pianist sent his assistant into the audience with a small wooden box containing slips of paper with a single musical note written on each such as: F, G, A#, B-flat, E.

Three people drew slips of paper and shouted out the notes, as the pianist wrote them down in a notebook he kept inside the Steinway. When he sat down on the bench, he looked at the notebook and played the three notes.

Then he turned to the audience and said, "This is what I've got. It's enough." The house lights came down, and using those three notes as a theme, he improvised a musical selection. It was marvelous.

Whatever you have now is enough. Begin to find this place you want to be your geography of place. You know where to start. Just thinking about it should make you happy. Get to work.

Self-Survey

Let's face it. No retirement expert knows the best place for you. The research says boomers want places that offer affordable housing, access to social and recreational activities, top-tier health-care services, and strong employment prospects. Nothing wrong with any of those things, but what if you only go to the doctor for an annual checkup, you don't want a job, and a rural farmhouse suits you just fine?

These 14 questions will generate ideas for *you* (ideas, not an exact place) and help you find a horizon—a stepping-out place for ideas to consider. If you end up with 10 ideas swirling around in your head, that's not a bad thing. If you have only one or two, that's fine too. Where might you most want to live? Why?

1. How important will work be in your future? What do you need to support this work? (Only an Internet connection? A place with job opportunities? A place to build a customer or client base?)
2. How important are outdoor activities and the natural environment? (Fishing, biking, hiking, golf, skiing, boating?)

3. What activities are important, and will it be easy to take part in them? (Knitting, yoga, intellectual pursuits, lifelong learning opportunities?)
4. To what degree do climate and weather matter? What climates do you like/dislike?
5. How much do cultural activities like art, film, theater, and music mean to you?
6. How important is being near family? Will extended visits work? What level of involvement in grandparenting is important?
7. Do you crave experiences? Is there a far-off adventure you want to have?
8. Do you thrive in a bustling city, suburb, or rural community?
9. Do you have health issues to consider? Do you need a place that hospitals/providers support?
10. What culinary needs do you have? Are you a foodie?
11. How might financial parameters affect your choices?
12. Do you like where you live now? Do you love it? What are the drivers? Does the place you're living now help or hinder your path to personal and work goals?
13. How might your needs change in the last third of life?
14. How might another place allow you to reach your potential to a greater degree?

Deal or No Deal

Most people can narrow down appealing places. "I told my wife it has to be a place where I can wear shorts year-round," said Ray (who was wearing shorts when he told me this). A place where Ray could *not* wear his shorts and be comfortable was his deal breaker. What's yours? A good way to cull wants and needs is to be clear about our Deal Makers and Deal Breakers.

What are the top two things I must have in a future place?

1. Deal Maker #1:
2. Deal Maker #2:

What are top two things that are so undesirable I'd never want to live there?

1. Deal Breaker #1:
2. Deal Breaker #2:

Well, now we're getting somewhere. What are you learning from this short go-to list of what you must have and what you don't want?

TWO FREQUENTLY ASKED QUESTIONS

These questions are often asked by those who are doing the work of geography of place.

1. *Will I know my geography of place when I see it?* Honestly, people sometimes do. They know. More than a few who are doing the work you are doing go on a trial visit to a place and purchase a house after the first two days. They stand on a piece of land for the first time, smell the air, and tell me "they just knew . . . that this was their place to be." And they were right!

   It also works in the opposite way. Regardless of the facts on the spreadsheet that look so good (climate, cost of living, cultural activities, transportation), when you are there, something isn't right. In fact, it's all feeling wrong. You don't feel safe, you feel like an outsider, or those traffic fumes are a big surprise. The "this is not it" feeling descended on me two hours after I landed in Fort Meyers, Florida, for an initial visit (I left on the next flight out to Atlanta) and in the middle of a fourth visit to Tucson, Arizona. What was it about these places that didn't click? Don't know, but they weren't the best places for me.
2. *How long will it take?* If you are working full time, caring for parents, or still raising children, this could be a process you will spread over several years. My interviews reveal that finding a geography of place can take two months to eight years.

7

THE SECOND PORTAL
Yield

If you don't like change, you're going to like irrelevance
even less.
—General Eric Shinseki, former US Army chief of staff

Slowly is the fastest way to get to where you want to be.
—André De Shields, American actor, singer,
dancer, director, and choreographer

Encouraging accomplished seniors to deliver "wisdom bombs" is the
idea behind "70 Over 70," a podcast that debuted in May 2021.
Max Linsky, cofounder of Pineapple Street Studios and cofounder of
Longform, talks to 70 remarkable people all over the age of 70, not just
about their past but about their current lives. These conversations are
about the big questions we ask ourselves no matter how old we are.
What does it mean to live well? What are we still searching for? How
do we make the most of our time left?

His first interview was with his dad, Marty, 80.

Max: Do you feel more alive or less alive or the same?

Marty: There is something about this time of life. You know, when
you get up, you look ahead to next week's schedule and um, there's
nothing on it and you got to figure out how you're going to fill it up.

Max: What do you—what do you mean?

Marty: I have to create a life. It's like waking up and having a clean
slate and saying what am I—what am I going to do today? It does
feel more like starting over again than I had anticipated. It also—it
also feels more glorious.

Marty goes on to say that one reason life feels so exciting is because he's still evolving, still learning. That's what this chapter is about. Evolving and learning how we can generate a better set of choices for engaging talents by focusing not on what we might do but on what we want to receive in return.

This chapter presents "Yield"—a new way to think and trigger ideas for the intersection of needs, desires, time, and talents. As we will see, this is contemplative work, and interesting things happen when we diverge from conventional approaches.

Finding a place for our interests and talents is cracking the code to remaining relevant. It's a little like getting your affairs in order.

WHAT DO YOU WANT IN RETURN?

In road transport, a yield sign asks you to let other road users go first. Motorists slow down, approach cautiously, and surrender the right-of-way, if necessary, when they see a yield sign. This red sign creates positive results in road safety in the United States; within a year of the sign's posting in 1950, the accident rate dropped dramatically. In European countries, the yield sign is more popular than stop signs.

As part of a constructive retirement toolbox, yield takes on a different definition. The word *yield* also means to produce, to provide, such as "The apple tree will yield a good crop." "Your future can yield promising results." In finance, "yield" refers to the earnings generated and realized on an investment over a particular period of time.

Unlike the road sign that alerts us to possible "surrender," identifying yield in late life is our beacon of triumph leading us to meaning and well-intentioned living. Using this concept of yield can save you from a life of boredom, wandering and getting too comfortable with less than you deserve.

The definition of work we covered earlier—the intentional commitment of time and talent whether paid or unpaid—describes the shape of earnest, wholehearted engagement in life after retirement. When Marty tells his son, "I have to create a life," he takes responsibility. That's a first step of gigantic importance for all of us. After that, we need to get scrappy and wrangle through a decision-making process to uncover an investment that is essential and critical.

As I wrote in chapter 4, work matters: For every pre-retiree or retiree, the takeaway is this: throwing away "work" as you create your life ahead is neither self-enhancing nor smart. Individuals who fail to redefine "work" and include it as part of the essential platform for daily living in retirement face a life crisis and gamble on future well-being.

The new start of this phase of life begins with a fresh start and a retirement problem: what will you do with all that time? Soon-to-be retirees as well as those already retired will ask this question in the earlier stages of retirement, and it will become more profound in the later stages.

"If you're getting close to that part of your life [retirement] and you don't know what you're going to do, treat it as a worrying sign," says Stewart Friedman, founding director of Wharton's Work/Life Integration Project.[1] "Don't assume it's going to be ok and that it's all going to work out. Figure this out now. Get busy."

Most of us do get busy with a bit of introspection and a list of possibilities. What will you do? It's not a trick question, and we don't treat it as one. We move quickly to options—be a travel blogger, work for a nonprofit, become an artist, double-down on a hobby, write a book, teach. Sometimes the idea seems to make so much sense and/or sounds so exciting, we jump right in. "Might work," we think.

And it might not.

"I always thought it would be interesting to teach," said Tim Wright, retired vice admiral of the Navy. The pitch to the dean of a small college was not a hard sell. Wright's successful career included a slew of commendations, experience as a battle group commander, two tours in Vietnam, and time spent as chief of naval education and training. That's just a sliver of what he could bring to the task of teaching college students. Oh yeah, I forgot to mention "fighter pilot."

Hired to teach Asia-Pacific Politics, Wright lasted one semester. He came to the lecture hall with enthusiasm, spent eight hours a day preparing, but concluded he didn't have the skill set. "I just wasn't good at it," he told me.

As we look at what we might do, skill sets are important in teaching and other endeavors. Interests, enthusiasm, curiosity, dormant desires, strengths, and hobbies are also useful avenues that can lead to options. But we can drown in options.

I like the approach of yield best. Yield helps us discover fulfillment in new ways with a structure of assessment based on what is to be gained versus what is given.

Here's how it works. Before we become too focused on what we'll do in retirement, first ask what we want in return. What might enhance your sense of self, purpose, and meaning? You have time, talents, wisdom, experience, and energy to invest. What do you want in return for your investment? What yield are you hoping for?

Do you need to generate income?

Do you desire to create legacy?

Do you want connection, respect, status, friendship, confidence?

Do you want opportunities in creativity, generosity?

Do you want geographic freedom?

Must the work produce continuous learning?

Do you seek a sense of community?

Do you want a stronger bond with family?

Defining yield helps us design a life of alignment. We are doing what we want to do with intention, and flowing back to us is confidence and meaning. Nothing feels "off." Establishing "my yield" worked so darn well when I changed careers in my 40s that I'm embarrassed to admit I failed to apply it 25 years later as retirement unfolded.

At 65, I felt a push to answer "What will I do?" My thinking was that as a smart, mature person, being confused seemed lame. I should know. Plus, every time I turned around people kept asking—What are you going to do now?

So I messed up. I jumped in with a list of possibilities right off the bat.

Here's the story: In midlife, I left my job as a middle school counselor, withdrew my retirement, and told my husband, "I have no idea what I am going to do, but there is no future here for me." I had never quit a job before, and it was scary, mostly because I was clueless about what I wanted to pursue. Work was a given, but figuring out what work

I now wanted was a mind-game of circles. Big circles, small circles, overlapping circles. (I bet you've done that exercise.)

On one of my long walks, I muddled through the current list of options. No clarity. No excitement either because I was frustrated. Halfway around the lake, I found the beautiful question. The Irish poet David Whyte tells us that the beautiful question is one that has the power to shift our thinking, catalyze inner change, and open us to new possibilities. He's right.

The beautiful question was not what might I do, but what did I want in return?

I knew those answers immediately.

Whatever the job or business model, the work must return:

1. pay for value (that teacher salary schedule set in stone was stifling to me);
2. control of my time; and
3. chances for creativity.

As I investigated numerous jobs and endeavors, I never veered from evaluating opportunities against that list. I went on to professional choices that held success. Most important, I was living in a deep well of happiness because I got back what I wanted.

Fast forward to my mid-60s, when extra innings of life spool before me. Again, I did want to invest my time (not all of my time, but some) and talents in engaging work in the future. But just like the pivot point in my 40s, I have no idea what that work might be.

But you can bet I'm busy working on it.

Instead of identifying what I want in return for my investment—my yield—which I had done before successfully, I did what most of us do. I assessed my strengths, looked to see what might be a good fit, then advanced to explore my options. The focus is entirely on the answer to "What do I want to *do* in retirement?"

One of the options I explored was a career as a professional mediator. I studied up. Professional mediation has a bright future. I interviewed individuals in this field, and they concurred this was a perfect fit for my skills. The plan entailed an 18-month certification program at

Harvard, volunteering to gain experience, and networking like crazy in my home territory of Northwest Florida to establish a reputation. Five years later plus a financial investment for that Harvard certificate, I'd be good to go in an interesting industry for as long as I wanted.

I loved this idea . . . until I couldn't love it.

Finally, when I returned to the concept of yield I discovered that the number one spot on my mid-60s yield list was "geographic flexibility." The new work had to be "work-from-anywhere." Just like my midlife yield list—earn money, have control of my time, and be creative—I wanted those same things in work after retirement. But now, I wanted to live part of the time in other countries.

Had I first moved in the direction of determining my yield, I'd never have wasted time on exploring mediation, as well as two other pathways deemed a "good fit" for my skills. "Geographic flexibility" was a deal breaker for all three ideas I pursued with vigor—professional mediator, college teaching, and an in-house corporate coaching position.

The encore career idea I loved most was mediation. There was another niggling thing I learned. Law firms told me they planned to keep the mediation work in-house (it's lucrative) and no matter how excellent I would become as a mediator, they wouldn't be referring business my way.

So not only was I exploring a profession that would not give me the number one thing I needed, it wasn't going to give me a great chance for pay for value, now number two on my yield list.

Yield is the one contribution to our future well-being that many individuals fail to master. Choices are the centerpiece of a post-retirement life, and yield helps you take a laser to the task of weighing options. Priorities can leap out when we ask ourselves what return on investment is most important.

Will the investment of starting a business have a greater return than the investment of grandparenting? Will time as a hospice volunteer have the same yield as learning to play the piano? Will venturing into a new field yield more than consulting in my present industry? Will a diverse portfolio for your investments of time and talents yield the best results?

Testing ideas against outcomes allows us to hone perspectives that will ensure that what we put on the "clean slate" of everyday living aligns with a deeper part of who we are. Asking what we want from our work also allows many, for the first time, to establish criteria for what may have been missing from life. People talk about how important it is to find a purpose. I think finding clarity is better.

It is an illusion that you can plan enough so that you can see the path all the way to the end. Yield is changing the framework of your future as well as loosening your grip on uncertainty. Transitions hold a difficult period as we move forward without clearly defined destinations. The in-between period is unpleasant. Yield is a tool that can diminish that foggy feeling from the inevitable pre-retirement question—What am I going to do now?

Aging and retirement are momentous events, and we are moved to take stock of our lives. Whatever the choices you consider to unlock potential, just make sure you get back what you want.

CATCH YOUR BREATH

Best-selling and critically acclaimed novelist Isabel Allende writes, "The greatest lesson that I could impart is one that I learned relatively later in life. Don't rush. There is time for everything."[2]

While we may or may not have time for everything, we can slow down in the time that we have. The Portal of Yield is one where contemplative work is done. We will determine how we live out our lives with meaning. This takes time.

Many pre-retirees and retirees choose retirement coaching or in-house programs or carve out time to explore with master teachers. The Modern Elder Academy—the first midlife wisdom school dedicated to transforming aging—opened their first campus in Baja California Sur, Mexico, in 2018. The brainchild of socialpreneur Chip Conley and cofounders Christine Sperber and Jeff Hamaoui, MEA provides an oceanfront environment for people to reimagine life as a time for learning, growth, and positive transformation through immersive workshops. Hamaoui explains that this community is to the 21st century what retirement communities were to the 20th—rather than leisure, the primary aspiration is to support flourishing resilience and connection. A new campus opened in Santa Fe, New Mexico, in March 2021.

Taking time to collect our thoughts will give us the best version of ourselves. An absence of any formal rites or routes of passage for those moving from retirement to the new phase in life is an incentive to creativity and individuality. Each of us can choose how we'd like to slow down, look around, play, and learn—with the intention of living a deeper life.

Susan Reece was a corporate warrior, highly respected and sought after. Seasoned with experience and education, she moved along the conveyor belt of executive suite success. Planes, trains, automobiles, relocations in a zigzag across global time zones—this was life. As with many in the C-suite, emotional exhaustion was just part of doing the job.

Susan had done some planning about the work she would do after she retired. In her last few years of work, she earned a certificate in financial therapy with thoughts of teaching. But retirement brought immediate tasks, and finding a destination for her time and energy for "work in retirement" took a backseat as she sold two houses and moved across country to be with her partner and into a new town where who she used to be didn't matter. Leaving behind an identity that had served her well was "surprisingly easier that I thought." When she began to hover over the question of what to do in retirement, she chose an idea she'd had forever. She'd take a gap year.

Although she gave herself permission not to be structured with goals, expectations, or rigid plans, that didn't happen. "I loved that idea, but of course I'm driven by control and success . . . so, yes, I had goals," she said. Her list included: bake biscuits, get a Bernedoodle puppy, do some writing, and get healthy. People laughed along with her as she described these "grand plans," but in her gap year—which she named "Curated Curiosity"—she checked off all those items.

When Susan dug out a values and mission statement written years ago, she realized that what she wanted many years ago was much the same as what she wanted for the last third of life—continue to learn and travel, spend more time on spirituality and health, and get involved in the community.

Today, Susan dabbles in ways to create the life she wants. She has a personal trainer, is on the board of two nonprofits, and designed a math curriculum for herself. "I do it every morning to keep my mind sharp," she said.

Is this work Susan's final destination for the future? Likely not. But slowing down gives her the needed space for the work of resizing and reshaping life. Susan is two years into her gap year.

For many it is just too difficult to be in a demanding work life and nail down what you might want in a different life. A gap year disrupts familiar patterns and allows for rest under the umbrella of "slowing down." The retirement gap year, also called the "Golden Gap Year," can be a time to tinker around with what you might want to do, complete things you never had time for, spend time with your family, or see the world. You can travel to test out a new retirement locale or put action into little things—like baking biscuits.

Slowing down allows reflection. Writing about a gap year for grown-ups, Marc Freedman, founder and CEO of Encore.org, tells the story of Anne Nolan, whose company was shut down, providing her a year's salary as severance. "That year of reflection was an important part of my journey," Nolan said. "Three months into the year, it just kind of hit me that I couldn't do another corporate job."

This is an important discovery. In Freedman's words, "It's time to align the ladder to a new wall."[3]

Nolan took a lot of long, reflective walks and got on the board of a homeless shelter, and five months later, when the president's position at the shelter became open, she applied for and got the job. She's been there for 10 years now, and while she's struggling with the financial implications, she still calls the move "the best thing I've ever done in my life."

Sabbaticals, mini-retirements, phased retirements, and gap years are not new concepts, but they are gaining in popularity. In Britain there are approximately 200,000 gray gappers each year. More and more people in their 50s and 60s are taking anywhere from a few months to a year off in company-sponsored sabbaticals or on their own. Many, like Susan, are calling the first part of retirement a gap year. No matter how we do it, adding time back into our lives can begin a journey not necessarily with lists but with reflection and learning more about ourselves. In this experience, one can also find a new strength or energy to continue the effort ahead—eager for change and a life of deep meaning. A second wind, so to speak.

On the horizon for many of us boomers is what is being hailed as the "second coming of age"—a second coming into our own. A generation "comes of age" when they become adults. Much like the first venture into adulthood (in the 1960s and 1970s), this second coming of age is grounded in the aging process and what we will make of it.

We are the aging boom. Our experiences will form the future—and not only for ourselves; we are changing the reality of what it means to live long. Your story is part of a new frontier with more possibility than you can imagine.

SETTLING FOR LESS

Most retirees will say they are happy no matter what. Retirement is often seen as crossing the finish line at the end of a long working career and picking up the trophy. We won! The retirement dream of the Golden Years—a time of life for leisure with financial security—is an idea that has been eclipsed. But here we are, trying our hardest to live up to feeling lucky and grateful, when in fact we feel ambivalence and angst. Retirement and happiness? It's complicated.

When people tell me the best part of retirement is spending time with grandkids, being on a vacation that never ends, or becoming the master of absolutely nothing, I wonder how much of our current cultural perspectives are at work in their lives. Where's the part of life in retirement about evolving and growing? When some tell me retirement is just a turn in the road, I wonder: where to? Because it doesn't seem like they have figured it out or that they are even getting ready to figure it out.

"I am bored as hell. B-O-R-E-D," says John, a successful attorney three months into his retirement. John's cure for his boredom will be travel. "Just as soon as COVID is over, I'm gone." On the other end of the continuum is Judy, an attractive 70-something who isn't bored. She's working on a home flip project and has a busy life. "I just feel invisible," she said, giving examples of not being listened to in book club or never being called by the pastor of the church she's been a member of since having babies. Like John and Judy, freedom in retirement holds challenges.

In a real sense, we get carried away with freedom. We can schedule too many trips, surrender to too many demands, commit to an overload of projects, and want to help everyone. We could also putter. Actually, we are puttering. We linger over breakfast and daily activities. We read. We get the mail. Screen time is up (seniors 65 to 74 watch four hours of TV), and exercise is down.

No matter what, we will tell the world we are happy perhaps for no other reason than it supports the narrative we have given ourselves. We boomers are goal-oriented, and "happy" is the goal. Many of us can frame events in our lives in positive ways so we appear to be living the dream, maxing out our potential, and reaching high levels of happiness. In some ways, it appears to me to be a coverup for a decline of relevancy. Our lives begin to reflect what others expect from us in retirement—and that's not much. There's a strong campaign out there to douse your drive, your ambition, and your self-esteem.

Ageism and stereotypes are erroneous perspectives that have a huge effect on our experience of getting older. These lead to misconceptions about our abilities and our approach to aging. If we internalize misconceptions about our capabilities and status, we might believe what we're hearing. Our self-confidence doesn't plummet—rather, it seems to ease out the back door—and we are kept from living a full life because we don't demand it for ourselves. We don't roar anymore.

While the elderly in a few countries still have influence and power and their vast knowledge is respected, you and I can just dream about that. In the Western world, the prestige associated with old age has declined. Power and prestige are held by those in the younger bracket. We are not revered.

Microaggressions—the subtle things people say and do that show bias against older people—are prevalent. Innocent statements that can be considered microaggressions when addressed to an old person are: *You're going to run the marathon? You listen to Pink? You have a girlfriend? You're in college? You're working? You are adorable.* (Adorable is not a term of respect.)

My own personal one delivered by my daughter: *You're getting your teeth straightened?*

Microaggressions imply that older people aren't up on technology, can't compete physically, are stuck in the past, are beyond the stage of learning, are no longer able to contribute to society, and have peaked in attractiveness and that their time for romance has long passed. Most microaggressions are subtle yet potent. Others are crafty. "OK, boomer" is a catchphrase used to dismiss or mock baby boomers and has gained heavy traction on the social app TikTok. It's like a verbal eye roll.

As soon as you hit 60, it is time to become ultra-cognizant of cultural messages that can lead to self-fulfilling prophecies. We can set ourselves up for a shallow life, one that is more like survival than living. We can be lonely not only from full connection with one another, but we can also be lonely if we disconnect from the fight for our best life. In other words, we can be lonely from ourselves.

After a 14-year hiatus, singer and songwriter Garth Brooks, 59, returned to huge success. In an interview with Gail King prior to the Kennedy Center Honors, Brooks reflected on the rest of his life. "You wake up in the morning and you're breathing. Then God's got a plan for you. Are you going to be a retired guy or a warrior? That's your question every morning."

You can be retired *and* a warrior. Deciding to thrive in the last third of life will take personal determination.

WILL YOU EVER NOT WORK?

While much about the evolution of this period of life remains unclear, a central defining feature is emerging. It is work.

Most of us are rolling up our sleeves to find work. The hottest demographic in the labor market is men and women working in their 70s, 80s, and beyond. Full-time, part-time, paid, or unpaid, the uptick in the percentage of people over age 65 who choose to keep working is big. According to a recent study by the AARP, nearly 80 percent of boomers are planning to continue in paid labor during their 60s and 70s.

While this new generation of aging boomers swaps that old dream of freedom from work for a new one built around the freedom *to* work—in new ways, on new terms, to new ends—the situation is far from idyllic. The elephant in the room is money. The "baby boomer retirement crisis" has been discussed so long we're sick of hearing about it.

But it is true. We might not have enough money to last a lifetime. Money and aging are sensitive topics, so I've saved this to the end. It's a bit of a rant. If I hear one more time that boomers didn't save enough money and didn't plan well, I'll—you know—*I'll scream.* The implication that we were irresponsible, lazy, or out to lunch galls me.

First of all, boomers are the wealthiest generation in history, owning roughly 70 percent of the wealth in the United States. And we're set to inherit $15 trillion in the next 20 years.[4] A study shows that millennials will hold five times as much wealth as they have today and the group is anticipated to inherit over $68 trillion from their baby boomer parents by the year 2030. This will represent one of the greatest wealth transfers in modern times. So boomers invested talents and produced gain.

Second, the boomers not in the wealthy group are more likely the ones who are worried about money. We did not commit a deadly sin. Many went to work every day and built a life for ourselves, put the kids through school, put money away in a savings account, and paid our taxes. And then we got divorced, hurt on the job, sick, or widowed. Or maybe none of that happened. Perhaps we had to recover from a natural disaster, pension cuts from a company bankruptcy, the 2008 financial crisis—or we were just plain unlucky.

A broken retirement system, a culture of privilege for youth, a financial crisis, the economy—these impact and change our financial future. If boomers need to or want to earn money as we age, those who seek ways to solve that problem should do so with pride and courage.

The end result may be that "financial compensation" is at the top of your yield list. So let's get clear on this. What could be better than investing time and talents that give meaning and make money? Sarah Wilson, *New York Times* best-selling author of *First, We Make the Beast Beautiful,* explores the path back to connection in a fractured world. She writes, "Love and work are sturdy and joyous things to cultivate in a lifetime. They take us on a morally straight path to a life of meaning."[5]

If working late in life can earn money for survival, peace of mind, maintaining a lifestyle, funding grandchildren, supporting worthy causes, and bankrolling new experiences, let's be ambitious about it. Whether or not finances in retirement will be a crisis for you is an individual matter. And while this is definitely not a third-world problem, it is, for many of us, our problem to solve.

Now to the question, "Will you ever really retire in the traditional way and live a life of pure leisure? Will you give up work?" The answer is for you to decide. Retirement age is increasing around the world. Your 80s are touted by some to be the new retirement age. Our privilege is that each of us has that choice.

Several weeks ago, I was introduced to Claudia, a beautiful woman in her mid-60s who is from Guadalajara. As operational manager for a screen company based in Mexico, her travels to the United States are frequent. She asked about the topic of this book, and I replied, "It's about life in retirement."

Her eyes lit up. "In Mexico we have no word in our language for 'retirement.' We will work forever."

Then she laughed and smiled, as if the thought of working forever didn't bother her at all.

WHAT MATTERS MOST

At the frontier of the last third of life, where we are now illuminates the path. This is not a strategic endeavor that ends up with a perfect map but takes a different form. Each of the Four Portals finds a new horizon to guide us. In this chapter, the return for value on work, space for contemplative work, and cultural challenges point us in the right direction.

Rate Your Working Decades

Many of us had jobs in our teens. Throughout our lives, work has changed, morphed, or sometimes disappeared. What was the return on that job you had as a teenager? How did that change life? Which decade gave the best yield for the investment of your talents? What decade of work yielded the most surprising results? Identify what we gained from work in the past to compare what we might want in return for work in the last part of life.

Hooked on Retirement

Day-to-day a blitz of images of older people in retirement come our way. You watched as your parents, aunts, uncles, and grandparents negotiated this passage. Bits of information now form the beginning of philosophy or perspective worth examining as we find ourselves at a major intersection of one of life's greatest passages. What words do you associate with this stage of life? How do you think you have been programmed to think about retirement? What are you learning from retired people you know? Do you think retired people are supposed to be happy no matter what? How can you reboot your perspective on retirement to benefit you?

Name Your First Chapter in Retirement

The initial months and years of retirement are a launch into the great unknown. The event might be worth a name. Susan Reece called her gap year Curated Curiosity. Small events in the beginning expanded into a more robust exploration—a useful springboard for what is to come. But that was Susan's theme. What is yours? What might you call your first chapter that will inspire and motivate your launch?

8

THE THIRD PORTAL

Freedom

Life loves to be taken by the lapel and told: I'm with you kid, let's go.

—Maya Angelou

There should be a place where only the things you want to happen, happen.

—Maurice Sendak, *Where the Wild Things Are*

" I think it takes about 65 years to find your way around the block," said singer, songwriter, poet, and novelist Leonard Cohen. Yes, we learn a lot in 50 or 60 years of living. Shifting out of parenting; leaving high-pressured, time-constrained, workaholic lifestyles; and rejecting yesterday's model of aging, we now head toward what is labeled the *Retirement Freedom Zone.*[1] Bound closely to this freedom are optimistic fringe benefits. According to the research, we associate retirement not only with the word "freedom" (55 percent) but also "enjoyment" (53 percent), and "stress-free" (43 percent).[2]

Will all this come true? We can make it so. At the start, we stand between two worlds—an old lifetime and a new lifetime—and although not the freedom of our youth, a blend of unregulated time that may include work and a yet-to-be-written future awaits. This is freedom laced with wisdom.

The portal of freedom is about fiercely owning your life. You can choose important pursuits, and you can grow into a person you want to be with pride. If that sounds like you're standing on the same freedom threshold of your 20s or 30s, take out a mirror. Looking back are the eyes of your Older Self.

This is life's final offer for a chance at grown-up desires. Just when is the magic time for stopping to shake things up and trying to get what you want?

It's not now.

THIS FREEDOM IS DIFFERENT

A shakedown cruise is a nautical term in which the performance of a boat is tested and the crew familiarizes themselves with a new vessel. That first outing, also called a maiden voyage, is a test of equipment, technology, and operating systems. The crew is put through the paces in anticipation of a life on the water.

For cruisers, the excitement of a shakedown cruise is palpable. Finally, we are on the water! But enthusiasm wanes because nothing ever always works or runs smoothly. The winch jams. The portholes leak. Sometimes you wish you had taken a bit more time to uncover the mysteries of that nautical chart or learn an additional knot or two.

There are stories of cruisers sinking their boats on a shakedown cruise. There are also stories of retirees who plunge into a life of freedom and still end up with common regrets at the end of life: not living one's dreams and aspirations, not living a life that feels true, and not allowing oneself to be happier.

The crisis of unfulfilled lives unfolds gradually, often with acquiesced boredom, a flimsy search for meaning, a lack of regard for good health, and indifference to a ticking clock. We succumb to the idea that a new future will be one of slow-moving ambition and then an even slower glide into comfort as the flush of freedom fades. Later in life, with decades still ahead, we lose our zest and hold onto standby status, hoping for the best.

The voyage into retirement life gives us a big breath of abandon. We have a notion—an inclination—that somewhere ahead we'll find something beyond our present lives. While life in retirement promises a sense of freedom, it is different from the freedom felt when we left home and went out on our own or took that great job with a corner-office view. Those earlier life stages reveled in an unending future and were mixed with bravado. (*You can do anything you want! You can reach any dream. Next time will be even better. You can win. You won! You are on the way.*)

That was then. At 60, a new spirit of aging exists along with the chance to redesign your life and promises, once again, freedom. But this freedom comes with the understanding that we *do* have limitations and circumstances.

- *The divorce hurt financially. So, no, you're not going to own a chateau in Italy.*
- *Your spouse lost interest in sailing. Do you want to single-hand that 42-foot sloop?*
- *Your current wife has sidelined your kids, and you miss your grandchildren. Are you up for the challenge of finding your way back into their lives?*
- *The hip replacement works fine, but is it good enough for your dream of reaching the Seven Summits in Ecuador?*
- *The law degree takes four years of hard work and will set you back financially. Is it worth it?*
- *The falling-out with your brother happened more than five years ago. Will you or won't you try to mend this relationship?*
- *Some of your friends found new partners online. But you are shy. As much as you'd like to find someone to share life with, you'll pass on trying. Good choice?*

Freedom at 20 and again at 60 has 40 years of living in between. Our past and present will determine how we use our freedom. While this new freedom can mean freedom *from* work and family responsibilities, we discovered in Portal Two: Yield that retirement also offers greater freedom *to choose* whether and how much one wants to work.

But freedom in retirement is so much more than work or no work. This is a chance to cast about with desires and intentions, though not everyone sees it that way. In a comprehensive survey of 9,000 adults in the United States and Canada, the majority (55 percent) viewed retirement as "a new chapter in life," while others saw retirement as a continuation of what life was (15 percent) or as time for rest and relaxation (22 percent). Only 8 percent viewed it as "the beginning of the end."[3]

Freedom is an operating system inherent in retirement life. But the algorithms—the data and useful information—used as input for the system are different.

- First, we are not invincible. Our freedom, layered within the moving parts of responsibilities and past events, now, more than ever, depends on health, vigor, vitality, and finances. The realities of age come to bear on how we will manage and spend our future time.
- Second, a boundary of limited time surrounds this time of freedom. While you may not make a daily habit of reading the obits, you are sure you are not going to live forever. Time is less permanent, more precious.

A different kind of freedom than that of our youth? Hell yes. This block of time knotted together with wisdom, a fresh start, and opportunity—often for decades—is even more glorious. But freedom in retirement disappears with a demise in health; becomes underutilized, ignored, lost forever with life's end; or easily fritters away.

THE TWO KINDS OF FREEDOM

Many look back five or six years after retirement to realize time has flown by and they haven't done anything significant. Suzanne, 70, is not lazy, disengaged, or unintentional with her freedom. Retired for four years from a portfolio career of real estate and retail store owner, she delivers food to families from the local food bank, is a prolific reader, and signs up for online courses—one after another—on writing, cooking, and art. "But I wonder sometimes," she says, "if I'm wasting time and not getting down to the real business of how I want to live my life."

The pandemic caused many of us to come to sudden understandings about our lives just like that "a-ha" moment of Suzanne's. The experience of lockdown magnified many small freedoms but curtailed other freedoms, causing us to tune into how we might live better. When it comes to late-in-life changes, the pandemic "forced many Americans to take a good long look at their working lives, their transition to the golden years, and what they ultimately want out of life."[4] Spending time with family and friends, always a priority for retirees, now becomes a top priority. And for the moment, globe-trotting may take a backseat as we explore the majesty of lands close to home.

Are you set to handle the newfound freedom of retirement? Freedom is a part of four fundamental shifts that take place in retirement—geography, identity, relationships, and pursuits. But freedom also stands apart as an integral and crucial component. What we do with freedom will define us. Thirty-one percent of new retirees (those who have been retired for less than five years) say they have struggled to find a sense of purpose.[5] And that struggle starts with how to spend their freedom of time.

There are two types of freedom, and you must make good use of both for an extraordinary life—"Go-After Freedoms" and "Self-Directed Freedoms." Over a long life, two issues—*What will you do? How will you be?*—are central to freedom and have been noted as questions "impossible to ignore over the course of a long life."[6]

First, the Go-After Freedoms

These Go-After Freedoms are foremost on an individual's mind: What shall I pursue now that I have time? Where shall I go? What do I want to see and experience? Maybe you want the freedom to restore an old automobile, learn a new language, cultivate an organic garden, read novels, enjoy new rituals of rest (a nap in the afternoon), renew energy through meditation or yoga every morning, or flatten your abs.

For sure, it is these exciting Go-After Freedoms that most individuals recite when telling others about retirement life. With time to create and live an interesting life, these items are commonly called the "Bucket List"—the personal list of things to do before you die.

A carefully crafted use of freedom should also include things we need to get rid of in our lives. Getting rid of anything that produces negative stress allows you to reuse time to create new synapses in your brain as well as activate the pleasure center. Just getting rid of a morning commute, the demands of child-rearing, or an incompetent coworker can reduce negative stress. But look harder and you'll identify stressors than have nothing to do with work.

Tangled up in our lives are a myriad of activities squeezing hours and days out of our lives. Isn't five years on the museum board enough? Why keep going to your giant-jerk brother's house for Christmas when you hate it? Are you overly generous with babysitting the grandchildren and secretly resenting it?

Older people in Blue Zones, the five places around the world where people consistently live more than 100 years, build more freedom into their lives by focusing on particular elements of life. One is "removing chronic stressors." The world's longest-living people do not pump iron, run marathons, or join gyms, but they do work in their gardens, pray, and take naps. People in the Blue Zones do not just live longer. "They live better," states Dan Buettner, Blue Zones founder, National Geographic Fellow, and multiple *New York Times* best-selling author. Buettner's life work is unlocking the secrets of extraordinary populations of longevity and happiness.

If we use newfound freedom to remove chronic stress, scientific and psychological research on aging in epigenetics confirms that our bodies and brains can regenerate some cells.[7] Choose activities that are important to you as well as focus on removing stress.

Second, Self-Directed Freedoms

These are freedoms used for something much deeper—an interior experience we can't (or shouldn't) ignore. The Self-Directed Freedoms offer us a chance to satisfy a deep yearning to become our best self. How do I want to be in this new life? How can my behaviors be improved? What actions do I want to take?

Let's face it. We've rearranged ourselves over the years. Who you are now and how you feel about yourself have a high correlation to self-confidence and happiness. Now we have a new chance to bring us back to the fullness of self, and that opportunity turns out to be critically important to older adults. While retirees want to spend time with loved ones (76 percent), many also want to spend time being true to themselves (67 percent).[8]

New research regarding the biochemistry and neurology of happiness confirms that "happiness" is a feeling of immense emotional and spiritual freedom—freedom to be who we are. An image of freedom is often Thelma and Louise driving off the cliff. Perhaps it is the *refusal* to drive off the cliff and instead start a conversation with ourselves over the direction of our lives that can provide a greater sense of spaciousness.

Most of us need a simpler identity. Complex identities bury us, and we become exhausted from the effort to sustain them, especially those that have others, and not us, at the center. I don't think identifying these freedoms "to be who you want to be" are so deeply buried into memory that one needs to write a life story, sit in a sweat lodge, or commit to long-term therapy in order to reclaim them. It does, however, require a truthful conversation.

Interior experiences may have outcomes obvious to only a few; still, we should not ignore their potent effect on how we feel about ourselves. And we cannot turn away from how our actions impact how we will measure our lives. While everyone may know from Facebook pictures that your dream of biking the Pyrenees came true, only a certain old friend will read the letter you wrote reaching out to make amends. Happiness in the last third of life benefits from deliberate decisions, no matter how small, to become more than we are.

Who you want to be still avails the power to change who you have been. You can find a simpler, more elemental identity truer to the template of your nature.

You can love like you have never loved before, forgive others despite your uncertainty of how to do it, and become ambitious for your talents. You can embrace generosity, open your heart and mind, and start giving every homeless person holding signs and standing on street corners the gift of your eye contact.

Bottom line: you can change.

Over the years of saying good-bye to my father after a visit, my hug ended with "Daddy, I love you." More often than not, an awkward silence followed. Other times, he'd whisper, "That's nice, Barbara." I knew my father loved me, and I accepted that this was just a part of the way things were. But at age 95, when he responded to my "I love you" with "I love you, too," I felt a warmth in my heart I had never known. From that moment on we found a span of time—albeit a short one—that held more affection in words and behavior than in my entire lifetime.

I do not know what unlocked my father's emotional response and generous spirit. But after a professional lifetime of helping leaders change their behaviors, I *do* know that it can—and does—happen. Behavior change can shape the course of life no matter at what age it happens. We can turn a switch somewhere deep inside, intentionally choose to be different, and recast ourselves.

Do you want to be more thoughtful or more generous? Will you decide to be more intuitive, caring, agreeable? More assertive, a better decision-maker, more energetic, more outgoing, orderly, hardworking, or organized? Could you become more resilient and worry less? More open-minded, curious, artistic, imaginative?

What's really at the core of this is the idea of fiercely owning your life—a life facing the finale of time? You don't need to wait until you're 80 or 90 to do this. This newfound freedom, seen as a value of time returned, is really more about switching the locus of control back to yourself for your *self*.

The work is not in strategy but rather in imagination and self-awareness. Determining desires for our future is the work in front of us.

CRACK OPEN YOUR WILD HEART

In graduate school, I was part of a group of 10 smart, capable individuals who were dutiful and obedient—checking off lists and courses, doing research (some of it stupid, in my opinion), writing papers, and worrying about our future. In our late 20s and early 30s, we weren't "failing" at living life, according to our favorite professor, but for certain there wasn't an adventurous soul in our bunch. This turned out to be unacceptable.

In this cherished class, no syllabus or list of recommended reading existed. No presentations or term papers were required. We listened to our professor talk about life—mistakes, regrets, limited horizons, unlived dreams, messing up badly but learning something. One day, at the end of class, the professor concluded with a wagging finger and a steady, raised voice: "You are lacking in a determined spirit to disengage from normalcy."

He began to give assignments. Elevators became human behavior laboratories.

- Assignment 1: Enter an elevator with four or more people, go to the door, turn around, and face the group. Keep ongoing eye contact. Do not move or talk.
- Assignment 2: Enter an elevator with one or two people. Do not inhabit your own space. Instead, stand very close to another individual. If asked to move, go stand close to the other individual.

Today, a stepped-up assignment might include going bare-breasted in those elevators. But, in Georgia at the time, unlike in other states, that was illegal. Our professor didn't want us arrested. All he wanted was to tickle our recklessness and allow us to break a few customary unwritten rules.

After a while, we took nervous delight in these activities. But it wasn't enough for the professor. Like a caring parent, our beloved teacher explained midsemester how he *still* feared we lacked definition for "getting out of our rut." So he assigned the following:

1. Sleep under a railroad trestle.
2. Make love in the woods.
3. Panhandle until you get $25.
4. Get drunk.

Strongly encouraged to do all four as soon as possible, we did not have to report back on completion of the assignment. Interestingly, we never shared our experiences with one another.

So, after all these many years, I will tell you that there's a ton of poison ivy along the wooded banks of the Chattahoochee River. (No drugs or alcohol were involved. *Could I hear a wild cheer here?*) And panhandling is not fun.

When I sense life getting dull, predictable, or constrained—when I allow life to be much less exciting than it could be—I hear my professor's scolding voice. I am thankful he chewed me out for not living fully. Who's chewing you out?

Other avenues present in all our lives can remind us to flirt with all kinds of possibilities in life. The joy of picture book bedtime reading is a renewed activity in my life. At the age of three, my grandson, Liam, was choosy about his books. If interest wanes while I read, he lands airplanes on the page or drag races Hot Wheels on the arm of the chair we share. But when we turn the first page of *Where the Wild Things Are*, the planes and cars go still.

He's rapt after launching into this imaginary place. And, it turns out, so am I. The author, Maurice Sendak, finally declares there is a place "to be so happily wild." Where is that place for you? Perhaps you need to re-wild. You can think of it as "controlled recklessness" or a small, very small act of rebellion—either one counts.

My husband, a pilot with Delta Air Lines for 34 years, wore a uniform and adhered to the strict rules on hair for the bulk of his life—first in the military, then with Delta. It took three years into his retirement to get what he wanted for himself—he grew a ponytail. The kids hated it. For a rule-following guy, this tiny bit of contrariness—the extent of my husband's wildness—made him very, very happy.

Some individuals chuck it all to be wild. Ben Saunders found himself scratching at the walls of his office for a wider space beyond and ended up in 10 weeks walking from the north coast of Russia to the North Pole and around to the north coast of Canada for another 10 weeks. Most of us aren't in that league of explorers. I love hearing about large-scale mental and physical challenges, but satisfying most wild hearts doesn't hinge on these. That may be comforting to some of you.

For many, wildness is a mystery. But if you are breathing just a little, getting things done, and calling it a life, you now have your chance to demystify it. Where is your wild heart? What makes up your wild heart? To discover the wild heart of your life, examine the orderly, controlled, managed life you live and then take steps to expand the scope of your existence. You'll be amazed at what you find.

To gain new insights into the role of freedom at this time in life you can also use an imaginative approach that asks you to find the "outlaw" in you. Each of us has a necessary outlaw in our imaginations and memories. We might have to cross a bit of unknown territory to get there, but we can cultivate a gleam in our eye, stray outside predictable, make sure no one really knows what we are up to, surprise others at the same time we surprise ourselves.

This rebellious spirit abides in each of us and is often gentle and playful. You might discover what was buried or walled off a long time ago that now needs to be investigated. Messaging your outlaw requires no follow-through other than to consider his/her ideas.

What does the outlaw in you say she wants to do with freedom in retirement?

Who does the outlaw say he wants to become?

As important as it is to believe we are capable of more in our endeavors, it is also important that we believe our lives can—and will—be more. Grow your options with a wild heart. But leave room for the unknowns. Years into retirement life you may be ambushed by desire. It happens.

AGING AND THE LOSS OF AMBITION

The idea that older adults can have a strong desire to seek new and exciting experiences is in short supply. More often we assume they "had their shot" and the remaining time is meant to make peace with what life gave them. Alongside this is the notion that once you raise your children, you can now live your dreams through their lives and their achievements.

Adopting a mindset with these beliefs may be your guide to life in retirement. Strong societal beliefs are in place, and filling up a gratitude journal is never a bad idea. We know that what makes us happy does change over time, but part of finding our happiness is letting go of others' expectations of us and figuring it out for ourselves. It is completely acceptable to let some dreams go that don't make sense. But staying open to our own development might be what ambition looks like as we age.

"I just see this time as one great adventure!" says Alan Work, 64, who sold his men's clothing store located on Palafox Street in Pensacola, Florida, two years ago. After a 35-year career in retail working six days a week, Alan plans to move to the mountains of North Carolina where he doesn't know a soul. His motivation? "I've just always wanted to live in the mountains," he told me. "And I'll make some friends."

Alan is a well-respected businessman with a ton of friends in his community. His long-held dream may not appear to have the risks of scaling Mt. Everest, but uprooting to resettle in a new place is taking a chance that the reward will be more than the risk.

In our 60s, 70s, and 80s, conventional wisdom is that we will become less driven and less motivated to want more for our lives. Aging often is characterized by a decline in ambition, motivation, and productive energy. Our capacity for big plans, awesome aspirations, and grand adventures can seem to run out of gas. "As we age, it's harder to have a get-up-and-go attitude toward things," says author Ann Graybiel.[9]

Desire, exclusive to human beings, can change as we age. Finding new sources and discovering ways of motivating yourself toward what you want is vital for an extraordinary life. We utilize a mere 10 percent of our brain power, and there's plenty of potential for our older years even as energy can dip and daily body aches occur. Because engagement is important for well-being and for learning, many of us need to find ways to jump-start ourselves and take charge of motivational challenges. One way to do this is to heed or probe a feeling of longing—earnest and deep, often wistful desire—seldom discussed or mentioned in planning a life in retirement.

"It seems to me we can never give up on longing and wishing while we are still alive. There are certain things we feel to be beautiful and good and we must hunger for them," George Eliot writes about longing. When were you last hit with intense longing? General malaise, discontent, envy, and depression are signs of uneasiness with life. You need not have any of those to feel longing. Longing is an invitation.

Fulfilling intense desires can be an internal battle. When my husband found himself trying on a Montecristi hat I had discovered at a men's upscale shop on Waikiki Beach, he was hesitant. He was afraid he would like it, and he knew this hat was not going to be in his usual price range. He put it on, looked in the mirror, and, sure enough, fell in love with this gorgeous Panama hat with the outrageous price tag. "I just can't do it," he replied when I asked if he was buying it.

We left and went to the bar. Over a scotch and soda, we talked.

Me: Do you love it?

Herb: Oh yes, I love it.

Me: Do you want it?

Herb: Yes, I want it, but it's a lot of money. I don't think I can do it.

Two scotches later and after a "but-if-it-makes-you-happy" talk from me, my husband went back to the hat shop and purchased the hat. We now call it the "mortgage payment hat." He wears it all the time, and it still makes him unbelievably happy.

Whether we long for stuff, experiences, or a change, paying attention to our wants is important. Life can teem with moments of intense and often surprising longing.

Here's how it happened to me not long ago: There was nothing not to like about my life in my late 60s. I lived by the water with a man I loved who loved me back. I biked, enjoyed good health and friends, traveled, and cherished my relationship with my beautiful daughter and her family. I finally had determined a path for my work in the future. Life was good.

A simple invitation to a place I'd never been began my undoing. It happened as I walked up a hill in a Mexican mountain town on a bright, sunny day. The experience was a strong stir that arrived with clear intent: *OMG, I want to live here.* I could have blamed the altitude.

My thoughts expanded: *I want months, not days, in a different culture. I want to better know individuals I'm meeting. I like all this walking on cobblestones in this old town where I buy beautiful flowers in the market for not a lot of money, buy fruit without stickers on them, listen to bells, and am the recipient of the shoeshine man's smile as he listens to my very bad Spanish.*

I also had to admit I liked daily life with a maid and gardener—both in the realm of possibility on my budget if living in Mexico. I've had extended stays of three or more months in Nicaragua, Chile, Argentina, and Ecuador. This was different. This longing of mine wasn't about a few months' stay. "A couple of years," I said to myself.

Returning home, I searched online for real estate. I have never returned from anywhere and done that. Where did my longing come from? I do not know. It simply arrived. I could have archived it. I did not.

In longing we move *from something to something we want that is often unexplained.* Longing may seem to make little sense. Longing can begin with a tiny notion. Longing can clang so loudly it hurts. Often we are determined to block out the noise of an unfulfilled whim or instinct. Perhaps you are good at this. Many of us are.

I visited San Miguel de Allende four more times to look beneath my infatuation. I took friends with me and watched as they never felt anything near my euphoria. Some liked it well enough. Others readily packed and would not return. Two friends who clearly loved the lives they created in San Miguel provided solace. One moved to San Miguel from Atlanta more than 10 years ago, and vibrancy radiated through the ends of her short red hair. The other sold her home on a coveted street with a view of the soaring pink spires of the neo-Gothic church in the town square and said, "It's the worst mistake I've ever made."

Perhaps you think it's crazy to harbor hopes and dreams in the last 20 years of life, let alone act on them. I can't honestly say I blame you. It complicates things and gets you all scaredy-cat. My husband and daughter were not wild about this idea from the beginning. Three months into my first year I received this text from my daughter: "Okay, Mom. I'm tired of this. We miss you. It's time to come home now."

It would behoove anyone turning 60 to get a good list of unfulfilled desires up against a realistic timeline of your life, which is now two-thirds done. You can become far less intimidated about changing up your life when you understand this is a smaller timeline than you've ever had to work with.

Eventually I realized that intense longing has bored holes into my good life more than once, as it most likely has with yours. My longing moments always begin with "Oh my god," because they upend me with surprise:

> OMG, I want to get married. *(1965 and again in in 1981)*
> OMG, I'd like to bike the Pyrenees. *(ongoing)*
> OMG, I want to have a baby. *(1969)*
> OMG, I have to go here (inspired by a picture of a place I'd never heard of: Oaxaca, Mexico). *(1988)*
> OMG, I've got to leave this job and do something else. *(early 1990s)*
> OMG, I want to get in that sailboat and see how far I can sail it (in my case, learn to sail it). *(2011)*

Action ensued on all of these except for that biking trip to the Pyrenees, which is a stretch for my capabilities (but I'm not dismissing it). Modified, it could happen. These longings turn out to be markers of change that made my life bigger and better.

Longing doesn't feel out of place as I age. It feels grand.

In an interview with Lydia, I asked why she chose to move from her home in Kentucky to live full time in Mexico. "It's my morning walk in my garden," she explained. "The flowers and the birds are just so beautiful."

"But didn't you have a beautiful garden in Kentucky?" I asked.

"Yes, I did," she replied. "But in this place, I feel different. I feel new."

Waiting for something "new" to appear in life is an option. But moving toward newness with our freedom—to choose a path out of your ordinary, do something different, make a first-time attempt—is an effort steeped in possibility for everyone.

Ken Dychtwald, foremost authority on aging and longevity, said, "I think it's really a psychological metamorphosis. During this transitional period, some people still feel unsettled, anxious or bored, but eventually they realize that 'I can be fresh. I can be new.'"[10]

To feel the newness of life after 50 or 60 years of living is extraordinary.

WHAT MATTERS MOST

Two threads of experiences make up a life—the internal and the external. When we think of life in retirement, we are most familiar with outer experiences—what we'll do, where we'll go, what adventures we'll have. We can still pay attention to often more subtle urges of our being asking us to integrate who we want to be with who we are now. Rather than choose indifference, we can find and face new ways of being ourselves.

In our maturity, we can experience newfound freedom, reclaiming wonder, awe, and delight that are rightfully ours in our later years.

Happy and Ambitious?

Hugh Grant, in his role as St. Clair Bayfield in the movie *Florence Foster Jenkins*, plays a failed English actor who recognized that his acting career had been only modestly successful and had little prospect of being anything more. His line, delivered deadpan by Grant, renders a subject to discuss and debate.

"Once freed from the tyranny of ambition, I started to live."

Did you have an ambitious young self? If ambition has an expiration date, when is or was yours? Can you be overly ambitious for your age? Staying open to our own development and being flexible to set our own path might be what ambition looks like as we age. What are your thoughts?

Doing Nothing

The Dutch have a name for doing nothing; it's called niksen. Some say we need more of it. Niksen literally means to do nothing, to be idle or doing something without any use. Just hanging around, looking out the window, lying on the bed looking up at the ceiling or listening to music while not doing anything else—this is niksen.

With more freedom, we have lots more time to "niks." This stress buster can inspire creativity and improve your problem solving. But while it's good for us, we can't do nothing all the time. Or can we?

How much niksen do you want or need in retirement life? How will you know when moments of doing nothing are more about just being lazy and not doing the work of finding a new life? Simply said, how will you use your time?

9

THE FOURTH PORTAL

Kinship

Some people go to priests; others to poetry; I to my friends.

—Virginia Woolf

Anyone who ever gave you confidence, you owe them a lot.

—Truman Capote

In the mid-1990s, Carl Kooyoomjian, newly hired vice president of global procurement at the Coca-Cola Company, set forth an initiative to change the structure and behavior of the corporate entity to the bottlers around the world. This change initiative—"moving forward to the future"—was deemed essential to the prosperity of the company. As the lead consultant, I worked with Carl and his senior team on two critical meetings that would determine the success or failure of the initiative.

After a difficult but ultimately victorious three-day meeting with a select group of bottlers, a second meeting with 60 members of the procurement team in Atlanta took place in a large hotel ballroom. Carl opened with "a picture of a more productive future" and emphasized how each person in the room had responsibility for this transformational change. The day proceeded with table topics, discussions, and reports back from small groups that included "things we do that destroy trust" and "how can we work together differently."

On the second morning, individuals took time to reflect and focus on what was vital for each of them to take into the future and what was important to leave behind. Some identified key partnerships, a spirit of collaboration, and a sense of humor to take forward, while leaving behind silo thinking, thin skins, boring meetings, and acceptance of status quo.

That afternoon, I asked Carl to offer comments. His inspiring message on how the secret to change is to focus all our energy not on the past but on building the future was a perfect finale to what only few in the room knew would happen next—a real-time event of moving to the future.

As the theme song from *The Bridge over the River Kwai* boomed over the speakers and the double doors in the back of the ballroom opened, everyone turned to watch three men wheel in a curved 30-foot wood walking bridge and position it over the threshold that spilled into the large reception area. Custom backpacks embroidered with "Moving Forward to the Future" were distributed as I instructed that we were now—indeed—leaving the past behind. "Put your personal items and the slips of paper identifying what you want to take to the future inside your backpack. Leave everything else."

Table by table individuals with backpacks slung over their shoulders marched over the bridge out of the ballroom through the reception area into another ballroom themed and decorated as "Our Future." As I write this, I hear in my head the triumphant music of *Bridge over the River Kwai* (bet you can too!). I recall the emotion and exuberance we all felt leaving that room. Of all the change initiatives I helped design and facilitate, this is the most memorable.

Your future of health and well-being depends on a change initiative—more personal perhaps—but just as critical. As you march over an imaginary bridge into your future, this chapter on the Portal of Kinship explores the social architecture that you have built over the past 20 to 40 years. You've invested in family, friends, and BFFs. These people are important. We know this. But now as we move into the future, we must do more.

In this last third of life, one of our responsibilities to ourselves is to examine, create, and maintain a framework of attachments that serves us well. Now is the time to deepen friendships; prune friendships; make new friends; establish different arrangements within marriages when necessary; set boundaries with parents, children, and siblings; and disengage with family members who treat us badly and are disrespectful. There is a lot to cover in this chapter.

ARE FRIENDS AND FAMILY MORE
IMPORTANT THAN EATING KALE?

If we didn't know it or believe it before the pandemic, the hard reality we learned from our self-imposed social isolation is that we need people in our lives. I mean real people, not images. We need to sit beside them, look into their eyes, and bear-hug some of them. Text, phone, and Zoom do not replace nearness or touch. Many of us now know this.

COVID-19 reduced social contact and may have intensified loneliness for many, but pandemic or no pandemic, simply growing older will bring social isolation to your door. That said, we must prepare for the inevitable loss of life within our circle of family and friends and be aware of the shrinking opportunities to engage with others to combat aging's inescapable curse. It's called the loneliness epidemic, and it's safe to say that no matter your age you can and do feel lonely.

In a graduation class of more than 800, my 50th high school reunion in Ohio was well attended. Two people I didn't know came up to me and said these exact words: "Thank you for saying hello to me in the halls." One described high school as "the most crushing years of my life." I'm sure I said hello to most everyone without ever knowing that this small gesture made life a little better for a lonely fellow student.

Harvard research suggests feelings of social isolation are on the rise and that those hardest hit are older teens and young adults. In a national survey, 61 percent of the respondents age 18 to 25 reported high levels of loneliness.[1] Perhaps your teenage years were different. Maybe you were overwhelmingly elected president of your class and got to pick from numerous invites to the prom. Good for you.

But now that you are older, social isolation is likely to become an inevitable part of your life. As we get older, our children move away; we lose touch with friends and don't make new ones. We are divorced, separated, and widowed. The result is that a whole bunch of us live alone. In the United States, older people are more likely to live alone than elsewhere in the world.[2] Nearly one-third of all seniors live by themselves, according to the US Census Bureau. That's close to 13.8 million seniors aging alone. And the number of people living alone in their 80s and 90s is set to soar.[3] While living alone doesn't automatically lead to senior loneliness, the two often go hand in hand.

Don't get me wrong. Many of us want to live alone. We like it. In conversations with men and women over 60, I can confidently report they wouldn't have it any other way. Sarah, a widow in her late 60s, has trouble with her knees but still sees the world as her oyster. When her son and daughter-in-law offered to put a tiny house in their backyard for her, she had a swift, straightaway response: "How sweet. How nice—but not in my lifetime. THANK YOU!"

I only live part of my time alone, but I, too, enjoy the heck out of it. I like my independence, not having to look at my husband's aviation art of divebombing P-47s, choosing my own Netflix series, and not cooking. Is this a gender thing? It appears so. Like Sarah, increasing numbers of older women are making a conscious decision to live by themselves—and enjoying it. The Administration on Aging found that 37 percent of women over 65 in the United States live by themselves, are happy about it, and wouldn't want to live any other way.

But despite the benefits or gender, a senior solo lifestyle has risks. If we aren't careful, we can become isolated, and that comes with consequences no one wants.

In the 2021 Annual Report on Retirement in the *Wall Street Journal*, Dr. Marc Agronin, geriatric psychiatrist at Miami Jewish Health, implores us to understand that lack of contact with people can possibly have a greater impact on mortality than smoking, obesity, and lack of physical activity.[4] Agronin lists smiles, touches, greetings, social pleasantries, and face-to-face talks that add sensory elements as the currency of a healthy mind and body and explains that the physicality of these interactions taps into the most primal centers in our brains that serve to reassure and soothe us, relax muscles, lower blood pressure and stress hormones, and increase endorphins.

Many seniors living alone maintain active social lives. They regularly see family and friends, book group travel adventures, actively nurture partnerships or marriages, and are involved in the community. Still, no one is exempt from feeling lonely.

Loneliness is the 70-year-old-woman who celebrates her birthday alone with no texts or calls from anyone. Loneliness is the man married to the woman who gives all of her love and time to grandchildren. Loneliness is the successful 65-year-old entrepreneur who slides a $10 million yacht into the water and calls his kids to go on a boat trip, but they're "too busy." Loneliness is the attractive, fit woman hiking in Chile with a travel group who wishes she could make a friend but doesn't know where to start. Loneliness is sitting at your kitchen table wanting to talk to someone who knows you well and realizing no one like that is in your life anymore.

Whether you live alone or not, growing and maintaining a strong social network is the work to be done. Friendships reduce the risk of mortality or developing certain diseases. Family can help speed recovery if you fall. A social relationship with a neighbor or fellow bird watcher reduces the risk of stroke. But most all, protect yourself from loneliness because the ache of loneliness hurts.

So is having coffee with a new friend more important than your yoga class? Yes. And should you visit your son even if your daughter-in-law will be her usual snippy self? Yes. And is inviting your sister who has undermined you for years—and still does—good for your new social structure? We'll get to that.

FRIENDSHIP MOUNTAIN

The word "friend" enters our vocabulary at age three and signals the beginning of a social structure that will be important until we die. My friends shape my life just as your friends shape yours. We talk and think through problems together—who to marry; what job to take; who to divorce; who to sleep with; who to keep seeing or stop seeing; how do deal with our mother; what to do with our son's new partner, a husband, ex-wife, or another friend. My conversations with friends have helped me make better judgments, and just as important, friends make me smile and laugh as life unfolds.

Most of us have different kinds of friends—fun friends, loyal friends, wild friends, and brutally honest friends. We also have friends who complain, brag, mooch, or generally fit the description of "flaky."

An illustration on the awesome website waitbutwhy.com divvies out the kinds of friends in our lives in a different way. The illustration is of a color-coded mountain—"Your Life Mountain"—dotted with tiny stick human images in three tiers that run parallel down the mountain with "You" at the top.

Tier 1. Your Closest Friends (not many here).

Tier 2. Your Pretty-Good Friends (a few more here).

Tier 3. Your Not-Really Friends (lots here).

At the bottom of the mountain and along the distant horizons, there are oodles of dotted human images labeled Acquaintances and Strangers.

While there are eight images at the top of the mountain in the area deemed "Your Closest Friends," experts insist that only one to three people could be in this area—absolutely no more. According to Laura Carstensen, PhD, founding director of the Stanford Center of Longevity, research supports that three close friends does seem to be the magic number.

Uh-oh. What if you don't have three? Many relationship experts suggest that having too few close contacts can be risky. "Fewer than three connections is just too few for comfort," writes Carstensen.[5] Social spheres generally contract with age, so you may have fewer friends at age 50 than you did at eight, but at this stage of the game, for lots of different reasons—death, a falling-out, loss of interest, geography, dementia, shrinking shared interests—you can be vulnerable to losing the whole top of your mountain.

One solution is to make new connections to take care of the ones you lose. But the nature of friendship is they don't automatically ignite, and making friends can be hard work. (This is another thing we'll talk about later.) Another key for a strong social network of friendships is to have a diverse mix of age. If all your relationships are with people your own age, you are vulnerable to losing the whole network.

But just adding anyone as friends is not a good solution and will not add to our health and well-being. Small social spheres do not pose a problem as long as the friendships have a strong, high-quality attachment. You want relationships that truly are a source of emotional enrichment.

Did you make enough friends for a lifetime? Probably not. But before making new friends, a look at those people you are calling "friends" is a good place to start. According to Carstensen, people engage in a natural pruning process as they age, removing people who are not so satisfying while retaining ones they enjoy. How are you doing with that?

WHEN OLD FRIENDS AREN'T THE
BEST FRIENDS ANYMORE

We assimilate into the narrative about friendships the idea that old friends carry far more status than other friendships. "Old" friends are special. They assume a grand, elevated status simply because they have endured. I know many people (and so do you) heading off to the annual weekend with "my grade school buddies," "my Air Force class," or "my college buds," who relish and hold these relationships in high esteem. We've known each other sooooo long!

Perhaps *Big Chill* moments aren't part of your life. Still, you've gotten the message that old friends are the best—better than new ones, precious even, with no apparent natural life cycle.

> Make new friends, but don't forget the old. One is silver,
> the other gold.
>
> —Unknown

Gold is one of the metals of antiquity, beautiful, currently 75 times more expensive than silver. I have gold jewelry pieces languishing in my top drawer in the form of one earring, a busted gold chain, and a wedding band from a previous marriage. These pieces—broken, outdated, and not meaningful anymore—could be melted down and redesigned or perhaps I don't need them in my life anymore. I must decide.

You decide every day who you want to be friends with and who you don't. You decide who to keep, where to put some distance, and whether you really want to go out with that group again.

"Friendships come with terms," Katherine, 40, my talented hair stylist, tells me. "I have an old friend who is never on time, talks over me, and forgets my birthday. Those are her terms, and for now, I accept those terms."

When a friendship—no matter how old—loses its luster or turns toxic and no longer yields significant returns, we must determine if that friendship is worth keeping. Are your old friends good friends? Are they worth keeping?

Having people who have known us for years is comforting. But let's be honest. Sometimes old friends are not worth keeping. One blogger said this about old friends: Your 18-year-old self knows them. Your 40-year-old self should not know them. This leads me to believe that checking in with your 60-year-old self about some of your friends could be enlightening.

In his book *Vital Friends: The People You Can't Afford to Live Without*, Gallup Organization's director Tom Rath undertook a massive study of friendship, alongside several leading researchers. The book recommends carrying out your own "friendship audit" in order to recognize which of your friendships provide you with the different things you need, then to sharpen each friendship in line with its strength and value. Judging friends in such a detached way may make us uncomfortable. Part of living an extraordinary life is an examination of your current friends.

Does there ever come a point in life where we learn who matters, who doesn't and who never did, who won't anymore and who always will? We don't seem to have a regular rite of passage into a retirement life where we step back and form some sort of picture of our friendships. We should.

The reality is some friendships necessitate boundaries; friendships may need culling; some friendships require slow ending; others could benefit from deepening; some friendships should never have begun; others need a clean, quick end.

We have a lot to decide about people we are calling friends. Furthermore, we need to make new friends. That can take a lot of time and be super daunting. Plus, as an older adult, it is harder.

FRIENDSHIP BOOT CAMP

"Do you want to play?" asks my three-year-old grandson when another toddler approaches the sandbox. What happens next is either heartwarming or heartbreaking. Sometimes there's no reply and nothing happens; other times the reply is "no," and then the child walks away. But when a stare softens between two toddlers, something magical happens and they begin to play together.

I have admired my grandson's patience and tenacity in many of these situations. Getting refused three times in a row would make me want to go home. But not Liam. He runs his truck through the dirt again and again until another child comes by and he asks for the fourth time, "Do you want to play?"

Our strong desire to connect is hardwired into each of us, but as we get older, it is increasingly difficult to form meaningful friendships. There are reasons for why it's harder to make new friends. First, we stay really busy and feel short on time. Second, we are rusty. Third, we don't make the effort. Fourth, we don't make it a priority.

So if friends feel harder to make, then we're less inclined to put in consistent time and effort. Children have friendships facilitated through play dates and school. In midlife our workplaces crackled with opportunities for friendships with coworkers and colleagues. But if you are 72 and need a new friend, it feels AWKWARD.

Given that manipulators, drama queens, and egomaniacs no longer make the cut, our pool of candidates for future friends is smaller. But if we pull back on the effort to restock friends, we may not have enough for a lifetime.

"You know I'm the last one left," said my father, 95, one afternoon in the new environment of a nursing home. "All my friends are gone." So true—he was last of the siblings, uncles, and grandfathers; last of the high school football team and the WWII army unit. Three days later my father introduced me to his roommate. "Barbara, this is Harry, my new friend." You can enter the kingdom of friendship with no age requirements or keys. The campaign for finding friends never ceases. Never. This is not a book on 10 ways to make friends or how to deepen friendships or be a great friend. The message here is that your best life needs people in it.

During an exploration of the Kinship Portal with a client, he whips out a color-coded list of friends. We are looking at it closely when he smiles and asks, "I have 570 Facebook Friends. Does that count?" I smile back. "It does not." Actually, that might not be true.

Do our digital connections count as friendships? The social media friends versus "real" friends debate is ongoing. Some argue that intimacy can exist in both digital and physical realms and that plenty of real relationships play out solely on the Internet. Most of us move fluidly between the social contexts of face-to-face encounters and the Internet. To dismiss online friendships is a mistake, some argue, saying that having a friend online is better than not having one at all. Life is lonely, they reason, and all connections have value.

Can a real relationship forge between people who never meet?

One part of the controversy is how online activity connecting people deludes us into thinking we have friends and obscures the importance of face-to-face interactions. Yes, we meet people online and exchange information. But that's all social media can transmit.

Susan Pinker, developmental psychologist and author of *The Village Effect: How Face-to-Face Contact Can Make Us Healthier, Happier and Smarter*, notes, "No body language, no pheromones, no touch." Experts like Pinker argue that social media is not good at deepening relationships.

The Internet has been part of our culture for more than two decades. It's in your pocket, on your wrist. Forty-five percent of those 65 and older report using social media.[6] Each of us will decide whether digital friends are a source for new friends that are real friends, how they fit into our lives, and what benefits we receive from the interaction.

MIDDLE RING FRIENDS

"So," I say to my husband as we enjoy sunset on the terrace of our new Panhandle dream home, "how many friends have you made this week?" The question lacks sweetness.

After two months in our chosen geography of place, we count using one index finger the number of people we can call "friend"—our architect. We had moved to a place where we knew no one. We needed friends, and finding them was more effort than we'd remembered. I'm more extroverted, but my husband is not off the hook. His strategy was cigars, scotch, and a local bar followed by golf, more scotch, and more cigars. It worked.

Today my husband has more friends than I do in Pensacola. Not "best friends." Not people who grew up like him. Not people he's tight with or gives bear hugs to. More like fist-bump people. Still, they stock life with social, happy, and meaningful interactions.

The Vanishing Neighbor, a book heralded as a lucid guide to more than 60 years of social science research, by Mark Dunkelman, Clinton

Foundation senior fellow and journalist, uses the metaphor of Saturn's rings to survey our relationships.

- In your inner ring are your most intimate relationships—family and close friends—people who love you no matter what.
- Your outer-ring relationships are relationship that are "passing to transactional"—a result of a single shared interest or experience. Examples are professional acquaintances, Parrot Heads, social media connections with people who share your passion for vigorous environmentalism, or the people in the reserved section of the Texas Rangers.
- Your middle-ring relationships are familiar but not intimate, "friendly" but not close: think of neighbors you wave to, the regulars at your Saturday cycling group, or members of your Bible-study group.

One of the most significant changes in the United States in recent decades, according to Dunkelman, is the decay in middle-ring relationships. Middle-ring relationships reverberate with diverse points of view, unlike affinity groups who are like-minded with similar values and beliefs.

There is an intimacy between you and your best friend and a yahooing alum. But folks in the middle ring have grown up differently. They may not be poles apart from our way of thinking, yet it's distinctive unlike what you're used to hearing. A middle-ring friend is one who can butt you up the side of the head with an idea you deem "strange," "way out," "silly," or "stupid." They can support their thesis. Discord and debate could show up. You might change your perspective or discover something new.

It is in middle-ring relationships where we learn to deal with and understand people who have different points of view. It's where we learn to question old ideas, stretch our minds, learn to empathize, and begin to accept that we live in a society of people with a variety of points of view.

The expat community is an incubator for middle-ring friendships. People choosing a lifestyle in another country leave family and friends and are challenged to build new lives in an unfamiliar culture. In Cuenca, Ecuador, a city with more than 4,000 expats, more than three-quarters of the people I met told me unsolicited, "I have more friends and have met more different, interesting people in three months than I had my whole life."

This community of assorted gringos—a retired dentist from Kansas; a teacher; a Kentucky couple, both artists; an Alaskan filmmaker; a truck driver—gather to exchange valuable information but also purposefully connect to create middle-ring friendships with potential for long-lasting intimacy.

Dunkelman argues that the rest of us are not going out of our way to find and cultivate middle-ring friends. We lack relationships with neighbors and don't talk to people with different points of view. The research clearly shows that over the past few decades, Americans socialized more with their families and others who live a few miles away but not with neighbors.

As we make efforts to fortify social networks, we'll want to consider diverse options in age, values, and points of view.

'TIL AGE DO US PART

At a time when divorce is becoming less common for millennials, so-called gray divorce is on the rise for baby boomers. "Gray divorce," also known as the "silver splitter" or "diamond divorce," is a term used to refer to the increasing trend of late-in-life divorces. According to the Pew Research Center, the divorce rate has roughly doubled since the 1990s for American adults ages 50 and older. And for those over 65, the increase was even higher—it more than tripled since 1990.[7]

What's going on? In the late 1970s and early 1980s, when the first boomers were between the ages of 29 and 39, the divorce rate peaked. Aging boomers then remarried only to have those marriages fail. Statistics show that in the United States 67 percent of second marriages fail, and 74 percent of third marriages end in divorce. It seems we are not risk-averse when it comes to walking down the aisle.

Some of the recent rising divorce rates can also be blamed on COVID. Unexpected in-home isolation put a sharper focus on marriages. I remember laughing when several women friends described how they felt in lockdown: "This togetherness is getting thin, and I'm tired of cooking." There is talk among relationship experts and family attorneys that more marriages may wilt post-pandemic.

A significant portion of couples over 50 who have been married for at least 30 years divorce—and not because of infidelity, abuse, arguing, or money. With longer lives and financial independence, a couple's choice of going separate ways most often is about a change in course for the time they have left. According to Dr. Vandervelde, psychologist and author of six books, including *Retirement for Two*, the number one reason people felt they might divorce after retirement was because they wanted to live in different places and have different lifestyles.[8]

When marriages get in the way of a desire to be near grandchildren, travel, enjoy a certain climate, or seek adventure, cutting marital ties can seem inevitable—and often is. But mostly, marriages are evaluated in terms of "my last chapter" or "my time." Seeking fulfillment and wanting different things in the last third of life becomes paramount. Vandervelde cites this issue of wanting to live in different places and have different lifestyles as a "difficult area in which to compromise."

But compromise is happening.

YOUR PLACE OR MINE

The trend of married but living apart, introduced in chapter 6, describes the growing number of married couples living in two different geographic places. Another popular relationship resolution the over-50 set seems to be leading is the Living Apart Together idea (LAT). Rather than marry or live together, many of them have separate homes and see each other several times a week. Partnered adults between the ages of 57 and 85 were twice as likely to have separate homes as to live together.[9] They say they are highly committed to each other but want that personal space and independence.

But LAT is also a lifestyle for couples who choose not to marry. Often couples who begin a relationship later in life are also keeping separate homes. Moving in together doesn't seem to be a prerequisite for these love partners who cherish private space and financial independence. When both partners keep separate homes, their finances, and their routines, romance can blossom.

The LAT movement is the relationship trend to watch as older couples, married or not, live out their last decades. When it comes to the research, having a partner blasts you in a stratosphere of positive paybacks. Studies indicate that people who are married live longer and enjoy better mental health and well-being. While that may be true, couples who choose to soldier on in a marriage that often feels lifeless, stale, or filled with conflict may regret not taking the opportunity longevity offers.

These changes in the way we look at marriage and late-in-life partnerships can be seen as ultimately healthy and refreshing. Couples can begin to openly talk to one another about what's working—and what's not. When people engage in a dialogue before retirement about what each wants in their last decades, marriage or a committed relationship can grow and deepen.

The work of the Kinship Portal is to be deliberate in choosing how to move forward, whether living apart or parting ways. Knowing that life is unpredictable and precious, either way becomes a new chapter in a longer life with possibilities for fulfillment.

THE FRACTURED FAMILY

Family is the single most important influence on a child's life. Families set the stage for future relationships and can be a source of affection, encouragement, and a sense of belonging throughout our lives. Everyone is born into a family, but not everyone ends up in an adult paradise.

Most of us have a bloodline squad with a couple of relatives who clash with our values; are disrespectful, controlling, manipulative, rude, or mean; or drive us crazy in some other way. Any family member can become a tormentor or behave in unacceptable ways to create spectacular toxicity. Given enough toxicity, the bond fractures—sometimes forever.

Families split apart in different ways. Parents watch grown children not get along and often witness brother and sister estrangement. You can be a conscientious parent only to find that your kid wants nothing to do with you when they're older. Perhaps you have a hateful sibling who has put a damper on a big bulk of your life, a parent who is abusive, or a stepdaughter who talks about you behind your back . . . and you've about had it.

We are all flawed. But when a family member creates so much stress, anxiety, and pain, we aren't letting it slide. We are cutting ties. One US study found that more than 40 percent of participants had experienced family estrangement at some point. In another study, more than a quarter of adults responding to a US survey by the Cornell Family Reconciliation Project reported being estranged from a family member.[10] The representational survey, which is the first of its kind, suggests by extension that tens of millions of Americans may be estranged from at least one relative.

"That number is probably low," said Karl Pillemer, professor of human development at Cornell University who lead the study. "People find this to be an embarrassing problem and feel too shameful to share."[11]

Of the parents who are estranged from adult children, more than one-third fall into the 70- to 80-year-old-age group. While traumatic childhoods are a reason given by adult children, the reasons are not so clear-cut in the majority of cases. Not feeling loved or nurtured, an incident that occurred years ago, or episodes that the parents may not even be aware of can also be the cause. Adult children often cut off their parents to protect themselves from a narcissistic personality, excessive neediness, or extreme negativity.

Whatever the reason, estranged parents don't have many others to talk to. Estranged from her daughter for more than 10 years, Beth Bruno writes that while her friends acknowledged the depth of her pain, their eyes would ask, "What did you do?"[12]

When parental-child relationships hit the skids, a grandparent's relationship with grandchildren may become collateral damage. There are times when parents are right to deny grandparents contact with grandchildren. Reasons that come to mind are sex offenders, alcoholics, substance abusers, not following safety rules established by parents, or undermining parental authority.

But those children of our children are mighty important to us in this season of life. We love them to the moon and back. Losing contact with grandchildren can bring up a stew of emotions, but eventually the outcome is plain and simple heartbreak.

Eighty percent of grandparents call their grandchildren a top priority in their lives. When asked what facets of life—health, home, work, leisure, giving, finance, family—is most satisfying, the number one answer was always "family." In fact, more retirees said "family" than all the other facets of life combined.[13]

What is fueling so much family estrangement? In the modern family, an obligation of honor and duty to family no longer is binding. The historian, Stephanie Coontz, director of education and research for the Council on Contemporary Families, states, "Never before have family relationships been seen as so inter-woven with the search for personal growth, the pursuit of happiness and the need to confront and overcome psychological obstacles."[14]

The most prominent path that comes between family members is often part of a painful history that proves just too hard to move on from. Five years ago, Vivien, 75, broke ties with her younger sister, 67. She describes early on petty grievances that stoked a progressive "mean streak in my sibling."

"My sister resented my hand-me-downs, refused to be my maid-of-honor, and worked hard to add drama to family events," states Vivien. "Being with her was like walking on eggshells." While there are brief moments of ambivalence, Vivien does not entertain a reconnection. "Honestly, my life is better without her in it."

Adult children who have divorced their parents say they did it for the good of their families or for their own good. A 2015 study found that 80 percent of individuals who cut ties with a family thought it had a positive effect on their lives. They reported feeling "freer, more independent, and stronger."[15]

This is not to say that when you decide to stop talking to your mother or you sever ties with a cousin, your life is void of negative consequences. The truth is you miss them, feel sad, often revisit the past to try to gain more understanding, and watch other family members take sides. Plus, family gatherings will be complicated or obsolete.

Deciding which friends to keep in or out of one's life as an important strategy for happiness was talked about earlier in this chapter. But culling family? That can be harder. Family defines us. Stories of family dysfunction can make us roar with laughter, weep with sorrow, or shrug our shoulders dismissively. Terminating relationships with "family" can feel morally and inherently wrong.

But when the bad outweighs the good, we must evaluate the health of that relationship for our own well-being. Deciding to manage the relationship is a brave step. You don't have to hate them. But when a burden to your sense of self and an unhealthy relationship result, you don't need them either. Age does not grant you respect, and not all people want what's best for you. That's your job.

Many of us will not find our biological family capable of change. But in the living of our remaining days, we need a family. Today the definition of family varies and moves in shifting patterns like the view into a kaleidoscope. Honestly, it's blurry.

DEFINING FAMILY TODAY

As a single parent with an only child for more than seven years, I had to come to terms with what felt like the smallness of a family. There was only she and I. As a family of two, we often lacked that "fun family" feeling, and family dinners sitting at a table are not something either of us can recall. When Elizabeth's third-grade teacher asked what her favorite television show was, my daughter said, "*60 Minutes.*"

"Why that show?" asked the teacher.

"Because that's the night my mom cooks and we eat dinner on the floor in front of the TV." My daughter's drawing of her family revealed the two of us as stick figures holding hands in front of an apartment building surrounded by a concrete parking lot. I was relieved. While we weren't exactly scripted into the sacred definition of family, we seem to have survived.

All this has changed, of course. Experts tell us that we are likely living through the most rapid change in family structure in human history. Whereas "family" was once a married man and a woman and children born in wedlock, that definition is now so much broader. What constitutes a family today?

- Nickie and Melina, lesbians, married, together 25 years, with two children, Grace and Lyle, and two dogs.

- Lillian and Jeff, married with two adopted children, three grandmothers, two biological mothers, and one biological father.
- Shawn and Tina, an over-70 cohabitating couple, with eight children and 21 grandchildren between them.

Bet you can add more examples from your own life to this list of family representations. The past 40 years have seen dramatic change in the shape of family life; the diversity of family structure is great. The consensus among researchers is that it is very hard to talk of a "typical family." They also agree that there is not so much the breakdown of the family as its reinvention.

We're talking a lot about family in this chapter for good reasons. As boomers we have adapted family to shape our aspirations of autonomy, self-definition, and emotional integrity. But while family is good for us and makes us happy, friends—good friends—may be better for us than family. Studies find that friendships, not family, were a stronger predictor of well-being at later ages.[16]

Taking that to heart, many are choosing their family to be a group of close friends who care for them and have their back. It's working great.

THE VOLUNTARY KIN MOVEMENT

A decade ago, 20 people over age 50 gathered in my home for a traditional Thanksgiving dinner, and one person, holding his wine glass high, renamed the holiday "Friendsgiving." Two of us hosting the event had invited people we knew who didn't have a place at a family table for one reason or another. Some of us had been friends for about two hours.

Today, seven in 10 young Americans aged 18 to 38 prefer Friendsgiving over a traditional Thanksgiving for reasons that fit most of us: "Because they don't have to bite their tongue around the dinner table or have to worry about offending a relative."[17]

It's one thing to substitute friends for family at the Thanksgiving table and quite another to plop them into a drawing of your family tree. But common ancestry is not a prerequisite for many as they choose individuals and consider them "My Family" regardless of their legal or blood connection.

These relationships, closer and more enduring than biology, are common within self-constructed families and are no less real or meaningful than conventional ones, according to Dr. Dawn Braithwaite, head of communication studies at the University of Nebraska. She and her colleagues call such families "voluntary kin."[18]

Nora Weaver, 70, has always had a family of birth and a family of choice.

She says: "Probably for 50 years or more, I have been surrounded by people I consider my Family of Choice. I'm very discriminating about the people about whom I feel this way. My closest friend is my 'sistie,' and I have a few good men friends that I consider 'bros.' I have lots of cousins of choice. These people and I have a level of intimacy, shared philosophy, and shared experience that is priceless to me."

It can be easy to assume Nora has no other family or is estranged from family. But that's not the case. Her biological family is two brothers with whom she is extremely close. "I love my tiny family, but we are a very small group."

Voluntary kin relationships serve important life functions: a sense of belonging, as well as financial and emotional relief. A core unit consists of hand-picked people who love and respect you and enrich your life. Knowing someone is there for you not out of some genetic obligation but because they genuinely care about you makes that bond infinitely more significant. What makes these relationships different from friendships is that they often become central to one's identity. Knowing these people want the best for you provides a reservoir of assuredness.

If you have friends (even one friend) who watches out for you, supports you, and can be there for you, you have an emotional family. Voluntary kin can increase feelings of belonging, foster emotional closeness, and become a person to turn to in case of crisis.

We've all heard someone say, "She's like a sister to me." Many voluntary kin relationships have been in place for a long time, or they grow out of a close relationship that has developed. But I'll be the first to tell you that if you begin now to make new friends or grow the ones you have, a family of your choosing could emerge. Friends I made after age 60 have blossomed or are on their way to being long-lasting friendships.

Choosing family might not be talked about much, but people are doing it.

SOLO SENIORS BY CHOICE OR CHANCE

I meet solo seniors everywhere—in airport lounges, at retirement centers, on trains, in the dentist's office, or at honky-tonk music venues. Some have family to rely on and some don't. When asked the number one thing that what would make life in retirement better, many individuals I interview reply, "I wish I could find someone to share my life with."

While a partner late in life is the wish for some, others find the idea outlandish. "Are you kidding me?" says Tara, 72 and divorced, as she fishes around in her backpack for the key to her Airbnb in Cuenca, Ecuador. "I love my life. I've got my freedom, a ton of friends, and my health."

As ridiculous as it may sound, these individuals who have no spouse, children, or close relatives nearby are often called elder orphans. No one I know is going to like that term. The term "elder orphan" was first coined by Dr. Maria Carney, chief of geriatric and palliative medicine at Northwest Health of Great Neck, New York, and a leading researcher. AARP picked up this phrase (they are also referred to as "solo agers"), and it's considered a sort of standard in the publishing sphere.

Carol Marak launched the Elder Orphan Facebook group that now has a membership of more than 9,500. Marak observes distinct differences in members. Those with children feel the most isolated and alone when distance keeps them apart from family. And those who never had children have learned to build social networks of friends.[19]

This population is hiding in plain sight. Over 20 percent of people older than 65 are or are at risk of becoming elder orphans. According to AARP, more baby boomers are aging alone than any generation in US history.

For many, like Tara, solo is a lifestyle choice and a final destination. For others, it's an unexpected development or unavoidable result of growing older. When a marriage ends with the death of a spouse, even when the death may be anticipated, the transition to widowhood can be traumatic. One day you're married; the next day you are single, alone, and grieving.

"The quiet is thunderous. The emptiness is total. The sadness is overwhelming," writes Joe Friedman four months after his wife of 44 years died. Widowhood has immediate and longer-term consequences, including finances, health and well-being, personal relationships, and sense of self.

In the 65-plus group, 32 percent of women are widows and 11 percent of men are widowers. Men do not expect to be widowers as much as women expect to be widows, and this is a high-probability event in later life, particularly for women.[20] Younger widows and widowers (aged 50 to 75) have a more stable social network compared to older ones (over 75) who typically experience a reduced sense of closeness to people, even in an existing social network. Thus, those widowed later in life, men and women, may be at greater risk to experience social isolation or loneliness on top of grief.

Whether or not they remarry, widows and widowers do have opportunities for satisfying relationships that provide companionship and often even romance. The Joe I know today is in a very different place than the man I met with constant tears in his eyes shortly after losing his wife. Joe met Linda four years ago, and they've been together ever since. "She's my SO [significant other]," he says when he introduces us. When his eyes follow her as she leaves the room, he winks at me and smiles. "It's good. She's my main squeeze."

Your Kinship Portal is vast and challenging. This chapter lays out reality along with a whoop-and-nudge reminder that we must strengthen, fortify, build, and improve our social structure for the remaining years of life. If it sounds like work, some of it is—but it's good work. People in our lives have been, are, and will be a significant source of deep love, joy, and caring, even as they sometimes create crisis, chaos, and angst.

If we focus only on the sections written about culling friendships, gray divorce, widowhood, and family estrangement, the Portal of Kinship may appear to be a sad, lonely one. Don't do that. Instead, take a look at a card that symbolizes how we can move forward in kinship knowing what we know with the uncertainty that prevails but with a spirit of adventure.

(Full disclosure: the closest I've ever been to a tarot reading is non-chalantly trying to listen in on someone else's reading in Jackson Square in New Orleans. So I'm not an expert in tarot, but I do love the artwork on the cards—especially The Fool.)

The Fool is one of the most well-known and best loved of the 78 cards in the tarot deck. On The Fool card, a young man stands at the edge of a cliff without a care in the world as he sets out on a new adventure. He is dressed in bright colors, and over his shoulder is a modest knapsack containing everything he needs. At his feet is a small white dog that encourages him to charge forward and learn the lessons he came to learn. He is seemingly unaware that he is about to skip off a precipice into the unknown. The mountains behind symbolize the challenges yet to come.

It is believed that this card is a symbol of ourselves and our own lives—of great potential and new beginnings. We have all been The Fool once or twice in our lives. Just like the young man, you are on the outset of another journey. The Fool encourages us to have an open, curious mind and a sense of excitement and not to miss any opportunity that may appear on the way.

WHAT MATTERS MOST

Soul-searching your friends and family may not feel good at first. But as we get older, our health and well-being depend on connections to other people. Friendships need culling or deepening. New friends are a must. Family can be minefield full of disappointment and frustration or a place of solace and support. While there are no clear timelines on the work to be done in this Portal of Kinship, we can and should begin.

Can Your Sibling Be Your Best Friend?

While people and friends come in and out of our lives, the bonds with siblings remain. One should not assume that a sibling will turn out to be a lifelong friend. But often a brother or sister is the person who knows and loves you best. If your sibling is your best friend, are you nurturing that relationship? Are you ignoring a sibling bond because of something that happened long ago? Will this relationship enlarge or diminish your life? Find a way to examine the natural bonds that tie you to these individuals.

Who Are You Going to Have Lunch With?

There is no automatic relationship generator in retirement. In *What Color Is Your Parachute in Retirement*, authors Richard Bolles and John Nelson point out that for some retirees, the television becomes an automatic relationship generator. Television and the Internet do not produce deep links into friendships that matter. What type of involvement would be good to explore for you to build connections face-to-face? Explore alumni organizations, faith communities, performing arts organizations, athletic teams, activism opportunities, lifelong learning events, forest bathing adventures, group travel, and your local Mahjong groups.

Hold a Deep-Thinking Group

The tradition of freestyle intellectual conversation lives on in Calcutta. The city has a lively oral culture. The word *adda* (pronounced AHD-da) is a practice of friends getting together for long, informal, and rigorous conversations. Exalted topics—life, philosophy, meaning, and death—are explored in meandering conversation. "How do others feel about aging?" "Is loneliness a natural part of growing older?" Do not depend on your book club or dinner group to get into deep conversations. Hold your own adda, salon, or deep-thinking group to expand your connections and hear other points of view.

Part III

YOUR NEW 25-YEAR LIFE

10

HOW NOT TO SQUANDER
YOUR LAST DECADES

Don't stop until you're proud.

—Anna Colibri

Being on the wire is living; everything else is waiting.
—Kurt Wallenda, American high-wire artist,
founder of the Flying Wallendas

The first week of the Tour de France 2021, the greatest cycling race in the world, was filled with tears. No one wept as deeply as Mark Cavendish, the British sprinter, who dropped to the pavement with a Stage 4 win, putting his head in his hands as tears streamed from his goggles and his body rocked with sobs.

Cavendish, 36, was never expected by anyone to be in the competition, including himself. His staggering comeback was hailed by NBC Sports commentator Chris Horner, retired professional road racing cyclist and the second-best climber in the world. "It's one of the greatest things I have ever seen, and I've been following cycling for many decades."[1]

How Cavendish got to this extraordinary moment is not a fairy tale but a lesson for doubters and cynics of what life can hold when we choose to try. Facing a 25-year life ahead, we can be intentional and make an effort or we can drift and ignore the passing of time. We can take a chance and try for what we want—a little or not at all.

What's most important for a well-lived life is to increase resolve late in life and raise the bar for our living. No matter how much life has given you or taken away, the future is now. Perhaps one of the most striking examples in moving forward is how Cavendish did not allow the washouts of his recent past nor the lack of a team of supporters deny him choice.

THE FEAR OF NOT TRYING

A world cycling champ with an illustrious career, Cavendish had had deep disappointments for a long time and had indicated his retirement in 2020. Plagued by underperformance, clinical depression, a lengthy bout of the Epstein-Barr virus in 2017–2019, and a series of heavy crashes, he raced in 2020, according to the experts, "like a shadow of himself."

No one had offered a contract for the 2021 Tour de France. The Tour, the most outstanding and highly respected bike riding competition in the world, is held in July, mostly in France, with 22 teams of nine riders. The route covers 3,500 kilometers with 21 stages—nine flat stages, three hilly stages, and seven mountain stages over 21 days. There are two rest days.

Winning even one stage at the Tour makes a rider's career; Cavendish's illustrious career included 30 stage wins, the first at the age of 23. But after five years without a win anywhere, and at 36, a relatively advanced age for a sprinter, no one believed in him. Many thought he was washed up and said so. Cavendish soaked in the messages, seemed resigned, and appeared to be bowing out. In October 2020, at the post-race interview after Gent-Wevelgem, a classic road cycling race in Belgium, Cavendish told reporters, "That's perhaps the last race of my career." He finished in 74th place.

The emotional Cavendish-comeback-moment revolves on an axis of the same elements that will make or break an extraordinary life in retirement—vital behaviors, habits, attitudes, and choices. Cavendish had nothing left to prove in his glittering career. Most of us facing the last third of life, with or without a string of successes, often feel a measure of contentment or at least acceptance of the life we've lived. We don't feel we need to prove much either.

In our 60s, 70s, and 80s, we don't give up on life nor live with dying on our minds. But we can, and often do, quietly choose to believe that what we've achieved is the finale of promise for ourselves. Any anxiety or resignation about living what feels a smaller life is easily hidden within a lively travel itinerary, volunteerism, helicopter grandparenting, or book club mania.

While Cavendish at one point appeared to be bowing out of cycling, retirees don't bow out of life. Many of us work double hard to appear fulfilled and look good. We zoom around to exotic places, proudly share the joy of genealogy with our loved ones, put our gratitude journals in overdrive, join the senior plastic surgery trend, and try to appear as comforted in our aging as Fonda and Hepburn waiting for the loons in *On Golden Pond*.

But Cavendish changed his future when he dropped a bombshell and asked for more than he thought he could deliver. Even though he was unsure of himself and had been written off by his team, "not trying" became unacceptable. "He came to my office," said Patrick Lefevere, the team manager, and said, "I don't want to stop like this. I want to come back." Lefevere didn't have a spot and that was that.

The surprise call came less than a week before the start of the race after sprinter Sam Bennet was dropped from the roster due to an injured knee. "Thank you. Thank you, I'll try as hard as I can," Cavendish told his boss. "I'm giving you the chance," replied Lefevere. "You can thank me with your pedals."[2]

And that's what he did. Cavendish bawled along with the entire team when he won Stage 4, his 31st win after 10 years. Two days later he won Stage 6. Four days after that he won Stage 10. Three days later he won Stage 13 to tie the world's record of stage wins.

Cavendish failed to honor the idea of retiring from cycling. You, too, can fail to honor the idea of retiring in the traditional way. No one expected to see him compete in the Tour de France. The brutal truth is that no one expects to see you strive for much in the last third of your life either. Who do you know in their 70s who openly talks about wanting more out of life and shares ambitions that make your jaw drop? How many of us are surprising ourselves late in life? How long has it been since you had butterflies in your stomach?

Stunning comebacks aside, when something appears beyond our grasp, cultivating a strength in spirit is just as critical as a game plan. Bike sprinting is a head game, according to Jason Gay, a *Wall Street Journal* sports columnist. "You've got to have ferociously strong legs, yes, and it helps to have talented teammates to deliver you close to the finish line, but in the final, furious meter, you have to *believe*, unequivocally, to barrel out of that blurry pack at 45 MPH and gun it for the finish, elbows wide, head over handlebars, brakes be damned."[3]

Belief is a strong force. Many of us struggle with believing in ourselves and the idea that we can build lives in our final decades that will be *our best yet*. The work of the Four Portals allows you to start from strength, but it takes more than a game plan.

Why is it important to believe in yourself? All of life, including the years ahead with all their ups and downs, will have times when we just don't think we can do it. Giving up or feeling incapable of creating change leads us to think *life is fine the way it is*. The problem with this, however, is that it means we become passive about exploring what the future could hold. We may even question if we are entitled to more in life. Self-belief at its core is realizing that you deserve an extraordinary life full of dreams, accomplishments, and happiness simply because you are alive.

Believing in ourselves triggers vitality and allows us to fall in love with life once again. All experiences shape us, and this one is worth every risk it could possibly harbor.

WHEN THINGS DON'T TURN OUT

When I asked Katherine, 64, what might get in the way of her hopes and dreams for upcoming life in retirement, she paused then repeated the question. "What might get in my way?" She weighed the request and looked upward to the corner of the room. When her eyes met mine, she stated soberly, "My husband."

While partners in life, family, and even friends often have roles that can influence many of our future decisions, they are not the ones who will sabotage an extraordinary life. Spoiler alert: it will be you. Through neglect, procrastination, or not trying, you can end up living an okay life but not a great one.

What's at the core of these crippling behaviors? Underlying wounds from the past or present never fully leave us. Biography affects judgment, and since we have all dealt with vulnerability, uncertainty, and failure in our lives, we can now spend our remaining decades in a limbo of doubt unless we free up the past.

Life in retirement asks us to build a future. We could avoid bold-ness in our aspirations simply because the road of the first half of life turned up sinkholes. Are the holes in your life too big to allow a dream to be reworked or revived?

One thousand mountaineers were on Mt. Everest at the start of the 2014 season; 600 were Sherpas. Sixteen climbing Sherpas were killed as a result of an avalanche, and when Mt. Everest "functionally" closed, not only had lives been lost but dreams shattered. A lot of people like Kent Steward, an American climber, had been preparing for this for years. Steward had summitted six of the highest peaks, five with his wife of 32 years, Julie. But Everest remained elusive; he had been unsuccessful in his attempt for Everest the previous year. Now his second chance was gone. Steward said, "If I don't make it to the top of Everest, I'm afraid there will always be a hole in my life, and frankly, that worries me."[4]

You and I may not know a carabiner from a wine opener, but we know disappointment and the feeling that we may never get over a loss. Bitter disappointment is the *sorrowful failing to satisfy one's hopes or expectations, great disillusionment*. The problem with bitter disappoint-ments is how they can affect how we feel about taking risks. The future we invent is best done on a foundation of hopes and dreams—exactly those things that may have gotten us those disappointments the first time around. Pipe dreams, castles in the sky, outlandish ideas—all may seem now best put away in the mind's attic.

My life's journey includes the lover who left (disappeared, actually), a job I deserved but wasn't offered, the busted business venture, a failed marriage, and the end of a friendship. I hurt just writing them. A few experts say disappointment is closely linked to unrealistically high expec-tations. I don't believe that's true. We've all tried our best in situations with reasonable hopes, but things didn't work out. It's not outlandish to expect that with genuine effort a marriage can last, your best friend will never need to be replaced, the land will produce a good crop, we'll keep our health, we'll hold onto some money, and the kids will turn out okay. By now, a few of your bitter disappointments have come to mind.

Facing a future of 20 to 30 years, the grandeur and enormity of our hopes and dreams is challenged by age, time left, and our appetite for desire. Can our dreams hold the hunger or grandness of our youth? Can you find new aspirations despite the holes left in your heart? Will new goals be as big or wild as those of your youth?

Stumbling is an inevitable part of living, but permanent injury to hopes and dreams is not. We may never get over painful disappointments. We carry them with us. And that's a good thing because they have made us stronger.

THE RULE OF LIFE: OUTLIVE THE BAD STUFF

Sometimes we don't really know ourselves until something bad happens. Hard luck, adversity, trials, and tribulations come our way. It's a mess. We survive, and as we overcome setbacks, we become resilient. I wasn't born resilient. Neither were you. You learn it. You develop it.

And if you've lived five or six decades or more, you've likely got it.

We've established that resilience is something older people are good at. Lucky us. Studies show that we are the more resilient age group, especially with respect to emotional regulation and problem solving. The American Psychological Association (APA) defines resilience as the "process of adapting well in the face of adversity, trauma, tragedy, threats or significant sources of stress."

As much as resilience involves "bouncing back" from difficult experiences, it can also involve profound personal growth. Resilience is not simply the ability to survive a difficult experience but the ability to adapt with circumstances in a way that enables one to emerge stronger, to thrive in the aftermath, and to integrate the lessons learned.

Misfortunes can make us strong. I know this to be true. I survived my misfortunes and learned from each one. Life got good again. Often life even got better than I could ever have imagined. Then, of course, something else would happen.

I am now, after seven decades, more resilient than ever. And so are you. Revisiting troubled times can be painful. In revisiting them, the emotions I felt can flood my heart. Sitting down with your past troubles can help you gain a better perspective on your future. It won't take you long to recall a couple of trying times in life.

Why revisit troubles? Because what I learned from each one either gave me a tool or fortified a mighty bastion of knowing that I am strong. In the face of a long future, being strong and staying strong are critical. We learn from troubled times. My vignettes pale in comparison to sufferings of life and death, but they are real and they are mine. You have yours; I have mine.

- Crossing the Gulf Stream with my daughter, Elizabeth, as we navigated (or rather, learned to navigate) a 42-foot sailboat south toward the Bahamas was cause for celebration. It was a short celebration. A day later bad weather stuck us in Frazier's Hog Cay, a small anchorage surrounded by uninhabited islands. Five days later we are running out of water, propane leaks from the stove, and power problems cause us to run the engine constantly.

  The winds howl and the rains come down from every directions. The portholes leak. We lie in our bunks and read and read and read. Early each morning Elizabeth dons foul weather gear, goes topside, and strings up a makeshift antennae to pick up two or three weather reports. Might we have a chance to clear the narrow exit at high tide and leave for Nassau 39 nautical miles away? No go. The seas are high, the winds too strong—day after day.

  And so each morning we head to our cabins and often slam the door. Not with anger toward each other but in despair. We can't get outside; the engine drones; and it's almost Christmas. We miss festivities and family. We are miserable.

  What I learned: There is a higher power overseeing the weather and my life. Call this what you want. I believe in my power, but this unseen power is bigger than my power. Often, I do my best, then I surrender.

- I'm 25, happy to be pregnant, and ready to deliver on the given "due date." The baby does not care about the "due date." Whoever made the mistake, I do not know, but instead of my gorgeous daughter arriving on March 12—her presumed arrival day—she arrives on April 12.

  That month of my life is wretched. I cry every day. I wail, "Why me?" People stop calling. My sister arrives with a basket of flowers and I sob. Watching the Academy Awards, I weep during every acceptance speech.

What I learned: Don't choose misery whenever possible. Crying does little good, and whining doesn't help at all. Today, I weep when it matters. If misery comes my way, I don't tend to stick around long but instead find a way to take a step forward—a small one will do.

- Dissolving a marriage that needs to end takes two and a half years. I am a schoolteacher who will become a single mom. Money matters. Most importantly, I am making a decision that has consequences for my daughter. I am scared. My confidence shakes, and I spend too much time second-guessing myself.

  What I learned: I must trust myself. My intuition told me this was the right and best thing for me and for my daughter. My intuition was right. I lose on the money front but gain in self-confidence.

- In 2004, Hurricane Ivan slams the Gulf Coast and takes away a lot of what is dear to me. I wish I had not left my grandmother's quilts under the bed downstairs where saltwater destroyed them. Although I have a structure left, I will be homeless for two and a half years, living with different people in various surroundings for free—a small bedroom, a garage apartment, a million-dollar house.

  Future finances are a big worry. How much out-of-pocket will it cost us in the rebuild? It will cost a lot.

  I hear the town's train at night and feel lonely. Often, I wake to find my husband sitting on the side of the bed with his head in his hands and I want to tell him everything will be okay, but I can't because I don't know that for sure.

  What I learned: People are generous and kind. They will help you. I learn there is goodness in the world. I also learn that sometimes the future matters less than the single moment in which I live.

With troubles and failures in our past, we cannot help but imagine a future without them. In my misfortunes, I took something away from each situation and locked it into my toolbox. I can deploy these at a moment's notice. This is a key to our resilience—in the midst of maddening times, we can learn more about ourselves, who we are, and how we are more courageous than we know.

The Dalai Lama once said, "When you lose, don't lose the lesson." The key to your future is to take what you've learned forward. Resilience? You've got that. We *can* push on.

Retirement offers us a huge step forward into a life we want to live. Unfortunately, our decision to retire may not be ours. Many who think they're going to finish out their work lives on their own terms are often surprised. And when that last day of work turns out not to be your idea, retirement well-being sputters and tumbles.

FORCED OUT

The firestorm controversy between the Federal Aviation Administration (FAA) and commercial airline pilots over the 1959 mandatory retirement age of 60 lasted half a century. "It's time to close the book on age 60," former FAA administrator Marion Blakey said in an annual speech on January 30, 2007.[5]

The age requirement for pilots was never based on any medical evidence. Pilots are required to pass an FAA-sanctioned medical exam every six months in order to remain on flight duty. Studies also showed that older pilots made no more mistakes than younger ones. While no pilot was ever granted a waiver from the age 60 rule, pilots *were* allowed to fly after suffering from heart conditions and alcohol abuse.

The mandatory retirement at age 60 became increasingly more difficult to defend. In 2007, the FAA adopted the new maximum retirement age of 65. Now, 14 years later, there's a newer retirement age on the horizon.

In 2021, the US airline industry is in the midst of a growing wave of retirements that will see thousands of commercial pilots turn 65 and forced out of the cockpit over the coming decade. The result is a massive pilot shortage made worse during a global pandemic when airlines stopped recruiting new pilots. This ultimately will limit the growth of the industry, and airlines are scrambling. United Airlines needs 10,000 new pilots over the next decade and has bought a flight school to help fill their ranks.

And there are rumors about a fresh debate over mandatory retirement of experienced pilots aged 65 with more than 40 years of professional experience—more than 20,000 hours of flying time—and who can easily pass an FAA first class physical. Could 67 or 70 become a new retirement age for pilots?

Age means a hard stop in certain professions—firefighters, law enforcement officers, and air traffic controllers all have to leave by a certain age. Americans assume that they have the right to make their own decisions about when to retire. But that's no longer the reality for many. The truth is it's getting risky.

Delores Richerson is a planner, and in 2017, her plan was to retire from her banking career in two years. As senior executive in charge of a region in the Southeast at 64 years old, she had formidable experience and a track record of success. When the bank began making strong suggestions that she consider leaving her VP post sooner rather than later, she was confused and taken aback. Why interrupt a high achiever with positive results? Why disrupt her team's plans for a smooth transition?

Delores loved her job and especially her people. "I loved them all," she said. "And we had outstanding performance every quarter." But the higher-ups kept pushing. Her age and salary were likely reasons. When the bank came through with an offer of two years' severance to depart two years before she planned, it became one of those "deals of a lifetime." She took it. They gave her a big party and she left.

And then she got mad.

Even with a formidable financial cushion, the exit to a long and stellar career didn't feel good. "I was angry for three months." Delores packed her bags for worldwide travel to try to get over it. But even when she tells me the story, her voice cracks and I can feel the pain. What starts out as a nudge from an employer can end up feeling like a great big kick.

Baby boomers have had a great run in the workplace, but the trend of older workers being pushed out is in full swing. New analysis by ProPublica and the Urban Institute shows more than half of older US workers are pushed out of longtime jobs before they choose to retire.[6] Laid-off people can find another job, but often that replacement job leaves little room for the individual to rebuild a career.

ProPublica describes how IBM has forced out more than 20,000 US workers aged 40 and over in just the past five years in order to "correct seniority mix." The company used a combination of layoffs and forced retirement as well as tactics such as mandatory relocation seemingly designed to push longtime worker to quit.[7]

IBM is no outlier in how it approaches shaping its workforce. Ideally, people retire when they are financially and psychologically ready. But often there's buzz in the air implying a certain "age of separation" or a culling of middle managers. Employers play a critical role in older adults' work and retirement decisions. While disbelief and anger may be an individual's first emotions when they realize they are not going to be able to exit on their own terms, sadness is close behind.

In onsite coaching sessions with Melody, 62, I was struck with the modern, brightly colored aesthetics of her corporate headquarters and with the young cadre of employees. This was a youthful company, casual but ambitious. When rumors began that company executives were having "to get rid of anyone over 50," Melody was concerned but not worried. She was a top performer.

Her retirement date was less than a year away when the first sign of trouble appeared. A performance review indicated problems. This had never happened before. She was stunned and distraught. Weeks later, she discovered she was not being included in certain meetings. In late November, she received the news from her boss about a reorganization: "Your position is being terminated." Melody's last day was December 31, two months shy of her planned retirement date.

The sting of Melody's unplanned departure amplified the pain of leaving behind a professional career she was proud of. Leaving our work often hurts. Leaving with a fresh failure or misfortune on your tail hurts more.

The beginning of an upbeat life in retirement was now gloomy, and the bad ending was followed by months of unease about the future and misgivings about the past. Eventually, Melody found firm footing and began to explore what she previously determined to pursue as part of her retirement life. She now teaches full time in a prestigious management program at a local university.

In corporate administrative jobs, retirements are legally supposed to be voluntary decisions made by employees, but more and more retirements are not freely chosen. Many older workers will have to weather an exit strategy not of their own making. Many will be let go of or fired yet say they "retired" to save face.

Knowing the reality of potential job loss can help us be prepared with backup game plans for an encore career and new work. If you land in a situation where you have no choice but to retire sooner than expected, you are not alone. A good 60 percent of workers are forced into early retirement according to data from Voya Financial.[8] While the coronavirus derailed careers of many individuals, more often it is the employer purging out older workers in favor of younger employers who require less salary or perhaps because the company wants to embrace a youthful culture.

Sudden retirement requires a look at finances, some careful planning, and renewed confidence in resilience. This hard reset in life is a way to go about being determined and hopeful for tomorrow's chance to try again.

FALL IN LOVE WITH LIFE AGAIN (WHAT NOT TO DO)

Whether you love fast food or not, McDonald's new 2021 commercial, "Two Chapters," highlights the marking of life with an event and some relevant philosophy for how to look at life. McDonald's assures that every person's life is split into two very different chapters. These two chapters exist before and after the moment when you finally have your first Big Mac. The spot ends with "The best chapter is the last."

Your appetite to get something going for more than what you think possible at this stage of life depends in large part on vital behaviors indispensable for finding one's best life. When my husband, Herb, and I mapped out a possible future marriage in front of George, a smart, competent psychologist in Atlanta, we began with admonitions—mild perhaps, but earnest—to set the tone for success.

Me: *I don't cook. I don't make beds. I don't do your laundry. I'll not turn over my paycheck. Do not parent my child.*

Him: *I don't do lawns. I don't fix things. I don't do early. I'll not turn over my paycheck. I don't want to parent your child.*

I am not a marriage expert, but we passed the 40-year mark, so I do think there's merit in crafting a life on what's *not* going to work. Below is a portfolio of five behaviors for our best third of life. Based on interviews, observations, research, and experience, people who master the transition of retirement and live an extraordinary life in retirement don't spend a lot of time and energy on these things.

1. **They don't disregard their hungry heart.**
   Even the most miserable of us has a hungry heart. Those who live best have high desire. What's in your hungry heart? If you soul has been asleep while you raised the kids, carved out a stellar career, and took care of aging parents, you can wake it up now.

   Google attracts top talent by hiring individuals not only for business acumen but for "passion, character, curiosity and someone who is engaged in the world around them." How do they determine an individual's curiosity and engagement in the world around them? Eric Schmidt, who served as CEO of Google from 2001 to 2011, uses the "LAX test": "You're stuck at the LAX airport with the candidate and after six hours, if you are still interested in talking to them, they pass. That's a very tough test."

   Could you talk about yourself for six hours? Imagine what you might learn. I bet hour five might hold something of what's in your hungry heart. If you allow yourself to listen to old longing and new yearnings, you begin to find horizons for the future. There are things you have in your heart that no one else does. Channel that. There are desires, hankerings, and thirsts that are yours alone. Find them.

2. **They don't watch and wonder. (They do things.)**
   Watch and wonder times are valuable. We've all benefited from being an apprentice to the mystery of life as it unfolds—observing, waiting, planning. But life in retirement might hold fewer years ahead. Time spent as merely a witness to life, stagnant or in boredom, confused and without direction, is time lost.

If I looked inside your life, would I want to live it? There's much to learn answering this question. The promise of renewal means it's time to test assumptions and try things out, not make a list of our strengths (which you've already done a hundred times).

The vast majority of academic studies show "virtually no relationship between age and job performance," says Harvey Sterns, director of the Institute for Life-Span Development and Gerontology at the University of Akron.[9] You can be successful in new work, continue upward in your current profession, write that novel, or lead that organization where you are not a volunteer no matter how old you are.

Individuals who create fierce identities may begin with moments of wonder, but they move to action sooner rather than later. You can be one of them. Or you can be one of many I meet who say, "I need to figure out what I want to do." Six months later, when I run into them again, they say, "I need to figure out what I want to do." It's cringe worthy.

3. They do not depend on others.

As a middle school counselor, I placed my hands on the shoulders of 11-year-old children in the hallways to let them know I was happy to see them in school. These children took hold of their lives despite lack of caring or competent parents, no supervision, little or no encouragement, and often scant financial support. They got themselves to school on time, completed homework, washed their clothes, occasionally took a bath, ate supper in their rooms while Mom and Dad screamed, followed the rules, and protected a place deep inside where a small "self" resided. No one within their family unit cared about their lives or offered guidance or support. They traveled life each day alone.

Do not tell me that navigating your adult life gets harder than that. Men and women in their late 50s, 60s, 70s, and 80s in far corners of the earth carve lives of meaning without anyone at their side—no one. Waiting for husbands, wives, partners, or friends to join us in living the life we want dangerously undermines life's capacity.

Your life offers a promise that is made upon truth and built with a future no other person has. The promise doesn't always include someone by your side. It takes courage to slip over the threshold of going it alone. But people late in life do it every day. All by themselves, they sit on buses that cross Chilean borders, hook casitas to cars and take off to National Parks, and occupy park benches in plazas throughout the world where no one speaks their language. They see, do, add new friends, cross culture divides, learn, and give back. This is not to say they wouldn't appreciate a companion. Many would. But a vibrant life may require doing some things alone.

4. **They don't base decisions on chronological age.**

When asked what age is old, respondents ages 50 to 64 said 72. The "emerging adults," ages 18 to 29, see it differently by a dozen years. They think old is 60. Being perceived as old is one issue. The bigger issue is what happens when *you* think you are old. Older adults who believe negative stereotypes about aging can undermine their own performance on memory tests. There is no telling how we limit ourselves in other ways. Research reveals we feel younger than our chronological age, but it's not enough to feel younger. We must *think* younger.

How do we keep thinking young? Recently I met an individual who shared his extraordinary successful tool that all of us can employ. Chuck Tessier, 65, is smart, gregarious, and warm and successful in urban developments throughout the Southeast. He makes sure he's clear-headed about his decisions. "I call it 'Twilight Savings Time,'" says Tessier. Instead of using his 65-year-old perspective, Tessier turns time back 10 years to consult with his 55-year-old self. "I view and assess all of my work and life decisions as if I were 10 years younger. It illuminates an entirely different thought." Might your younger self offer a different point of view than your real-age self? I'm pretty sure it would.

5. **They don't try to shape a statement of life's purpose.**

I've already hammered away on how life purpose works for some but not everyone. But let's be clear that many, many experts talk about life purpose as the be-all-end-all to a fulfilling life. You've got to figure this out (and write it down), they say, or you are in trouble. Life will forever be devoid of meaning and you're not going anywhere without a purpose. Pretty terrifying. Pretty much baloney.

Here's the truth: life purpose statements, much like company mission statements, are lame. I earned good money to help organizations and teams figure one out. The results were contrite prose posted somewhere, bloated with words like "be the best," "give back," and "make the world a better place." Many people revisit a personal mission statement written more than 20 or 30 years ago. But first they have to find it, which tells me it has been inconsequential.

Call it purpose, mission, vision, mantra—this unnecessary endeavor limits your potential and wastes precious time. Skip it. Individuals who live their best lives engage in often lofty goals but simultaneously mine relationships, act on curiosity, find and treasure beauty, and acquire serenity. In other words, they lead lives bigger than one statement could ever hold. Your purpose in life is to express your fullest potential and live deliberately. Your purpose is to become who you are, express your gifts, and use your time wisely. That's it.

WHAT ARE YOUR INTENTIONS?

During watch on a night crossing of the Mona Passage, I sat glued to the cockpit's radar screen, where a troubling scenario brewed. Radar images showed a sailboat ahead on a potential collision course with what appeared to be an exceptionally large ship.

The Mona Passage, 80 miles wide and one of the most difficult stretches of water in the Caribbean, is a key shipping route between the Atlantic and the Panama Canal. Fraught with tidal currents, fishing nets, and rough waters, navigating it requires sailors to be vigilant. My screen had tracked this large, yellow, blurry blob—possibly a military vessel, cruising ship, barge, oil tanker, or freighter—moving fast in an erratic, zigzag course that could present immediate danger.

For more than an hour, the sailor on the boat ahead tried every 10 minutes to contact the large vessel on the VHF using the proper protocol—giving his boat name, coordinates, and course direction—and asking for the vessel to identify itself. There was never a radio response, but often the boat would increase speed and choose another course—sometimes a more dangerous one.

Big ships cannot stop on a dime, and big ships often will not stop. Most containerships and cruise ships travel at speeds around 24 to 30 knots. On this night, our sailboat and the other sailboat traveled at seven knots. Big ships do not turn well, and often the beam angle from their radar is too high for them to see a small craft. The nautical Rules of the Road may not apply, but the rule of BIG applies. Hailing the ship to let her know you are there and hoping the ship's pilot will answer is your best course of action.

With positions getting closer together, the situation grew more uncomfortable. I began checking course changes, as I suspected the sailor ahead was doing, but the Mona Passage is narrow. Even dealing with this ship's large wake could be problematic.

Sailing at night with a full moon lighting the way had been a glorious discovery for me. But this dark night's passage, full of uncertainty, was hair-raising. When the VHS call was finally answered, I remember thinking that the guy on the sailboat should take this ship's captain to task for his negligence. That sailor did not. He chose to ask the most important question—in the calmest way I ever could have imagined. It was the only question that mattered.

"Sir," he said, "what are your intentions?"

Life is mysterious, but we've all built one. The hope for the last third of life is to build your best life yet, *but hope will not make it happen.* What are your intentions?

You may be surprised to find how quickly daily routines of life in retirement will absorb your waking hours. You may be surprised how easily it will be to neglect hopes and dreams. You may be surprised to find how quickly you start to see life in terms of other people's expectations rather than your own. You may be surprised to find out how often you plop in front of the TV. You may be surprised at how the months will turn into years.

Thoreau said, "The mass of men lead lives of quiet desperation." Sooner or later, we define ourselves by our actions. With each decision, we tell ourselves and the world who we are.

Late adulthood is a wonderful thing—and brief. Be swift. Make haste.

WHAT MATTERS MOST

Making choices that sometimes are not well thought out will waste your time, sap your motivation, and deplete your confidence. One of the very best things you can do is to focus. You can get side-tracked doing what a million experts tell you to do. What give us the ability to live an extraordinary life is the idea of devoting all our efforts to explore just one thing at a time. Give your full attention to only one of the Four Portals or a sole idea that has struck a chord while reading this book. Ditch your impulse to make a list of twenty things to do.

What Unconsciously Wastes Your Time

Aside from the obvious—social media, procrastination, TV, inter-ruptions—there are tons of other ways we waste time that are harder to spot. We don't deliberately set out to waste time, and often we are not fully aware of where we are losing minutes of our day. Which one of these is not serving to maximize your most valuable resource: focusing on the wrong priorities, few boundaries, holding grudges, micromanag-ing others, complaining, gossiping, indecisions, or being too available? Can you give up one of these? Two?

Scrap the Little Plans

Here's a lesson many of us learn too late in life: small dreams push us forward for a while but are not remarkable enough to give us a reason to bound out of bed each morning and roar. Our dreams are often two sizes too small. Finish life using all your talents and potential. What would give you a BIG sense of accomplishment? How could you make a BIG impact on someone? What does your neighborhood, community, or the world need now that could be a BIG contribution you could make? What can make you roar?

11

THERE WILL BE WINNERS

> You think the dead we loved truly ever leave us? You think that we don't recall them more clearly in times of great trouble?
>
> —Albus Dumbledore, *Harry Potter and the Prisoner of Azkaban* by J. K. Rowling

> If I know this is the last time I see you, I'd tell you I love you and would not just assume foolishly you know it already.
>
> —Gabriel García Márquez, *One Hundred Years of Solitude*

At 65, my mother traded power and influence in a top-level government position securing parts for US defense systems for a daily pack of Winstons and a Bingo card. After rising from the stenographer pool in the 1960s to management in the 1980s; she was retiring from work she loved. Remember, when I asked her why, she said, "Because that's what people my age do." Well, she also added: "Anyway, your father needs my company."

The latter part of that answer made no sense. My parents hadn't spent a significant amount of time together for more than 40 years, and that was good news for a marriage not made in heaven. My father's night shift assembly-line work began at 4 p.m., the same time of day that my mother's work ended.

Nevertheless, she retired. I watched her do it, and I learned from it. In psychology this is referred to as "observational learning," which is also sometimes called "shaping" or "modeling." A tremendous amount of learning happens through this process. At any point in life, we learn directly and indirectly from others. We observe and process to find something of value we can add to our own parenting, marriage, friendships, and life's journey. What we learn might be what not to do, what to do more of, what to change, and what to try.

While my mother inspired me throughout my life, she did not show me how to live in the fullness of a life after age 65. In my view of Mom's retirement life, she lost more than she gained. Yes, there was a nice government pension, card club, annual trips to the Kentucky Derby and Las Vegas, visits from her four children and grandchildren, good health, and Bingo nights.

Still, it didn't make for ongoing vitality. Most days were filled with black coffee, television, and more and more Winstons. During phone calls, when it was my turn to ask, "So what's going on with you?" the answer was always "Not much, Barbara." I think we both knew in our hearts that life was unfolding in ways that made it seem that the best years of my mom's life were behind her.

Mom died quickly at 75 of a brain aneurysm.

Watching this play out, I could have learned to give more serious thought to and be more intentional about my life in retirement, but I did not. *Almost* living a future of neglected potential and lowered expectations—just like Mom—nearly happened to me. Luckily, as you know, I self-corrected but only after a lot of wasted time—precious time.

We are surrounded by people in retirement transitions that spin into lifestyles. They are a formidable force for our perceptions of aging as we forge a path forward. If we watch the choices and actions of others—whether we know them or not, whether from the past or present—these models of life can show us what our own last third of life can be. Their narratives offer incentives, clear-sightedness, and resolve about what might be good for us to do, sidestep, or avoid altogether.

My dentist shapes his future life using the conscious assimilation of information from comrades. I ask Dr. Scott Booker, in his 60s with a full head of sandy hair and a full-time practice, when he'll retire. He scoots over from the monitor of my X-rays to quip, "Not me! I may cut back. But I've watched too many of my colleagues go downhill fast after they quit working."

With intention, observational learning can be powerful. Role models are people whom we admire and who exhibit admirable strength and skills. Role models are also those who make mistakes and exhibit flaws, albeit in deeply human ways with lessons for those of us watching.

We can find individuals to learn from anywhere—in the neighborhood, on the tennis court, at a book signing, in an online art class, or in history. Closer up are our friends, family, and colleagues who serve as models.

Just in case you're thinking of role models as all those other people and not you, let's get this right. At this moment, others are not only watching you live life but also making a memory of you doing it.

You are a role model whether you like it or not.

Grandchildren, children, nieces, nephews, and friends observe your choices, your attitude, and your day-to-day activities. The clues and lessons *from your life* can make them big winners in this new world of longevity. Our efforts to live an extraordinary life in retirement bestow an abundance of wisdom upon those with chances to live even longer lives.

But we can do much more than model behavior. This final chapter illuminates the privilege of living long with a call for transparency. Let's start talking about our long life. Let's expose our thoughts, fears, plans, hopes, and challenges to one another. Let's have conversations with friends and our spouse or partner.

Let's ask our children, adult grandchildren, and young people we know how they see their long lives playing out. Let's help them see possibilities. Let's encourage them to ask questions about our lives and give us ideas so we can become more fully engaged.

Living longer and better lives is not just about us. It's about *all* of us.

HARVEST THE PAST

Long before the idea of living to age 100 was a reality, individuals nurtured grit with wisdom and molded their spirit of aging. A memory or a new discovery of how others before us aged and created productive lives sparks an explosion of emotions as well as substantial influence.

My mother instilled in me the idea that I was beautiful and strong. She taught me to find sunshine when all I could see was a heavy downpour of despair. Her positive, dynamic, and constant influence shaped most of my life, but when it came to living well in retirement, she gave me little to go on.

Gradually unearthing a memory of another person helped crystallize a vision for living that I badly needed in my struggle to find a path forward in my mid-60s. The past is always present in our lives, and lucky for me, I had a grandmother who could show me more.

As the oldest of four, I was granted long summer visits to my father's mother who lived alone in a house built by the coal company in Webb Holler in eastern Kentucky. For a month or more, from the time I was 12 years old until I turned 16, I slept many summer nights with Grandma in a cedar bed so high I had to get a running start to leap onto it. A light dangled from the center of the ceiling on a black cord and moved in circles when turned on, making shadows across the framed pictures of two babies lost shortly after birth that hung above the bed. I never did find out about much about those children.

Self-reliance shaped Grandma's spirit, and every day was an opportunity to better a life in a corner of the world where hardship appeared regularly. When the sun made it over the mountain mid-morning, the day filled naturally without a written to-do list—more gardening, snakes to kill, a half mountain of brush to clear, flowers to coax into more blooms, chickens to feed, and food to gather and can. With a hand-fed wringer washer and baskets of wet clothes to lug from the back porch to the clothesline in the front yard, washing clothes took the whole day.

In her late 70s, Grandma rose early during our summers together and spent two hours in the garden before breakfast. Born in 1881, she was a schoolteacher until she married and raised four children on miner's pay. But the garden of food and flowers was work she loved and always would. All meals were farm-to-table fare—sweet corn, beets, potatoes, zucchini, radishes, carrots, beans—cooked on a coal stove until her bachelor son bought her an electric one, which she didn't much like.

When evening came, I wrote postcards to movie stars asking for an autographed picture and helped myself to chewy caramel creams from the glass candy jar. In a brown, overstuffed, made-to-look-like-velvet chair with wide rolled arms ordered from the Sears Roebuck catalog, Grandma read her Bible.

Away from the chaos and noise created by my siblings, these visits were heaven for me. It was so quiet I could hear the creek at the edge of the yard running morning, noon, and night. When I turned 16, I needed a summer job to earn money and summers with Grandma ended.

She died at 83. My dad dug up all her purple peonies and transplanted them to Ohio. They bloomed every year. They were gorgeous. Years later, I'm 65 and struggling to piece together my years ahead. Slowly but surely, I remember Grandma and how she set about her work late in life without reciting a daily affirmation, a purpose statement, a motivational video, or a self-help book. Forty-five years later, magically, her example presented to me an illustrated promise for my future and a shape for what my life could be.

We are challenged to create "older selves" and discover how we might best fit in the world. Those who have gone before us offer intimate portraits in a quest for self-knowledge.

Many, like newly retired Christy Emmanuel, 63, trace family roots in a way that can seem obsessive, and they listen closely to understand how potent the past can be. When a treasure trove of ancestral records—books, photographs, letters, diaries, news clippings, historical records—appeared on Christy's doorstep from the wife of her mother's first cousin (whom she had never met), Christy was hooked. She picked up the research to discover riveting stories of her forebearers and in four months covered the first nine generations, among them 132 family members, many immigrants from England, France, and Germany.

"These people lived inventive, purposeful lives and were highly accomplished. These pioneers—my people—were guided by courage and resilience in the face of much adversity. Frankly," she adds. "I am awestruck."

While my relatives dug for potatoes or coal, Christy's graduated from medical school, ran sawmills, and published books. No matter the contrast or complexity, they all survived hard times, had failures to overcome, and often triumphed. These histories are parts of our personal stories that can give us a boost in core identity, connection, and compassion—specifically self-compassion—which we can use to encourage and coax ourselves to greatness.

TODAY'S SUCCESSFUL AGING ROLE MODEL—YOU

Each Sunday, I look forward to the weekly episode of *60 Minutes* to see who will wither under the tough questioning of Leslie Stahl, the award-winning journalist with a storied career that has spanned more than 50 years. First, I'll check out her choice of earrings, lipstick, and hairstyle. Leslie likes shiny dangle earrings and bright lipstick color, often too bright. While always a version of blonde, she never sticks to one haircut. Leslie Stahl, 80, appears not to have a stylist and impresses me to death.

Married for more than 40 years, this 12-Emmy-winning correspondent has one daughter, two grandchildren and lots of self-control—at least in those interviews with Yasser Arafat, Boris Yeltsin, and multiple US presidents, including Donald Trump, who walked out. But get her started on talking about those grandchildren, and she's effusive.

Stahl shows no signs of slowing down or forfeiting her commitments either to her work or grandparenting. Stahl has a down-to-earth presence, a nuts-and-bolts approach to her work, the respect of colleagues, and a competitiveness I admire. She is my ace-in-the-hole role model. I'm sure she doesn't know this.

Role models are everywhere. They can stimulate our thinking, invite possibilities, and light a fire in our belly. We dare not underestimate the power of a role model; we cannot underestimate nor fail to understand that *we are role models with that power.*

Individuals adopt positive views on aging through role models. In a study of successful aging role models,[1] individuals ages 18 to 99 were asked whether they had a role model of successful aging. Eighty-five percent of participants had at least one role model. The most common role models were a family member, followed by a friend, and more rarely a famous figure. And here's a gem for you: the most mentioned models from family were parents and grandparents. Hence many of us have a chance to serve and influence two generations.

Baby boomers have rewritten societal rules at every stage of life, and retirement is no different. We are trailblazers at the forefront of defining retirement as a new phase in life that can bring freedom, intentional living, enjoyment, and higher levels of well-being.

While it helps to have someone to watch live an active and high-quality life, what's even more valuable is to be in conversation with that someone. We've all had that moment when we'd give just about any-thing to pick the brain of a person we admire. With more knowledge and experience than we have, that person could shine a light on what we've been wondering about.

There's a lot to talk about when it comes to a long life, but con-versations aren't often happening. The days we spent sharing our hopes and dreams for the future with our partner may be long past and need to be revived. Heart-to-heart talks with one another about aging and navigating life need a boost.

Most important are those conversations with those who are clos-est to us. Do children want to talk to parents about their choices in a retirement life? Are parents sharing what they want to accomplish late in life with children? Should they? Who seeks more information on life in retirement? What generation *wants* to talk about it? We'll get to all this.

The answers might surprise you.

THE MIGHTINESS OF TALK

In an era of increased longevity where "long-life learning" inspires colleges and universities to focus on helping us grow whole while we grow old, financial planning and wealth management industries adopt a holistic approach as a winning model for the future. Today, boot camps for alumni on navigating the last third of life abound, and successful retirement planning is not a single piece of financial advice but a mar-ketplace focused on helping clients uncover lifestyle goals and imagine their retirement lives.

These new forms of education and business are winning models for *more* interaction, *more* connections, and *more* communication. They exemplify exactly what we need *more of* in our personal relationships, within our families, friendships, and communities.

You would think as individuals on the threshold of one of the most difficult and important transitions in life, boomers would be in deep discussion about growing older, trying to learn a thing or two from one another—a chat over coffee or glass of wine about how easy it is to be confused about what you want when time is running out in life. Nope, not happening. We are more likely to be open to reviewing the results of our bone density scans than engaging in a meaningful conversation about a disappointment that has currently wreaked havoc with our self-confidence.

Are these topics too difficult to talk about? Maybe. We construct walls around certain parts of our lives, often keeping private about money, dying, and death. We often hide our insecurities, keep our vulnerabilities to ourselves, and choose not to disclose our longings for the future.

As we age, we become weary of commitments made a lifetime ago, find ourselves unclear and less motivated to achieve, and feel stretched of hope and tired of letting go of dreams, or worse, having them snatched away by circumstances. These may be tough issues for us to share. Yet sharing thoughts and ideas as well as vulnerabilities can help build psychological resilience, including the development of a sense of growth and purpose.

If we can destigmatize these conversations—even just a little—we can help one another and those who will maneuver through long lives in the future. We can chat or go deep. We can listen and talk. With everyone's wisdom on the table, we can expand our knowledge, learn from one another, and grow into better lives.

The human brain is a time traveler and looking to the future is, at times, what we do. We all, at some point in our lives, think about growing old and life in retirement.

What's on our minds?

PERSPECTIVES OF LIFE AFTER 65 FROM THREE GENERATIONS

While generational labels may seem like we're singing the Alphabet Song, this still is a good foundation as we begin to understand how we are similar and different in our views of the future. The breakdown by age looks like this: baby boomers are currently between 57 and 75 years old; Gen X is currently between 41 and 56 years old; Gen Y (more often called millennials) are currently between 25 and 40; Generation Z (Gen Z) is between 6 and 24 years old; and since no letter follows Z, the newest batch of babies will be called Generation Alpha (Gen A).

Retirement means different things to different generations. In the hearts and minds of three generations—millennials, Generation X, and baby boomers—the word "retirement" is most often associated with "freedom," despite concerns about whether it is financially attainable.

To help us better understand one another and begin a dialogue about aging and retirement (which I'll implore you to do), each generation's views on aging and retirement are worth a look. Research provides these key aspects to highlight similarities and differences:[2]

- **Long Lives and Long Retirements**. All three generations are already thinking in terms of longer lives. Almost one in five millennials (17 percent) are planning to live to age 100 or older, compared with Generation X (11 percent) and baby boomers (9 percent). Millennials are the first generation in human history who can not only anticipate reaching the age of 90 in large numbers but who also will spend about one-third of their life as "old people." An implication for increased longevity is potentially more time spent in retirement.

- **Positive Views of Retirement**. All three generations have positive visions of retirement, albeit with legitimate concerns related to financial security and declining health. Millennials (34 percent) are more likely to dream of working in retirement (e.g., pursuing an encore career, starting a business, continue working in the same field), compared with baby boomers (26 percent) and Generation X (25 percent). Many millennials also envision a flexible transition into retirement that differs from prior generations when retirement was marked by an abrupt stop to work.

- **Retirement Dreams**. The top three retirement dreams—traveling, spending more time with family and friends, and pursuing hobbies—are common across the generations. However, some retirement dreams differ across generations. Baby boomers (31 percent) are more likely to dream of doing volunteer work, compared with Generation X (25 percent), and millennials (23 percent).

- **Retirement Fears**. Retirement fears are shared across generations. The top retirement fear is outliving savings and investments followed by those that are health related. Other fears shared by the three generations include finding meaningful ways to spend time and stay involved and being laid off—not being able to retire on their own terms.

- **Fears of Aging**. Gen Xers share a range of fears about aging, with more than half (56 percent) saying they're afraid of getting old, and 70 percent thinking about their own mortality more now than they did 10 years ago.

  When it comes to aging, Gen Xers are more worried than boomers about loneliness (19 percent versus 15 percent, respectively), looking older (12 percent versus 6 percent), and having less sex (10 percent versus 5 percent).

- **A Focus on Generation X**. Boomers are parents of Generation X and most of the millennials. But it is Gen Xers in the prime of life—who are juggling demanding careers while taking care of their aging parents, their own children, and themselves—who are neglecting their health and making poor lifestyle choices, setting themselves up to fall short of reaching old age.

  Looking ahead 20 years from now, Gen Xers expect to be working (46 percent), caring for their parents (22 percent), caring for grandchildren (35 percent), and even supporting adult children (14 percent). Half of Gen X expect to be helping family members with health costs.

  An MDVIP Health and Longevity Survey reveals that more than half of Gen Xers (53 percent) want to live past the age of 90, including more than a quarter wanting to live past 100. But only half (55 percent) of Gen Xers—versus 72 percent of boomers—have had an annual physical exam in the past five years. Two out of three Gen Xers admit they could be doing a better job of exercising regularly (67 percent), eating well (66 percent), maintaining a healthy weight (63 percent), and managing stress (66 percent). Health experts agree that it is not too late for this generation to take control of their health and change their behavior to make a positive impact on the future.

No matter the differences in age, our concerns and hopes for our future give us plenty to talk about. How many of us wish for conversations we did not have with people we loved who are gone? Why didn't we ask about their hopes and dream, challenges, and joys and heartaches? While aging and views about retirement are highly personal in nature, what survives from our lives will become a tether to those left behind. Not talking about our lives will mean that those who have many spent years with us will not have really known us.

I WISH I KNEW MORE ABOUT YOU

Gabriel García Márquez was a celebrated author, referred to as one of the best Spanish-language novelists, and the winner of the Nobel prize for Literature for *One Hundred Years of Solitude* in 1982. In his son's book, *A Farewell to Gabo and Mercedes: A Son's Memoir of Gabriel García Márquez and Mercedes Barcha*, he writes of his regret: "I didn't ask them more about the fine print of their lives, their most private thoughts, their greatest hopes and fears."

In his personal reflection, Rodrigo García recalls one of his father's sayings. "Everyone has three lives: the public, the private and the secret." At the funeral within the grandiose halls of Palacio de Bellas Artes in Mexico City, yellow butterflies were thrown into the air. Yellow was García Márquez's favorite color, and the author was regularly seen with a yellow rose in his lapel. His son gazed into the throng of people in attendance, wondering who might be part of his father's secret life.[3]

I share in this son's regret of not asking more about a parent's life. Or my Aunt Naomi's life or my Uncle Snooks's. What about you? The person you would like to talk to may have been pleased to have talked about their journey and what they learned along the way.

Why didn't I ask? Why didn't you? Why aren't we asking now?

At the end of my presentations about *Leading and Living Boldly in Your 100-Year Life*, the most frequently asked question is "How can I talk to my dad/mom about the life he/she is living in retirement?" The question is always asked with care and concern. Granted, it may mean that the questioner's parents are in for some unsolicited feedback on their choices in retirement life. But maybe not. The result could be kind advice, a new perspective, or, better yet, a helping hand.

Turns out, despite their relatively young age, millennials have a high desire to explore the future and are most open to talking. This group is three times larger than Generation X. You may also recall my story about the millennial who called his mom after a presentation to ask, "Mom, I've got to talk to you. Are you leading an extraordinary life?" When the conversation turns to longevity, millennials (Generation Y, sometimes called "echo boomers" because they are the children of the baby boomers), who face six decades of work instead of four, are surprisingly engaged in the topic of retirement.

One in five millennials (21 percent) frequently discuss savings, investing, and planning for retirement with family and friends, a significantly higher percentage than that of the older generations. In contrast, almost a third of Generation X (31 percent) and baby boomers (32 percent) "never" discuss it. Almost three in four (72 percent) indicate they do not know as much as they should about retirement investing—and just as many (72 percent) would like to receive more information and advice from their employers on how to achieve their retirement goals.[4]

This data does not indicate directly that younger generations want to talk to parents or grandparents about aging and retirement, but the topic is on their minds. You could open up a conversation with your child by saying, "Lately I've been thinking I might be watching too much TV and need a new interest." Or "I'm thinking I need to start eating better food. What do you think?"

New doors can open as you age, and at times your kids can keep the doors ajar as you amble through to explore a new terrain. Writing this book was extremely important to me and proved a weighty project with moving parts and needed resources. When finding the right editor proved troublesome, Elizabeth, my daughter, said, "Mom, I'll do it for you." While I value my abilities to manage my own affairs and knew that my daughter's time was jam-packed with a demanding real estate career and raising two children ages 8 and 9, I agreed. So, between the cello and Mandarin lessons, a crazy hot housing market, and her own life, my daughter, *who knew how much this book meant to me*, stepped up to the plate.

What do you have that may be decades in the making that's important to you? Have you told your children? Purposeful sharing with your children helps dreams come true. At the least, sharing possibilities out loud can make them feel more real and cause you to gain more energy to pursue certain ones.

After retiring, Russell Ellis got into stone carving, then modeling clay, then steel work and painting. A celebrated architecture professor at the University of California–Berkeley and later a vice chancellor, Russell never bit down on any one thing until a muse came calling in the form of songs. He didn't just get songs in his head; he got whole orchestrated movements.

Russell didn't know a thing about the music industry and called on musician friends to help. But his children also had contacts, and he exploited all of them. At 85, he celebrated his first-ever album "Songs from My Garden," with 11 original songs.[5]

Russell, who has concluded his brief recording career, says the experience of doing something that involves others "can get you unstuck in life and make you feel better about yourself." He also adds that doing the album "made me a kinder person." The best part, however, is that he relished having "my kids' clear respect and support."

FIVE WAYS TO MAKE A CONVERSATION ON AGING AND RETIREMENT MEANINGFUL

The TED Talk format is a short, carefully prepared talk that is no longer than 18 minutes and delivered without notes by a single presenter. They are scripted and carefully rehearsed, often for months. Talking to your kids, grandkids, parents, spouse, partner, or friend about their future and retirement life . . . is the opposite of a TED Talk.

The outcome you want is *talking together*. But even more than an exchange of words, you want a meaningful conversation and an action that carries power and possibly delight. A meaningful conversation is one where you learn something. When a conversation allows you to better understand something important about yourself, the other person, or the world, then it becomes meaningful. Most of us are hungry for an opportunity to share what we're thinking, to clarify and explore things that matter to us.

This is a conversation, not a discourse, diatribe, or debate. And since it is not about money, sex, parenting, death, or dying, it should not be awkward or laborious. Participants are allowed the freedom to express themselves and the interaction is characterized by co-creation.

But while everyone struggles with what's next, some just don't want to talk about it. Or they do want to talk, just not *with you*. Family dysfunction can run deep or just deep enough to disallow this conversation even if you want it. But as we've seen, the data tells us that the future is thought about by all of us, so it can be worth trying. Mutual understanding and connection feel good and are important to our well-being, but each of us makes decisions based on the context of the situation.

Use these guidelines to start a dialogue in your relationships about how to live long lives:

1. **Don't Dismiss Small Talk**. Many of us may want to leave behind the shallows of small talk in lieu of a BIG TALK. This is not a BIG TALK. While a deeper discussion might be the end goal, don't dismiss small talk altogether. It can set the scene, establish rapport, and evolve to the more substantive conversations. An article on longevity, a story in the media on health and living long, an anecdote about a friend of yours who enrolled in law school at 60—these are conversation starters.

2. **Go Slow, Be Present, Be Open**. Take it easy on your expectations. This is not therapy. Initially, do this face-to-face if possible. Listen more than you talk, and be willing to share something about yourself. Self-disclosure is a key step in developing intimacy, so exposing a small part of your inner self leads to better, more meaningful conversation. No need to peel back to the core of the onion right away. A fear, a value or belief, something that happened to you in the past—that's enough to get started.

3. **Steer Clear of Ouchy Questions.** *Ouchy* questions. You know them. *Where's your life headed? What are the biggest goals in your life? Who are you really?* Even to ask about anyone's hopes and dreams for the future is too big to process. A better question is "What might you be curious about doing if you had more time?" Thought-provoking questions are appreciated. A study in 2017 by psychologists at Harvard University found that people

who ask questions tend to be better liked by their conversation partner than those who don't.[6] (A list of good questions appears in the "What Matters Most" section at the end of this chapter.)

4. **A Learning Frame of Mind**. Get ready to learn. Adopt a learning frame of mind. In an educational context, meaning can be derived from an exchange not only of personal information but also about an interesting or important topic or issue. Imagine a good conversation with reciprocity not only of what you know is true for you but what might be true for the other person.

5. **Unpack It and Get Back in the Game**. Holding onto a conversation when participants have signaled an end, perhaps nonverbally, is not a sign of respect. And if they abruptly remember a Zoom call they need to be on or a flight to catch, let it be over—even if you want it to go on. What's important is advancing and legitimizing meaningful conversation—bit by bit.

THE UNDERSIDES OF WORDS

Though conversations will not be enough to resolve ageism and dispel the narrative much of our world has about aging, we can learn from one another and reorient life enhancement for ourselves, friends, family, and younger generations simply through a good talk.

The Judds were the best mother-daughter duo of the 1990s with 14 number-one singles on the Billboard Country Chart. Their song "Love Can Build a Bridge," written by Naomi Judd, along with John Jarvis and prolific songwriter Paul Overstreet, won the Grammy for Song of the Year in 1992. Within its slow cadence, the message is that words are singularly the most powerful force available to humanity. Conversations create unforgettable moments through human connection.

Ready or not, our transition begs us forward, and as we go, we can expand our capacity to be courageous. Let's talk about aging and how we can live an extraordinary long life.

Don't you think it's time?

WHAT MATTERS MOST

Her Nickname Is "Hurricane"

The gift was a small paperback book, *My Magic Moments—A Nature Journal*, for my granddaughter—a sweet gesture by a new neighbor. The introduction was written by Julia Hawkins. No one in our family had ever heard of Ms. Hawkins. But at the Sunday dinner table, where age spans 8 to 76 years, no one could stop talking about her.

Ms. Hawkins, a star of the track and field world, holds the world record in the 100-meter dash for the 100-and-over age group. At 101, she ran her first race, setting a running record in the 100-meter dash, and earned her nickname, "Hurricane."

An avid bicycle rider, she found it increasingly difficult when it came to shifting gears, so she started running—at age 100. And not without a few concerns. "I was afraid of falling down, of embarrassing my family and even of dying. I even took care of a few things at home in case I didn't come back. But I looked that fear in the face and I ran."[7]

It's hard to imagine anyone not being inspired by Ms. Hawkins. When you decide to initiate conversations on growing older, you don't have to start with you and your story—start with someone else's. The interesting, casual conversation about someone else's life just may begin more talk and openness about aging. Communication could naturally move to other topics such as the power of role models, fears about growing old, or ageism itself.

Where to Begin Talking about Our Long Lives? 14 Great Questions

Let's overcome our reluctance to initiate and begin to hold conversations on living long with an important skill—asking good questions. We like question-asking people who think before they ask, then listen before they respond. Often, a respectful look into someone's eyes with care or a nod of the head is much better than a verbal response.

If you're ready to step up to the plate, be your best self, and take the lead, these questions can help guide a meaningful conversation with just about anyone.

1. What would you like to make time for in your later years?
2. If retirement is a door that you walk through, imagine walking back through it to answer the question "How was it?" What will you say?
3. How might your children, spouse/partner, or friends see you living a long life?
4. If you're in a life-story writing class, what should be in the introduction to "Part III: Your New 25-Year Life"?
5. What habit would you most like *not* to take into your later years?
6. What characteristic of yours will help you lead an *extraordinary* life after 65?
7. What does successful aging mean to you?
8. What nickname would you like to earn for yourself in the last third of life?
9. What are you doing now to impact your future in a positive way?
10. What ritual or tradition could you add to celebrate long lives?
11. What's one regret you have that you can keep from being a *big* regret?
12. Who are you talking to about life in retirement?
13. Who are role models for life ahead?
14. How is the culture of living longer changing you and your life?

ACKNOWLEDGMENTS

What makes the jukebox play is life's starts and stops, all kinds of people, a good story, and a little bit of heart. This venture is awash in all of these and supported by a troupe of individuals generous with time and truth, brimming with encouragement.

A friend is a friend, but what makes one darn special is when they listen to what's on your mind and never fail to ask, "How's the writing?" Through inquiry and a poke or two, this project was enriched by a posse of smart individuals. My wholehearted thanks to Dee Dee Kincade, Deanna Berg, Julie Auton, Thelma Kidd, Carol Osborn, Susan Reece, and Sara Fountain.

A prolific and successful writer who encourages from afar is one of my life's blessings. For her friendship and spirit, and for many years of encouragement, I am grateful to Casey Hawley. Gratitude to fellow writers Christy Emmanuel, ReAnn Scott, and Mona Pineda for giving their talents and resources. Philomena Madden's punctuation obsession makes her any writer's dream friend, but she also graces my life with laughter and honesty. I owe her.

Long bicycle rides with Marny Needle were needed for exercise, as well as time to explore our experiences coaching leaders to higher performance, often returning me to the keyboard with a better way to express an idea. I appreciate her.

As COVID-19 raged and travel ceased, my expat community stayed in touch, sending poetry, emojis, and great articles I was bound to miss. With appreciation to Nora Weaver, Carol Jackson, and Marvin Berk. Shout out to Beverly Moor, who wanders through life with a skip in her step. As a creative artist of many-layered surfaces, her assurance that the muse would always return buoyed my spirit.

Writers have different environment requirements to enhance the flow and quality of their writing. I do best when the doors have handles, fans work, and my art is on the walls. With two moves in one year, John O. McGuire Jr. continuously showed up at my door, cheerfully asking, "Where's my list?" No one could love and appreciate a son-in-law more than I do. My admiration for Teresa dos Santos knows no bounds. As the recipient of her design acumen, my space harbors harmony. I am indebted.

Thanks to Herb Ludwig II, my stepson, for cheerful invites to far-away places ("You've got to come to Iceland! You must see Croatia!") and for his charitable giving of Marriott Points that jog me into the big, wide world.

One thing I know for sure is having partners to dance with into the publishing world is invaluable. Vibrant, thoughtful, and smart, my agent April Eberhart smoothed the way with persistence and hard work. I am happy to have found her. My thanks to Suzanne Staszak-Silva, senior executive editor at Rowman & Littlefield Publishing, for her patience and guidance. I treasure Karen Sale, CEO, Essex River Consulting, who curates and aligns my online presence with professional expertise.

And lucky me, to have found gifted Janie Townsend, a crackerjack master of efficiency, to put the finishing touches to the manuscript.

Gather all the stars in the sky and none will outshine my pride in Elizabeth Pagano McGuire. Her talents lie at the tipping edge of a strong core of integrity, love, and generosity. My daughter read every word of this book—except these—then descended with her award-winning journalism skill set. Together, we know I could never have done this without her.

"Without Elvis none of us could have made it," said Buddy Holly. I owe a debt to writers and scholars who do and have done so much to elevate the importance and value of productive long lives. My thanks to: Chip Conley, Marc Freeman, Laura Carstensen, David Whyte, and Daniel Pink.

This book highlights a generation that is resourceful, unafraid of hard work, competitive, and in pursuit of excellence. Boomers are at the forefront of the longevity revolution. My sincere gratefulness to all those who gave time and transparency to interviews. Heroes all.

I am singularly fortunate to share life with a guy who puts up with my writing about him and defends my honor to the Liar's Club at the Cigar Factory. Herb Ludwig, my husband, bookends my personal and professional life with freedom and love.

—Barbara Pagano
Nashville, Tennessee
February 2022

NOTES

CHAPTER 1

1. Katherine Ellison, "With the Novel Coronavirus, Suddenly at 60 We're Now 'Old,'" *The Washington Post*, June 27, 2020, https://www.washington post.com/health/with-the-novel-coronavirus-suddenly-at-60-were-now-old/2020/06/26/16b1406c-afea-11ea-8f56-63f38c 990077_story.html.

2. Emily A. Vogel, "Millennials Stand Out for Their Technology Use, but Older Generations Embrace Digital Life," Pew Research Center, September 9, 2019, https://www.pewresearch.org/fact-tank/2019/09/09/us-generations -technology-use/.

3. Nicole F. Roberts, "Forget Generational Stereotypes, Baby Boomers are Just as Addicted to Smart Phones as Millennials," *Forbes*, May 6, 2019, https://www.forbes.com/sites/nicolefisher/ 2019/05/06/forget-generational -stereotypes-baby-boomers-are-just-as-addicted-to-smart-phones/ ?sh=526abb 904f89.

4. BBC News, "People Aged 65–79 'Happiest of All,' Study Suggests," accessed February 2, 2016, https://www.bbc.com/news/uk-35471624.

5. Joseph F. Coughlin and Chaiwoo Lee, "The Revealing Words People Use to Describe Retirement," *Wall Street Journal*, November 17, 2019, https://www.wsj.com/articles/the-revealing-words-people-use-to-describe-retirement -11574046240.

6. TED, "The Psychology of Your Future Self | Dan Gilbert," YouTube, June 3, 2014, video, 6:49, https://www.youtube.com/watch?v=XNbaR54Gpj4.

7. Institute for the Future, "The American Future Gap, Survey," accessed 2021, https://www.iftf.org/americanfuturegap/.

8. TED, "The Psychology of Your Future Self."

9. Holly Harris and Michael A. Busseri, "Is There an 'End of History Illusion' for Life Satisfaction? Evidence from a Three-Wave Longitudinal Study,"

Journal of Research in Personality 83 (December 2019), https://doi.org/10.1016/j.jrp.2019.103869.

10. Next Big Idea Club, "Next Big Idea Club with Daniel Pink Welcome," YouTube, February 26, 2019, video, 0:44, https://www.youtube.com/watch?v=hc5l5lH6K6k.

11. World Regret Survey, accessed 2021, https://worldregretsurvey.com/.

12. Makenna Berry, "90 Percent of Us Have Big Regrets: Dealing with It Is a Crucial Skill for Healthy Living," *Unbound* (blog), Saybrook University, January 20, 2011, https://www.saybrook.edu/unbound/90-percent-us-have-big-regrets-dealing-it-crucial-skill-healthy-living/.

13. Aaron Becker, *Journey* (Somerville, MA: Candlewick Press, 2013).

CHAPTER 2

1. *American Perception of Aging in the 21st Century: The NCOA's Continuing Study of the Myths and Realities of Aging* (Washington, DC: National Council on Aging, 2002).

2. Andrew Scott, "Living Longer: Our 100-Year Life," *After the Fact* (podcast), February 1, 2019, hosted by Dan LeDuc, MP3 audio, 18:58, https://www.pewtrusts.org/-/media/assets/2019/02/atf-transcript_episode-48.pdf.

3. Department of Economic and Social Affairs, *World Population on Ageing 2019* (New York: United Nations, 2020).

4. Chris Johns, editor, "This Baby Will Live to Be 120," *National Geographic*, May 2013.

5. Pew Research Center, "Living to 120 and Beyond: Americans' Views on Aging, Medical Advances and Radical Life Extension," August 6, 2013, https://www.pewforum.org/2013/08/06/living-to-120-and-beyond-americans-views-on-aging-medical-advances-and-radical-life-extension/.

6. Maura Judkis, "Why 30-Year-Olds Are Smashing Cake into Their Faces. Yes, Just Like Babies," *The Washington Post*, June 9. 2016, https://www.washingtonpost.com/news/food/wp/2016/06/09/why-30-year-olds-are-smashing-cake-into-their-faces-yes-just-like-babies/.

7. Emily Laber-Warren, "You're Only as Old as You Feel," *The New York Times*, October 17, 2019, https://www.nytimes.com/2019/10/17/well/mind/age-subjective-feeling-old.html.

8. William J. Chopik, Ryan H. Bremner, David J. Johnson, and Hannah L. Giasson, "Age Differences in Age Perceptions and Developmental Transitions," *Frontiers in Psychology* 9, no. 67 (2018), https://doi.org/10.3389/fpsyg.2018.00067.

9. Julia Angwin, Noam Scheiber, *The New York Times*, and Ariana Tobin, "Dozens of Companies Are Using Facebook to Exclude Older Workers from Job Ads," ProPublica, December 20, 2017, https://www.propublica.org/article/facebook-ads-age-discrimination-targeting.

10. Beth McEvoy, "Westbrook Grandmother Can't Stop Turning Heads in Her Swimsuit," Maine News, December 12, 2019, https://www.newscenter maine.com/article/news/local/westbrook-grandmother-cant-stop-making -headlines-in-her-swimsuit/97-557907709.

11. Thomas Armstrong, *The Human Odyssey: Navigating the Twelve Stages of Life* (New York: Ixia Press, 2019).

12. The Longevity Project, "Laura Carstensen," accessed 2021, https://www .longevity-project.com/speakerblog/laura-carstensen.

13. *The New Map of Life: 100 Years to Thrive*, Stanford Center on Longevity, November 2021, https://longevity.stanford.edu/wp-content/uploads/2021/11/NMOL_report_FINAL-5.pdf.

CHAPTER 3

1. Ken Dychtwald and Robert Morison, *What Retirees Want: A Holistic View of Life's Third Age* (Hoboken, NJ: Wiley, 2020).

2. Glennon Doyle, *Untamed*, (New York: Dial Press, 2020).

3. Audrey Hamilton, "Self-Esteem Declines Sharply Among Older Adults While Middle-Aged Are Most Confident," American Psychological Association, 2010, https://www.apa.org/news/press/releases/2010/04/self-esteem.

4. Lyn Chapman, Kerry Sargent-Cox, Mark S. Horswill, and Kaarin J. Ansley, "The Impact of Age Stereotypes on Older Adults' Hazard Perception Performance and Driving Confidence," *Journal of Applied Gerontology* 35, no. 6 (January 2014): 642–52.

5. Doyle, *Untamed*.

6. Catherine Winter, "11 Examples of Life Purpose Statement That You Could Adopt," *A Conscious Rethink* (blog), January 26, 2021, https://www .aconsciousrethink.com/14552/life-purpose-statement-examples/.

7. Olga Khazan, "Find Your Passion Is Awful Advice," *The Atlantic*, July 12, 2018, https://www.theatlantic.com/science/archive/2018/07/find-your -passion-is-terrible-advice/564932/.

8. Cal Newport, *So Good They Can't Ignore You: Why Skills Trump Passion in the Quest for Work You Love* (New York: Grand Central Publishing, 2012).

9. Tasha Eurich, "What Self-Awareness Really Is (and How to Cultivate It)," *Harvard Business Review*, January 4, 2018, https://hbr.org/2018/01/what -self-awareness-really-is-and-how-to-cultivate-it.

10. Benjamin Franklin, *Poor Richard's Almanack* (New York: Peter Pauper Press, 1980).

11. Ferris Jabr, "Does Self-Awareness Require a Complex Brain?" *Brainwaves* (blog), *Scientific American*, August 22, 2012, https://blogs.scientificamerican.com/brainwaves/does-self-awareness-require-a-complex-brain/.

12. Hamilton, "Self-Esteem Declines."

13. Philippe Rochat, "Five Levels of Self-Awareness as They Unfold Early in Life," *Consciousness and Cognition* 12 (February 2003): 717–31.

14. Herminia Ibarra, *Working Identity: Unconventional Strategies for Reinventing Your Career* (Boston: Harvard Business Press, 2004).

15. John LaRosa, "$10.4 Billion Self-Improvement Market Pivots to Virtual Deliver During the Pandemic," MarketResearch.com, August 2, 2021, https://blog.marketresearch.com/10.4-billion-self-improvement-market-pivots-to-virtual-delivery-during-the-pandemic.

CHAPTER 4

1. Transamerica Center for Retirement Studies, *19th Annual Transamerica Retirement Survey* (Los Angeles, CA: Transamerica Center for Retirement Studies, 2019).

2. Michelle Silver, *Retirement and Its Discontents: Why We Won't Stop Working, Even If We Can* (New York: Columbia University Press, 2018).

3. Merrill Lynch Bank of America Corporation and Age Wave, *Leisure in Retirement Beyond the Bucket List*, May 2016, https://agewave.com/wp-content/uploads/2016/05/2016-Leisure-in-Retirement_Beyond-the-Bucket-List.pdf.

4. Bruce Feiler, *Life Is in the Transitions: Mastering Change at Any Age* (New York: Penguin, 2020).

5. Gallup, *State of the Global Workplace: 2021 Report*, available at https://www.gallup.com/workplace/349484/state-of-the-global-workplace.aspx#ite-350777.

6. Karla L. Miller, "'Micromanaged and Disrespected': Top Reasons Workers Are Quitting Their Jobs in 'The Great Resignation,'" *The Washington Post*, October 7, 2021, https://www.washingtonpost.com/business/2021/10/07/top-reasons-great-resignation-workers-quitting/.

7. Ben Casselman, "Record Number of American Workers Quit Jobs in September," *The New York Times*, November 12, 2021, https://www.nytimes.com/2021/11/12/business/economy/jobs-labor-openings-quit.html.

8. Vipula Handhi and Jennifer Robinson, "The 'Great Resignation' Is Really the 'Great Discontent,'" Gallup Workplace July 22, 2021, https://www.gallup.com/workplace/351545/great-resignation-really-great-discontent.aspx.

9. Ian Cook, "Who Is Driving the Great Resignation?" *Harvard Business Review*, September 15, 2021, https://hbr.org/2021/09/who-is-driving-the-great-resignation.

10. Tom Rath and Jim Harter, *Welbeing: The Five Essential Elements* (New York: Gallup Press, 2010).

11. Ibid.

12. Paul Deer, "How Long Will $1 Million Last in Retirement?" *Daily Capital*, September 21, 2021, https://www.personalcapital.com/blog/retirement-planning/can-you-retire-with-a-million-dollars/.

13. Tara Siegel Bernard, "'Too Little Too Late': Bankruptcy Booms Among Older Americans," *The New York Times*, August 5, 2018, https://www.nytimes.com/2018/08/05/business/bankruptcy-older-americans.html.

14. Emily Zulz, "Americans Would Rather Talk About Sex or Death than Retirement," ThinkAdvisor, August 27, 2014, https://www.thinkadvisor.com/2014/08/27/americans-would-rather-talk-about-sex-or-death-than-retirement-2/.

15. Merrill Lynch and Age Wave, *The Financial Journey of Modern Parenting: Joy, Complexity and Sacrifice*, October 2018, https://business.bofa.com/content/dam/boamlimages/documents/articles/ID18_0983/the_financial_journey_of_modern_parenting_finalpdf.pdf.

16. Michael Hyatt, "Why Retirement Is a Dirty Word," Michaelhyatt.com, August 18, 2014, https://michaelhyatt.com/retirement/.

CHAPTER 5

1. George Michelsen Foy, "Humans Can't Plan Long-Term, and Here's Why," *Psychology Today*, June 25, 2018, https://www.psychologytoday.com/us/blog/shut-and-listen/201806/humans-cant-plan-long-term-and-heres-why.

2. Laura Carstensen, "We Need a Major Redesign of Life," *The Washington Post*, November 28, 2019, https://www.washingtonpost.com/opinions/we-need-a-major-redesign-of-life/2019/11/29/a63daab2-1086-11ea-9cd7-a1becbc82f5e_story.html.

3. Stephen F. Barnes, *Third Age—The Golden Years of Adulthood*, San Diego State University Interwork Institute, 2011, http://calbooming.sdsu.edu/documents/TheThirdAge.pdf.

4. P. A. Gooding et al., "Psychological Resilience in Young and Older Adults," *International Journal of Geriatric Psychiatry* 27, no. 3 (March 2012): 262–70, https://pubmed.ncbi.nlm.nih.gov/21472780/.

5. Bruce Feiler, *Life Is in the Transitions: Mastering Change at Any Age* (New York: Penguin Press, 2020).

6. Thomas Moore, *Care of the Soul: A Guide for Cultivating Depth and Sacredness in Everyday Life* (New York: HarperCollins, 1992).

7. Katherine May, *Wintering: The Power of Rest and Retreat in Difficult Times* (London: Rider, 2020).

8. Lynda Gratton and Andrew Scott, *The 100-Year Life: Living and Working in an Age of Longevity* (London: Bloomsbury, 2016).

CHAPTER 6

1. Merrill Lynch Bank of America Corporation and Age Wave, *Home in Retirement: More Freedom, New Choices*, 2015, https://agewave.com/wp-content/uploads/2016/07/2015-ML-AW-Home-in-Retirement_More-Freedom-New-Choices.pdf.

2. Daniel Gilbert, *Stumbling on Happiness* (New York: Vintage Books, 2007.)

3. Richard Florida, *Who's Your City? How the Creative Economy Is Making Where You Live the Most Important Decision of Your Life* (New York: Basic Books, 2009).

4. Dan Buettner, *The Blue Zones of Happiness: Lessons from the World's Happiest People* (Washington, DC: National Geographic, 2017).

5. Merrill Lynch Bank of America Corporation and Age Wave, *Home in Retirement*.

6. Maria Zamudio, "Growing Number of Americans Are Retiring Outside US," *PBS News Hour*, December 28, 2016, https://www.pbs.org/newshour/world/growing-number-americans-retiring-outside-u-s.

7. Staff Writer, "Numbers of Americans Retiring Abroad Soaring, as Cost of Retiring Stateside Also Soars: Report," *American Expat Financial News Journal*, September 25, 2019, https://americanexpatfinance.com/news/item/267-numbers-of-americans-retiring-abroad-soaring-as-cost-of-retiring-stateside-also-soars-report.

8. Lottie Gross, "The World's Friendliest Cities—as Voted by You," *Rough Guides* (blog), February 24, 2021, https://www.roughguides.com/articles/the-worlds-friendliest-cities-as-voted-by-you/.

9. Center for the Study of Long Distance Relationships, "Long Distance Relationship Frequently Asked Questions 2018," https://www.longdistance relationships.net/faqs.htm.

10. Nanci Hellmich, "How Retired Couples Can Live Happily Ever After," *USA Today*, February 12, 2014, https://www.usatoday.com/story/money/personalfinance/2013/11/05/retirement-couples-happy/2918023/.

11. Roberta K. Taylor and Dorian Mintzer, *The Couple's Retirement Puzzle: 10 Must-Have Conversations for Creating an Amazing New Life Together* (Naperville, IL: Sourcebooks, 2014).

12. Michelle Schroeder-Garner, "The Honest Truth about Van Dwelling: Answers to the Most Common Van Life Questions," *Making Sense of Cents*, March 4, 2021, https://www.makingsenseofcents.com/2019/09/van-dwelling.html.

13. Jessica Bruder, "The New Nomads: Living Full-Time on the Road," *The Saturday Evening Post*, June 28, 2018, https://www.saturdayeveningpost.com/2018/06/the-new-nomads/.

14. Rachel Levin, "When the Techies Took over Tahoe," *Outdoor*, April 15, 2021, https://www.outsideonline.com/adventure-travel/news-analysis/tahoe-zoomtown-covid-migration/.

CHAPTER 7

1. Knowledge@Wharton, "The Retirement Problem: What to Do with All That Time?" January 14, 2016, https://knowledge.wharton.upenn.edu/article/the-retirement-problem-what-will-you-do-with-all-that-time/.

2. Isabel Allende, interview by Mia Funk, *The Creative Process*, accessed 2021, https://www.creativeprocess.info/interviews-1/isabel-allende-mia-funk.

3. Marc Freedman, "A Gap Year for Grown-ups," *Harvard Business Review*, July 14, 2011, https://hbr.org/2011/07/a-gap-year-for-grown-ups.html.

4. Filip Lau and Lester Lam, *The Second Coming of Age: Understanding Baby Boomers . . . and How to Cater to Them*, ReD Associates and Cognizant Digital Works, 2016, https://www.cognizant.com/whitepapers/the-second-coming-of-age-codex2239.pdf.

5. Sara Wilson, *This One Wild and Precious Life: The Path Back to Connection in a Fractured World* (Sydney: Pan Macmillan Australia, 2020).

CHAPTER 8

1. Merrill Lynch Bank of America Corporation and Age Wave, *Leisure in Retirement Beyond the Bucket List*, May 2016, https://agewave.com/wp-content/uploads/2016/05/2016-Leisure-in-Retirement_Beyond-the-Bucket-List.pdf.

2. Transamerica Center for Retirement Studies, *19th Annual Transamerica Retirement Survey* (Los Angeles, CA: Transamerica Center for Retirement Studies , 2019).

3. Edward Jones and Age Wave, *The Four Pillars of the New Retirement*, 2021, https://www.edwardjones.com/sites/default/files/acquiadam/2021-01/Edward-Jones-4-Pillars-US-report.pdf.

4. Laurent Belsie, "Why Pandemic Forced Baby Boomers to Rethink Retirement Plans," *The Christian Monitor*, June 1, 2021, https://www.csmonitor.com/Business/2021/0601/Why-pandemic-forced-baby-boomers-to-rethink-retirement-plans.

5. Edward Jones and Age Wave, *The Four Pillars of the New Retirement*.

6. Lynda Gratton and Andrew Scott, *The 100-Year Life: Living and Working in an Age of Longevity* (London: Bloomsbury, 2016).

7. Kevin McCormack, "De-stressing Stem Cells and the Bonnie & Clyde of Stem Cell," *The Stem Cellar* (blog), CIRM, February 5, 2021, https://blog.cirm.ca.gov/tag/wnt/.

8. Ken Dychtwald and Robert Morison, *What Retirees Want: A Holistic View of Life's Third Age* (Hoboken, NJ: Wiley, 2020).

9. Anne Trafton, "Study Helps Explain Why Motivation to Learn Declines with Age," *MIT News*, October 27, 2020, https://news.mit.edu/2020/why-learn-motivate-age-decline-1027.

10. Dychtwald and Morison, *What Retirees Want*.

CHAPTER 9

1. Colleen Walsh, "Young Adults Hardest Hit by Loneliness during Pandemic," *The Harvard Gazette*, February 17, 2021, https://news.harvard.edu/gazette/story/2021/02/young-adults-teens-loneliness-mental-health-coronavirus-covid-pandemic/.

2. Pew Research Center, "Religion and Living Arrangements Around the World," December 12, 2019, https://www.pewforum.org/2019/12/12/religion-and-living-arrangements-around-the-world/.

3. Jennifer Molinsky, "Housing Perspectives," Joint Center for Housing Studies of Harvard University, August 7, 2020, https://www.jchs.harvard.edu/blog/designing-senior-housing-safe-interactions-age-covid-19.

4. Marc Agronin, "What Covid-19 Taught Us About the High Cost of Isolation," *The Wall Street Journal*, April 10, 2021, https://www.wsj.com/articles/covid-19-isolation-11618005941.

5. Laura Carstensen, *A Long Bright Future* (New York: PublicAffairs, 2011).

6. Brooke Auxier and Monica Anderson, "Social Media Use in 2021." Pew Research Center, April 7, 2021, https://www.pewresearch.org/internet/2021/04/07/social-media-use-in-2021/.

7. Stacy Francis, "'Gray Divorce' Rates Are Exploding Due to This Perfect Storm," *Kiplinger*, April 12, 2021, https://www.kiplinger.com/personal-finance/602589/gray-divorce-rates-are-exploding-due-to-this-perfect-storm.

8. Maryanne Vandervelde, "Are You Emotionally Ready to Retire? Eight Questions to Ask Yourself," *The Wall Street Journal*, April 1, 2021, https://www.wsj.com/articles/ready-to-retire-emotionally-11618007274.

9. Clare Ansberry, "More Older Couples Stay Together Because They Live Apart," *The Wall Street Journal*, July 28, 2019, https://www.wsj.com/articles/more-older-couples-stay-together-because-they-live-apart-11564311602.

10. Christine Ro, "The Truth About Family Estrangement," *BBC Future*, March 31, 2019, https://www.bbc.com/future/article/20190328-family-estrangement-causes.

11. Karl A. Pillemer, *Fault Lines: Fractured Families and How to Mend Them* (New York: Avery, 2020).

12. Beth Bruno, "Encouragement for Mothers Who Are Estranged from Their Child," *Medium*, October 8, 2019, https://bethbruno2015.medium.com/encouragement-for-mothers-who-are-estranged-from-their-child-e089964cb426.

13. Ken Dychtwald and Robert Morison, *What Retirees Want: A Holistic View of Life's Third Age* (Hoboken, NJ: Wiley, 2020).

14. Joshua Coleman, "A Shift in American Family Values Is Fueling Estrangement," *The Atlantic*, January 10, 2021, https://www.theatlantic.com/family/archive/2021/01/why-parents-and-kids-get-estranged/617612/.

15. Amy Morin, "How to Know When to End a Relationship with Family," *Verywell Family*, March 4, 2020, https://www.verywellfamily.com/cutting-ties-with-family-4781962.

16. William Chopik, "Are Friends Better for Us Than Family?" *MSU Today*, June 6, 2017, https://msutoday.msu.edu/news/2017/are-friends-better-for-us-than-family.

17. Zoya Gervis, "Most Young People Enjoy 'Friendsgiving' More Than Thanksgiving," *New York Post*, November 18, 2019, https://nypost.com/2019/11/18/most-young-people-enjoy-friendsgiving-more-than-thanksgiving/.

18. Dawn O. Braithwaite, Betsy Wackernagel Bach, Leslie A. Baxter, Rebecca DiVerniero, Joshua R. Hammonds, Angela M. Hosek, Erin K. Willer and Bianca M. Wolf, "Constructing Family: A Typology of Voluntary Kin," *Journal of Social and Personal Relationships* 27, no. 3 (April 2010): 388–407.

19. Carol Marak, "What We All Need to Know About Solo Aging," *Next Avenue*, October 10, 2018, https://www.nextavenue.org/challenges-solo-agers/.

20. Administration on Aging, *2017 Profile of Older Americans*, developed by the Administration on Aging, Administration for Community Living, and US Department of Health and Human Services, April 2018, https://acl.gov/sites/default/files/Aging%20and%20Disability%20in%20America/2017OlderAmericansProfile.pdf.

CHAPTER 10

1. NBC Sports Commentary, "Tour de France," *NBC Sports Channel*, June 29, 2021.

2. Daniel Ostanek, "Lefevere: The Whole Staff Was Crying after Cavendish's Tour de France Stage 4 Win," *Cycling News*, June 29, 2021, https://www.cyclingnews.com/news/lefevere-the-whole-staff-was-crying-after-cavendishs-tour-de-frace-stage-4-win/.

3. Jason Gay, "The Emotional, Outrageous Comeback of Mark Cavendish at the Tour de France," *The Wall Street Journal*, July 9, 2021, https://www.wsj.com/articles/mark-cavendish-tour-de-france-stage-wins-record-34-eddy-merckx-11625855896.

4. Bhadra Sharma and Ellen Barry, "Climbers Leave Everest Amid Regrets and Tensions Among Sherpas," *The New York Times*, April 24, 2014, https://www.nytimes.com/2014/04/25/world/asia/climbers-leave-everest-amid-regrets-and-tensions-among-sherpas.html.

5. Beatrice Kathleen Barklow, "Rethinking the Age Sixty Mandatory Retirement Rule: A Look at the Newest Movement," *Journal of Air Law and Commerce* 60, no. 1 (1994), https://scholar.smu.edu/cgi/viewcontent.cgi?article=1367&context=jalc.

6. Peter Gosselin, "If You're Over 50, Chances Are the Decision to Leave a Job Won't Be Yours," ProPublica, December 28, 2018, https://www.propublica.org/article/older-workers-united-states-pushed-out-of-work-forced-retirement.

7. Ibid.

8. Maurie Backman, "What to Do if You're Forced into Early Retirement," The Motley Fool, March 4, 2018, https://www.fool.com/retirement/2018/03/04/what-to-do-if-youre-forced-into-early-retirement.aspx.

9. Anne Tergesen, "Why Everything You Know about Aging Is Probably Wrong," *The Wall Street Journal*, November 30, 2014, https://www.wsj.com/articles/why-everything-you-think-about-aging-may-be-wrong-1417408057.

CHAPTER 11

1. Daniela S. Jobb, Seojug Jung, Amanda K. Damarin, Sheena Mirpuri, and Dario Spini, "Who Is Your Successful Aging Role Model?" *The Journal of Gerontology, Series B* 72, no. 2 (March 2017): 237–47.

2. MDVIP, "Health Longevity Not So Much Reality for Generation X," Business Wire, January 31, 2017, https://www.businesswire.com/news/home/20170131005473/en/Health-and-Longevity-Not-So-Much-a-Reality-for-Generation-X.

3. Rodrigo García, *A Farewell to Gabo and Mercedes: A Son's Memoir of Gabriel García Márquez and Mercedes Barcha* (London: HarperVia, 2021).

4. MDVIP, "Health Longevity.

5. Chris Colin, "It's Never Too Late to Record Your First Album," *The New York Times*, August 17, 2021, https://www.nytimes.com/2021/08/17/style/adult-record-first-album.html.

6. Shankar Vedantam, "People Like People Who Ask Questions," *NPR*, November 29, 2017, https://www.npr.org/2017/11/29/567133944/people-like-people-who-ask-questions.

7. Bill Shafer, "103-Year-Old Runs into History," Growing Bolder, Facebook (video), June 20, 2019, https://www.facebook.com/GrowingBolder/videos/608999532923015/.

BIBLIOGRAPHY

Administration on Aging. *2017 Profile of Older Americans.* Developed by the Administration on Aging, Administration for Community Living, and US Department of Health and Human Services. April 2018. https://acl.gov/sites/default/files/Aging%20and%20Disability%20in%20America/2017Older AmericansProfile.pdf.

Agronin, Marc. "What Covid-19 Taught Us About the High Cost of Isolation." *The Wall Street Journal,* April 10, 2021. https://www.wsj.com/articles/covid-19-isolation-11618005941.

Allende, Isabel. Interview by Mia Funk. *The Creative Process.* Accessed 2021. https://www.creativeprocess.info/interviews-1/isabel-allende-mia-funk.

American Perception of Aging in the 21st Century: The NCOA's Continuing Study of the Myths and Realities of Aging. Washington, DC: National Council on Aging, 2002.

Angwin, Julia, Noam Scheibr, *The New York Times,* and Ariana Tobin. "Dozens of Companies Are Using Facebook to Exclude Older Workers From Job Ads." ProPublica, December 20, 2017. https://www.propublica.org/article/facebook-ads-age-discrimination-targeting.

Ansberry, Clare. "More Older Couples Stay Together Because They Live Apart." *The Wall Street Journal,* July 28, 2019. https://www.wsj.com/articles/more-older-couples-stay-together-because-they-live-apart-11564311602.

Armstrong, Thomas. *The Human Odyssey: Navigating the Twelve Stages of Life.* New York: Ixia Press, 2019.

Auxier, Brooke, and Monica Anderson. "Social Media Use in 2021." Pew Research Center, April 7, 2021. https://www.pewresearch.org/internet/2021/04/07/social-media-use-in-2021/.

Backman, Maurie. "What to Do If You're Forced into Early Retirement." The Motley Fool, March 4, 2018. https://www.fool.com/retirement/2018/03/04/what-to-do-if-youre-forced-into-early-retirement.aspx.

Barklow, Beatrice Kathleen. "Rethinking the Age Sixty Mandatory Retirement Rule: A Look at the Newest Movement." *Journal of Air Law and Commerce* 60, no. 1 (1994). https://scholar.smu.edu/cgi/viewcontent.cgi?article =1367&context=jalc.

Barnes, Stephen F. *Third Age—The Golden Years of Adulthood.* San Diego State University Interwork Institute, 2011. http://calbooming.sdsu.edu/documents/ TheThirdAge.pdf.

BBC News. "People Aged 65–79 'Happiest of All,' Study Suggests." Accessed February 2, 2016. https://www.bbc.com/news/uk-35471624.

Becker, Aaron. *Journey.* Somerville, MA: Candlewick Press, 2013.

Belsie, Laurent. "Why Pandemic Forced Baby Boomers to Rethink Retirement Plans." *The Christian Monitor,* June 1, 2021. https://www.csmonitor.com/ Business/2021/0601/Why-pandemic-forced-baby-boomers-to-rethink -retirement-plans.

Berry, Makenna. "90 Percent of Us Have Big Regrets: Dealing with It Is a Crucial Skill for Healthy Living." *Unbound* (blog), Saybrook University, January 20, 2011. https://www.saybrook.edu/unbound/90-percent-us-have-big -regrets-dealing-it-crucial-skill-healthy-living/.

Braithwaite, Dawn O., Betsy Wackernagel Bach, Leslie A. Baxter, Rebecca DiVerniero, Joshua R. Hammonds, Angela M. Hosek, Erin K. Willer, and Bianca M. Wolf. "Constructing Family: A Typology of Voluntary Kin." *Journal of Social and Personal Relationships* 27, no. 3 (April 2010): 388–407.

Bruder, Jessica. "The New Nomads: Living Full-Time on the Road." *The Saturday Evening Post,* June 28, 2018. https://www.saturdayeveningpost.com/ 2018/06/the-new-nomads/.

Bruno, Beth. "Encouragement for Mothers Who Are Estranged from Their Child." *Medium,* October 8, 2019. https://bethbruno2015.medium .com/encouragement-for-mothers-who-are-estranged-from-their-child -e089964cb426.

Buettner, Dan. *The Blue Zones of Happiness: Lessons from the World's Happiest People.* Washington, DC: National Geographic, 2017.

Carstensen, Laura. *A Long Bright Future.* New York: PublicAffairs, 2011.

———. "We Need a Major Redesign of Life." *The Washington Post,* November 28, 2019. https://www.washingtonpost.com/opinions/we-need-a-major -redesign-of-life/2019/11/29/a63daab2-1086-11ea-9cd7-a1becbc82f5e _story.html.

Casselman, Ben. "Record Number of American Workers Quit Jobs in September." *The New York Times,* November 12, 2021. https://www.nytimes .com/2021/11/12/business/economy/jobs-labor-openings-quit.html.

Center for the Study of Long Distance Relationships. "Long Distance Relationship Frequently Asked Questions 2018." Accessed 2021. https://www.longdistancerelationships.net/faqs.htm.

Chapman, Lyn, Kerry Sargent-Cox, Mark S. Horswill, and Kaarin J. Ansley. "The Impact of Age Stereotypes on Older Adults' Hazard Perception Performance and Driving Confidence." *Journal of Applied Gerontology* 35, no. 6 (January 2014): 642–52.

Chopik, William. "Are Friends Better for Us Than Family?" *MSU Today*, June 6, 2017. https://msutoday.msu.edu/news/2017/are-friends-better-for-us-than-family.

Chopik, William J., Ryan H. Bremner, David J. Johnson, and Hannah L. Giasson. "Age Differences in Age Perceptions and Developmental Transitions." *Frontiers in Psychology* 9, no. 67 (2018). https://doi.org/10.3389/fpsyg.2018.00067.

Coleman, Joshua. "A Shift in American Family Values Is Fueling Estrangement." *The Atlantic*, January 10, 2021. https://www.theatlantic.com/family/archive/2021/01/why-parents-and-kids-get-estranged/617612/.

Colin, Chris. "It's Never Too Late to Record Your First Album." *The New York Times*, August 17, 2021. https://www.nytimes.com/2021/08/17/style/adult-record-first-album.html.

Cook, Ian. "Who Is Driving the Great Resignation?" *Harvard Business Review*, September 15, 2021. https://hbr.org/2021/09/who-is-driving-the-great-resignation.

Coughlin, Joseph F., and Chaiwoo Lee. "The Revealing Words People Use to Describe Retirement." *Wall Street Journal.* November 17, 2019. https://www.wsj.com/articles/the-revealing-words-people-use-to-describe-retirement-11574046240.

Deer, Paul. "How Long Will $1 Million Last in Retirement?" *Daily Capital*, September 21, 2021. https://www.personalcapital.com/blog/retirement-planning/can-you-retire-with-a-million-dollars/.

Department of Economic and Social Affairs. *World Population on Ageing 2019.* New York: United Nations, 2020.

Doyle, Glennon. *Untamed.* New York: Dial Press, 2020.

Dychtwald, Ken, and Robert Morison. *What Retirees Want: A Holistic View of Life's Third Age.* Hoboken, NJ: Wiley, 2020.

Edward Jones and Age Wave. *The Four Pillars of the New Retirement.* Edward Jones, 2021. https://www.edwardjones.com/sites/default/files/acquiadam/2021-01/Edward-Jones-4-Pillars-US-report.pdf.

Ellison, Katherine. "With the Novel Coronavirus, Suddenly at 60 We're Now 'Old.'" *The Washington Post*, June 27, 2020. https://www.washingtonpost

.com/health/with-the-novel-coronavirus-suddenly-at-60-were-now-old/
2020/06/26/16b1406c-afea-11ea-8f56-63f38c 990077_story.html.

Eurich, Tasha. "What Self-Awareness Really Is (and How to Cultivate It)." *Harvard Business Review*, January 4, 2018. https://hbr.org/2018/01/what-self-awareness-really-is-and-how-to-cultivate-it.

Feiler, Bruce. *Life Is in the Transitions: Mastering Change at Any Age.* New York: Penguin Press, 2020.

Florida, Richard. *Who's Your City? How the Creative Economy Is Making Where You Live the Most Important Decision of Your Life.* New York: Basic Books, 2009.

Foy, George Michelsen. "Humans Can't Plan Long-Term, and Here's Why." *Psychology Today*, June 25, 2018. https://www.psychologytoday.com/us/blog/shut-and-listen/201806/humans-cant-plan-long-term-and-heres-why.

Francis, Stacy. "'Gray Divorce' Rates Are Exploding Due to This Perfect Storm." *Kiplinger*, April 12, 2021. https://www.kiplinger.com/personal-finance/602589/gray-divorce-rates-are-exploding-due-to-this-perfect-storm.

Franklin, Benjamin. *Poor Richard's Almanack.* New York: Peter Pauper Press, 1980.

Freedman, Marc. "A Gap Year for Grown-ups." *Harvard Business Review*, July 14, 2011. https://hbr.org/2011/07/a-gap-year-for-grown-ups.html.

Freeman, Daniel, and Jason Freeman. "Is Life's Happiness Curve Really U-Shaped?" *The Guardian*, June 24, 2015. https://www.theguardian.com/science/head-quarters/2015/jun/24/life-happiness-curve-u-shaped-ageing.

Gallup. *State of the Global Workplace: 2021 Report.* Available at https://www.gallup.com/workplace/349484/state-of-the-global-workplace.aspx#ite-350777.

García, Rodrigo. *A Farewell to Gabo and Mercedes: A Son's Memoir of Gabriel García Márquez and Mercedes Barcha.* London: HarperVia, 2021.

Gay, Jason. "The Emotional, Outrageous Comeback of Mark Cavendish at the Tour de France." *The Wall Street Journal*, July 9, 2021. https://www.wsj.com/articles/mark-cavendish-tour-de-france-stage-wins-record-34-eddy-merckx-11625855896.

Gervis, Zoya. "Most Young People Enjoy 'Friendsgiving' More Than Thanksgiving." *New York Post*, November 18, 2019. https://nypost.com/2019/11/18/most-young-people-enjoy-friendsgiving-more-than-thanksgiving/.

Gilbert, Daniel. *Stumbling on Happiness.* New York: Vintage Books, 2007.

Gooding, P. A., et al. "Psychological Resilience in Young and Older Adults." *International Journal of Geriatric Psychiatry* 27. no. 3 (March 2012): 262–70. https://pubmed.ncbi.nlm.nih.gov/21472780/.

Gosselin, Peter. "If You're Over 50, Chances Are the Decision to Leave a Job Won't Be Yours." ProPublica, December 28, 2018. https://www.pro-publica.org/article/older-workers-united-states-pushed-out-of-work-forced-retirement.

Gratton, Lynda, and Andrew Scott. *The 100-Year Life: Living and Working in an Age of Longevity.* London: Bloomsbury, 2016.

Gross, Lottie. "The World's Friendliest Cities—as Voted by You." *Rough Guides* (blog), February 24, 2021. https://www.roughguides.com/articles/the-worlds-friendliest-cities-as-voted-by-you/.

Hamilton, Audrey. "Self-Esteem Declines Sharply Among Older Adults While Middle-Aged Are Most Confident." American Psychological Association, 2010. https://www.apa.org/news/press/releases/2010/04/self-esteem.

Handhi, Vipula, and Jennifer Robinson. "The 'Great Resignation' Is Really the 'Great Discontent.'" Gallup Workplace July 22, 2021. https://www.gallup.com/workplace/351545/great-resignation-really-great-discontent.aspx.

Harris, Holly, and Michael A. Busseri. "Is There an 'End of History Illusion' for Life Satisfaction? Evidence from a Three-Wave Longitudinal Study." *Journal of Research in Personality* 83 (December 2019). https://doi.org/10.1016/j.jrp.2019.103869.

Hellmich, Nanci. "How Retired Couples Can Live Happily Ever After." *USA Today,* February 12, 2014. https://www.usatoday.com/story/money/personalfinance/2013/11/05/retirement-couples-happy/2918023/.

Hyatt, Michael. "Why Retirement Is a Dirty Word." Michaelhyatt.com, August 18, 2014. https://michaelhyatt.com/retirement/.

Ibarra, Herminia. *Working Identity: Unconventional Strategies for Reinventing Your Career.* Boston: Harvard Business Press, 2004.

Institute for the Future. "The American Future Gap, Survey." Accessed 2021. https://www.iftf.org/americanfuturegap/.

Jabr, Ferris. "Does Self-Awareness Require a Complex Brain?" *Brainwaves* (blog), *Scientific American,* August 22, 2012. https://blogs.scientificamerican.com/brainwaves/does-self-awareness-require-a-complex-brain/.

Jobb, Daniela S., Seojug Jung, Amanda K. Damarin, Sheena Mirpuri, and Dario Spini. "Who Is Your Successful Aging Role Model?" *The Journal of Gerontology, Series B* 72, no. 2 (March 2017): 237–47.

Johns, Chris, editor. "This Baby Will Live to Be 120." *National Geographic,* May 2013.

Judkis, Maura. "Why 30-Year-Olds Are Smashing Cake into Their Faces. Yes, Just Like Babies." *The Washington Post,* June 9, 2016. https://www.washingtonpost.com/news/food/wp/2016/06/09/why-30-year-olds-are-smashing-cake-into-their-faces-yes-just-like-babies/.

Khazan, Olga. "Find Your Passion Is Awful Advice." *The Atlantic*, July 12, 2018. https://www.theatlantic.com/science/archive/2018/07/find-your -passion-is-terrible-advice/564932/.

Knowledge@Wharton. "The Retirement Problem: What to Do with All That Time?" January 14, 2016. https://knowledge.wharton.upenn.edu/article/the -retirement-problem-what-will-you-do-with-all-that-time/.

Laber-Warren, Emily. "You're Only as Old as You Feel." *The New York Times*, October 17, 2019. https://www.nytimes.com/2019/10/17/well/mind/age -subjective-feeling-old.html.

LaRosa, John. "$10.4 Billion Self-Improvement Market Pivots to Virtual Deliver During the Pandemic." MarketResearch.com, August 2, 2021. https://blog.marketresearch.com/10.4-billion-self-improvement-market-piv ots-to-virtual-delivery-during-the-pandemic.

Lau, Filip, and Lester Lam. *The Second Coming of Age: Understanding Baby Boomers . . . and How to Cater to Them.* ReD Associates and Cognizant Digital Works, 2016. https://www.cognizant.com/whitepapers/the-second-coming-of-age -codex2239.pdf.

Levin, Rachel. "When the Techies Took over Tahoe." *Outside*, April 15, 2021. https://www.outsideonline.com/adventure-travel/news-analysis/ tahoe-zoomtown-covid-migration/.

Longevity Project. "Laura Carstensen." Accessed 2021. https://www.longevity -project.com/speakerblog/laura-carstensen.

Marak, Carol. "What We All Need to Know About Solo Aging." *Next Avenue*, October 10, 2018. https://www.nextavenue.org/challenges-solo-agers/.

May, Katherine. *Wintering: The Power of Rest and Retreat in Difficult Times.* London: Rider, 2020.

McCormack, Kevin. "De-stressing Stem Cells and the Bonnie & Clyde of Stem Cell." *The Stem Cellar* (blog), CIRM, February 5, 2021. https://blog.cirm.ca .gov/tag/wnt/.

McEvoy, Beth. "Westbrook Grandmother Can't Stop Turning Heads in Her Swimsuit." Maine News, December 12, 2019. https://www.newscenter maine.com/article/news/local/westbrook-grandmother-cant-stop-making-h eadlines-in-her-swimsuit/97-557907709.

MDVIP. "Health Longevity Not So Much Reality for Generation X." Business Wire, January 31, 2017. https://www.businesswire.com/news/ home/20170131005473/en/Health-and-Longevity-Not-So-Much-a -Reality-for-Generation-X.

Merrill Lynch Bank of America Corporation and Age Wave. *Home in Retirement: More Freedom, New Choices.* Merrill Lynch Bank of America Corporation,

2015. https://agewave.com/wp-content/uploads/2016/07/2015-ML-AW-Home-in-Retirement_More-Freedom-New-Choices.pdf.

———. *Leisure in Retirement Beyond the Bucket List.* Merrill Lynch Bank of America Corporation, May 2016. https://agewave.com/wp-content/uploads/2016/05/2016-Leisure-in-Retirement_Beyond-the-Bucket-List.pdf.

Miller, Karla L. "'Micromanaged and Disrespected': Top Reasons Workers Are Quitting Their Jobs in 'The Great Resignation.'" *The Washington Post,* October 7, 2021. https://www.washingtonpost.com/business/2021/10/07/top-reasons-great-resignation-workers-quitting/.

Molinsky, Jennifer. "Housing Perspectives." Joint Center for Housing Studies of Harvard University, August 7, 2020. https://www.jchs.harvard.edu/blog/designing-senior-housing-safe-interactions-age-covid-19.

Moore, Thomas. *Care of the Soul: A Guide for Cultivating Depth and Sacredness in Everyday Life.* New York: HarperCollins, 1992.

Morin, Amy. "How to Know When to End a Relationship with Family." *Verywell Family,* March 4, 2020. https://www.verywellfamily.com/cutting-ties-with-family-4781962.

NBC Sports Commentary. "Tour de France." *NBC Sports Channel,* June 29, 2021.

Next Big Idea Club. "Next Big Idea Club with Daniel Pink Welcome." YouTube, February 26, 2019, video, 0:44. https://www.youtube.com/watch?v=hc5l5lH6K6k.

Newport, Cal. *So Good They Can't Ignore You: Why Skills Trump Passion in the Quest for Work You Love.* New York: Grand Central Publishing, 2012.

Ostanek, Daniel. "Lefevere: The Whole Staff Was Crying after Cavendish's Tour de France Stage 4 Win." *Cycling News,* June 29, 2021. https://www.cyclingnews.com/news/lefevere-the-whole-staff-was-crying-after-cavendishs-tour-de-frace-stage-4-win/.

Pew Research Center. "Living to 120 and Beyond: Americans' Views on Aging, Medical Advances and Radical Life Extension." August 6, 2013. https://www.pewforum.org/2013/08/06/living-to-120-and-beyond-americans-views-on-aging-medical-advances-and-radical-life-extension/.

———. "Religion and Living Arrangements Around the World." December 12, 2019. https://www.pewforum.org/2019/12/12/religion-and-living-arrangements-around-the-world/.

Pillemer, Karl A. *Fault Lines: Fractured Families and How to Mend Them.* New York: Avery, 2020.

Rath, Tom, and Jim Harter. *Wellbeing: The Five Essential Elements.* New York: Gallup Press, 2010.

Ro, Christine. "The Truth About Family Estrangement." *BBC Future*, March 31, 2019. https://www.bbc.com/future/article/20190328 -family-estrangement-causes.

Roberts, Nicole F. "Forget Generational Stereotypes, Baby Boomers Are Just as Addicted to Smart Phones as Millennials." *Forbes*, May 6, 2019. https://www .forbes.com/sites/nicolefisher/ 2019/05/06/forget-generational-stereotypes -baby-boomers-are-just-as-addicted-to-smart-phones/?sh=526abb904f89.

Rochat, Philippe. "Five Levels of Self-Awareness as They Unfold Early in Life." *Consciousness and Cognition* 12 (February 2003): 717–31.

Schroeder-Garner, Michelle. "The Honest Truth about Van Dwelling: Answers to the Most Common Van Life Questions." *Making Sense of Cents*, March 4, 2021. https://www.makingsenseofcents.com/2019/09/van-dwelling.html.

Scott, Andrew. "Living Longer: Our 100-Year Life." *After the Fact* (podcast), February 1, 2019. Hosted by Dan LeDuc, MP3 audio, 18:58. https://www .pewtrusts.org/-/media/assets/2019/02/atf-transcript_episode-48.pdf.

Shafer, Bill. "103-Year-Old Runs into History," Growing Bolder, Facebook (video), June 20, 2019, https://www.facebook.com/GrowingBolder/videos/ 608999532923015/.

Sharma, Bhadra, and Ellen Barry. "Climbers Leave Everest Amid Regrets and Tensions Among Sherpas." *The New York Times*, April 24, 2014. https:// www.nytimes.com/2014/04/25/world/asia/climbers-leave-everest-amid -regrets-and-tensions-among-sherpas.html.

Silver, Michelle. *Retirement and Its Discontents: Why We Won't Stop Working, Even If We Can*. New York: Columbia University Press, 2018.

Staff Writer. "Numbers of Americans Retiring Abroad Soaring, as Cost of Retiring Stateside Also Soars: Report." *American Expat Financial News Journal*, September 25, 2019. https://americanexpatfinance.com/news/item/267 -numbers-of-americans-retiring-abroad-soaring-as-cost-of-retiring-stateside -also-soars-report.

Taylor, Roberta K., and Dorian Mintzer. *The Couple's Retirement Puzzle: 10 Must-Have Conversations for Creating an Amazing New Life Together*. Naperville, IL: Sourcebooks, 2014.

TED. "The Psychology of Your Future Self | Dan Gilbert." YouTube, June 3, 2014. Video, 6:49. https://www.youtube.com/watch?v=XNbaR54Gpj4.

Tergesen, Anne. "Why Everything You Know about Aging Is Probably Wrong." *The Wall Street Journal*, November 30, 2014. https://www.wsj.com/articles/ why-everything-you-think-about-aging-may-be-wrong-1417408057.

Trafton, Anne. "Study Helps Explain Why Motivation to Learn Declines with Age." *MIT News*, October 27, 2020. https://news.mit.edu/2020/ why-learn-motivate-age-decline-1027.

Transamerica Center for Retirement Studies. *19th Annual Transamerica Retirement Survey.* Los Angeles, CA: Transamerica Center for Retirement Studies, 2019.

————. *What Is "Retirement"? Three Generations Prepare for Older Age, 19th Annual Transamerica Retirement Survey of Workers.* April 2019. https://transamericacenter.org/docs/default-source/retirement-survey-of-workers/tcrs2019_sr_what_is_retirement_by_generation.pdf.

Vandervelde, Maryanne. "Are You Emotionally Ready to Retire? Eight Questions to Ask Yourself." *The Wall Street Journal,* April 1, 2021. https://www.wsj.com/articles/ready-to-retire-emotionally-11618007274.

Vedantam, Shankar. "People Like People Who Ask Questions." *NPR,* November 29, 2017. https://www.npr.org/2017/11/29/567133944/people-like-people-who-ask-questions.

Vogel, Emily A. "Millennials Stand Out for Their Technology Use, but Older Generations Embrace Digital Life." Pew Research Center, September 9, 2019. https://www.pewresearch.org/fact-tank/2019/09/09/us-generations-technology-use/.

Walsh, Colleen. "Young Adults Hardest Hit by Loneliness during Pandemic." *The Harvard Gazette,* February 17, 2021. https://news.harvard.edu/gazette/story/2021/02/young-adults-teens-loneliness-mental-health-coronavirus-covid-pandemic/.

Wilson, Sara. *This One Wild and Precious Life: The Path Back to Connection in a Fractured World.* Sydney: Pan Macmillan Australia, 2020.

Winter, Catherine. "11 Examples of Life Purpose Statements That You Could Adopt." *A Conscious Rethink* (blog), January 26, 2021. https://www.aconsciousrethink.com/14552/life-purpose-statement-examples/.

World Regret Survey. Accessed 2021. https://worldregretsurvey.com/.

Zamudio, Maria. "Growing Number of Americans Are Retiring Outside US." *PBS News Hour,* December 28, 2016. https://www.pbs.org/newshour/world/growing-number-americans-retiring-outside-u-s.

Zulz, Emily. "Americans Would Rather Talk About Sex or Death than Retirement." ThinkAdvisor, August 27, 2014. https://www.thinkadvisor.com/2014/08/27/americans-would-rather-talk-about-sex-or-death-than-retirement-2/.

INDEX

ABOUT THE AUTHOR

In her late 50s, Barbara, along with her daughter, Elizabeth, set out for a six-month sailing adventure on their 42-foot sailboat, *Revival*. Together they sailed alone for more than 2,000 miles.

Neither woman was an experienced sailor. Two weeks before departure, Barbara flunked out of navigation school (the test was difficult), and Elizabeth returned from Orlando with certification from a one-week sailing school. Pushing a little boat through water was hard work, especially for two inexperienced sailors. Barbara learned how by doing it.

Eight years later, that learn-by-doing approach yielded significant returns as Barbara faced the challenge of creating a postretirement life. The transition should not have been so hard.

Her story and motivation to help others inspired the launch of www.YourExtraordinaryLifeAfterRetirement.com, which gives post-50 individuals tools and strategies to design and live fulfilling lives in the last third of life. With graduate degrees in counseling and human behavior as a solid base, Barbara curates research and produces content on aging, retirement, un-retirement, productive longevity, well-being, and happiness.

Barbara's strong desire to engage in life fully is one of her extraordinary gifts. But it is her excellence as a teacher that impacts others. With groundbreaking clarity and a refreshing, experienced voice, people listen to her and they profit from it.

Formerly an executive coach and seasoned speaker, Barbara has motivated thousands of senior leaders and middle managers to higher levels of performance in work and life. Her previous book, *The Transparency Edge: How Credibility Can Make or Break You in Business* (2004), was chosen by *Fast Company* magazine as a "Book of the Month." Written with her daughter, Elizabeth, an award-winning business journalist, the book was translated into four languages, including Spanish and Chinese, and was among Bookscan's list of 50 best-selling new business books in America. Also, it hit #7 on Barnes & Noble's list of best-selling business ethics books.

A fierce advocate for the sabbatical movement, Barbara is cofounder of YourSABBATICAL.com, a research and strategy firm with tools and resources for assessing the value of existing or new sabbatical programs in corporations and that offers current trends and best practices in sabbatical initiatives. YourSABBATICAL.com was a 2009 winner of the Moving into the Future Award present by the Conference Board. Barbara is coauthor of *The Ultimate Toolkit for Writing and Presenting a Killer Sabbatical Proposal Your Boss Can't Refuse* and *The Comprehensive Sabbatical Program Toolkit: A How-To Guide for Implementing Your Company's Sabbatical Strategy.*

Articles by and about Barbara have been published in *Fast Company, Investor's Business Daily, Consulting to Management,* the *New York Times,* and *American Executive,* among others. She is a highly rated speaker, is past president of the Georgia Speakers Association, and was previously named one of the top three speakers in Atlanta.

Barbara's personal practice of designing three-month or more solo work/life adventures in falling-down beautiful colonial cities in Latin and South America is indicative of how the last third of life can combine freedom, work, and joy. She has lived and worked in Nicaragua, Chile, Ecuador, Argentina, and México.

When not speaking, coaching, or writing, Barbara takes tap-dancing classes and will trade in her ten-year-old bike for an electric bike to ascend those hills on the Natchez Trace Parkway near her home in Nashville.